HANDFULS ON PURPOSE

SERIES VII

BY
Pastor JAMES SMITH
Author of "A Survey of the Wondrous Cross,"
"Spiritual Patterns" etc.

WM. B. EERDMANS PUBLISHING COMPANY
Grand Rapids   **Michigan**

American Edition

———

Published in 1947, by

WM. B. EERDMANS PUBLISHING CO.
by
Special Arrangement with

PICKERING & INGLIS, LTD.
14 Paternoster Row, London, E.C.4
229 Bothwell St., Glasgow, C.2
Manchester—Newcastle—Liverpool—Edinburgh

This printing, August 1963

PHOTOLITHOPRINTED BY CUSHING - MALLOY, INC.
ANN ARBOR, MICHIGAN, UNITED STATES OF AMERICA
1963

Guide to Series 1 to 12

SERIES 1 to 10 .. By Pastor JAMES SMITH
SERIES 11 and 12, .. By ROBERT LEE
SERIES 13, .. COMPLETE INDEX TO SERIES

PREFACE.

IT is with deep thankfulness to the Giver of every good gift that we send forth this SEVENTH Series of "Handfuls on Purpose." It is very gratifying to us that the interest taken in them has been steadily growing since the first; and as they have been the means of leading many Christian workers into a closer study of the Word for themselves, we rejoice, as this was one of the chief objects of their publication.

We hoped at first to publish, perhaps, *four* volumes of these Outlines Studies, thinking that they might be quite sufficient to cover the whole Bible in the manner in which we had purposed to deal with it. But this is now Volume *Seven*, and we have only managed to get about half through the Book. Although we have made some gallant attempts to get over the ground more quickly, yet, somehow, the further we go, the attractions to linger becomes growingly powerful.

We should like, if the Lord will, to issue other three volumes, and so complete the blessed task that has been on our heart to do unto His Name. But perhaps this will depend on whether our many friends, who have hitherto received them gladly, will care to continue their favour to such an extent. For the many grateful expressions that reach us of the helpfulness of these books, we seek to praise Him, from whom all blessings flow.

JAMES SMITH.

INDEX OF SUBJECTS.

INDEX OF SUBJECTS—Continued.

INDEX OF TEXTS.

INDEX OF TEXTS—Continued.

Handfuls on Purpose

𝔒𝔩𝔡 𝔗𝔢𝔰𝔱𝔞𝔪𝔢𝔫𝔱 𝔒𝔲𝔱𝔩𝔦𝔫𝔢𝔰

STUDIES IN JOB

JOB'S CHARACTER

JOB 1. 1-10

"My strength is as the strength of ten
Because my heart is pure."—TENNYSON

THIS book, supposed to have been first committed to
writing by Moses, is regarded by many as the
oldest in the world. Its object is to set before us the trial
of an "upright man." Job himself is quite unconscious of
the fact that he is being used by God as an object-lesson to
all generations; he knows nothing at all about the con-
ference that has taken place concerning him, recorded in
verses 7 to 12. The days of Job were probably about the
time of Abraham, as in the book there is no mention of
Israel, the Tabernacle, the Temple, or the Law. The
book is of great value as a revelation of the forces that are
at work against the life of the righteous. All the characters
are representative: Job, the servant of God; Satan, the
adversary; the three Friends, the wisdom of the world;
Elihu, the wisdom of God; God, the Judge of all. That

Job was no mythical character is clearly proven in Ezekiel 14. 14 and 20, when his name is mentioned by Jehovah Himself. As the teaching of this book is centred in the *person* of Job, we shall try and grasp its leading principles through this *man*, that they may, if possible, become more interesting and powerful in our own individual lives.

I. He was Perfect. "Perfect and upright, one that feared God, and eschewed evil" (v. 1). "There is none like him in the earth" (v. 8). As a man, he was all that a man in those days could be in holiness of character. That there was "none like him in the earth" is not his own testimony, but the statement of Him who knows what is in man. "The Lord knoweth them that trust in Him" (Nahum 1. 7). He was perfect, not in the sense of being sinless, but in the sense of being *plainly* (Heb.) devoted to God and to righteousness. He was transparently upright, according to his knowledge and ability. He walked in the light, although that light may have been but twilight. Like an honest man, Job straightened himself up, morally, before God and men. His character is in strong contrast to the multitude of men who, like the woman in the Gospel, are so "bowed down" with the love of the world, and the fear of man, that they can in no wise lift themselves up. Love and lust are fetters that bind the souls of men as with iron bands.

II. He was Rich. "His substance was 7000 sheep, 3000 camels, 500 yoke of oxen," etc.; "so that he was the greatest of all the men of the east" (v. 3). Good men are not always rich; but God had surely put a premium on the goodness and faithfulness of Job, by allowing *him* to become the wealthiest man in the country. The *best* man will always be the richest, if not in material goods, certainly in the more enduring treasures that are spiritual and Divine. Although there was a gulf of agony between Job's present and future life, yet he found that it paid to be righteous. The *perfect* man will be upright, will fear God and hate evil, if all his worldly possessions should need to be sacrificed for this end. If his riches increase—even spiritual riches—he sets not his heart on *them*.

III. **He was Wise.** "Job rose up early in the morning and offered burnt-offerings for all his family, for he said, It may be that my sons have sinned and cursed God in their hearts. This did Job *continually*" (v. 5). These family gatherings, for social enjoyment, were in themselves a good testimony to their upright and priestly father. Those seven sons must have been well brought up, when they sought so often the fellowship of one another, and did not fail to give their three sisters a special invitation to their parties. Job did not forbid such festivities, but he knew human nature too well to suppose that there was no moral danger connected with such seasons. "It may be that my sons have sinned." When it is a question of pleasure-seeking it is so easy to forget God, and to act in such a way as to dishonour His holy Name. So Job, as priest in his own family, offers a sacrifice for each of his sons. As a wise father, he is most concerned that his sons should be kept right with God. It is not enough for the "perfect man" that his family should be healthy and happy and prosperous in the world; he longs intensely, and spares no sacrifice, that they might *each one* live and walk in the fear and favour of God. *Sin* against God is that one thing which his upright soul has learned to hate.

IV. **He was Protected.** "Hast Thou not made an hedge about *him*, and about his *house*, and about *all that he hath* on every side?" (v. 10). His person, his family, and his property, were hedged about by the special care of God. Three circles of defences had been raised about him. He and his were as the vineyard of the Lord (Isa. 5. 1, 2).

Satan seems to have known more about the impregnable
position of Job than Job himself. His fear of God had
made him safer than he thought. The God of yesterday
is the same God to-day. We cannot see that "angel of the
Lord that *encampeth round about* them that fear Him," but
the Devil does. Hedges of the Lord's making are too thick
even for the cunning hand of Satan. Satan's testimony to
the security of God's children is of great value. Without
God's permission his great power is utterly useless against
the man that is hiding in the bulwarks of his God. "God
is our refuge...therefore will not we fear."

V. He was Marked. "The Lord said unto Satan,
Hast thou *considered* My servant Job...Then Satan
answered, Doth Job fear God for nought?" (vv. 8, 9).
Job, being a perfect and upright man, was an object of
special consideration to the Lord and to Satan. He was a
marked man for the favour of the Lord, and for the envy
and hate of Satan. Both God and the Devil marks the
perfect man (Psa. 37. 37). The divine consideration
is all for our safety and usefulness—the Satanic consideration is how to disturb and destroy. Is it not true in a
sense, of every "perfect man in Christ Jesus," that they
become the special objects of assault by the powers of
darkness? When Joshua, the high priest, was seen
"standing before the angel of the Lord," Satan was seen
"standing at his right hand to *resist* him" (Zech. 3. 1).
Why was Satan so desirous to have Simon Peter that he
might sift him as wheat? Did he dread lest that warm
impetuous nature should be wholly yielded to the cause of
Jesus Christ? Those whom Satan and his host takes no
trouble at must be accomplishing very little for God.
Heaven and Hell marks the holy man. Put on the whole
armour of God, that ye may be able to stand against the
wiles of the Devil.

JOB'S ADVERSARY.

JOB 1. 6-22; 2. 1-10.

"When the fight begins within himself
A man's worth something."—BROWNING.

JOB'S case was typical. Ye have *heard* of his patience, as ye have *seen* the faith of Abraham, and the meekness of Moses. Job's desperate struggle is allowed to take place in the open arena, that we might learn the secret of resistance. It is a battle between the best of men and the worst of enemies. Satan does his best to crush and overthrow the integrity of this "perfect man" who has been incased with the special providence of God, and who can offer but a passive resistance. Although God's environments were everything that could be desired, he was not proof against the powerful temptations of the Devil. The environments of Christ Himself did not save Him from Satanic assaults. Job had a good house, and a good income, but houses and wages are not everything that men need, if they would stand firm against all the deadly wiles of the Devil. About this enemy of all righteousness, let us not forget—

I. **His Personality.** According to the teaching of Scripture there is but one Devil, but many demons. The apostles and evangelists in referring to him always speak in the singular, and this they do about thirty times. "Get behind Me Satan" could never be said of a mere impersonal influence. He is a *liar* from the beginning, an influence cannot lie. Only men and devils can lie. All lying is devilish, and devilishness proves there is a Devil.

II. **His Origin.** "The Lord said unto Satan, *Whence comest thou?* Then Satan answered, From going to and fro in the earth, and from walking up and down in it" (v. 7). The same mystery that hangs over the fact of sin, hangs over the origin of Satan. When our Lord says

that he was a murderer, and a liar, *from the beginning*, it is
difficult to believe that he has ever been anything better.
According to his own confession, his sphere of work is
"going to and fro in the earth." His domain is the world,
and his condition is one of eternal restlessness. That
Satan and his demon host are the disembodied spirits of
a pre-Adamic race, that brought the condemnation of God
upon them because of sin, is a theory not without some
attractions.

III. **His Object.** His unwavering purpose is to set
God and man at variance (v. 11). In his devilish business
he is, alas, too often successful. Before he attempted
the separation of Job from his God, he had succeeded
with Adam and with Cain, and afterwards with Saul
and with Judas, and a multitude of others. There is
no man in all the earth that annoys Satan so much as the
"perfect man." He directs all his energy against the
praying, sacrificing man. While Jesus Christ was on the
earth, the forces of Hell were continually meeting Him in
one form or another. The names given to Satan in the
Scriptures are strongly indicative of his character and
purpose. He is the *Adversary*; the *Accuser* of the brethren;
the *Murderer*; the Prince of *darkness*; the Prince of *this
world*; the roaring *lion*. He is the god of this lost world;
the ruler of its darkness. He is the opposer and the
accuser of the brethren; the liar against the truth, and the
murderer of souls. "*Resist* the Devil, and he will flee
from you" (James 4. 7).

IV. **His Power.** That Satan is capable of great power
as well as great wrath is unquestionable. But he is utterly
powerless to touch a child of God, or anything that he has,
without His permission. Satan was allowed to send his
messengers, one after another, to buffet Job, just as he was
afterwards permitted to do with the Apostle Paul (2 Cor.

12. 7), and blessed be God, with much the same result. Although the Devil may be allowed at times to sift, he is not allowed to devour the wheat: "Behold all that he hath is in thy power; only upon himself put not forth thine hand" (v. 12). So far, but no farther. Then when this adversary made his second challenge, the Lord said, "Behold *he* is in thine hand, but save his life" (chap. 2. 6). It was a long rope this roaring lion got, and he used every inch of it. He had got access to everything but the spirit of this evil-hating man, and having received liberty to exercise his fiendish art, we soon discover where the secret of his power lies. He finds his mighty weapons in the Sabeans, the Chaldeans, the lightning, and the wind (vv. 15-19). That he should be able to commandeer such forces is a revelation of his wonderful power and resources. The Devil has two arsenals, one in the heavens, and the other in the earth, namely, the *elements*, and the *hearts* of ungodly men. Such an enemy is not to be trifled with.

V. His Manner of Working. His first act is, to get himself away out of the presence of God. "So Satan went forth from the presence of the Lord" (v. 12). Satan, and all his host, seen and unseen, whether they be men or demons, love the darkness rather than the light, because their deeds are evil. He has a great task before him— to break down a perfect man's confidence in his God— so he waits for the best time to make the attack. That opportune day arrived when Job's "sons and daughters were eating and drinking in their eldest brother's house" (v. 13). To get at Job, the Devil had to break down the outside fences first; this he did by prevailing upon *men* to steal his oxen, his asses, his camels, and to kill his servants. Little, perhaps, did these men think that when they were helping themselves to the property of Job, they were the agents of the Devil carrying out his diabolical ends. The same spirit is *now working* in the children of disobedience (Eph. 2. 2). Ungodly men are tools lying ready at hand for the work of Satan. He entered Judas just because he was a fit person for the accomplishment of his 'fiendish purposes against the Son of God. He sent *fire from the heavens*, and burned up the sheep, to make Job believe that it was a judgment from God. Satan surely thought this was a master-stroke, when the servant whom he had spared to carry the tidings went and said, "The *fire of God* is fallen from Heaven, and hath burned up the sheep" (v. 16). If Satan can only get God's people to believe when the time of affliction and testing comes, that God is against them, he has gained a victory. He was very careful to spare one, who might run to Job, saying, "I *only* am escaped *alone* to tell thee." The *I*'s here are most emphatic. The *method* he adopted in breaking the news to Job was in itself devilish. The Devil's wheat is all bran. King Canute promised to make the man who would kill King Edmund, his rival, the highest man in England; he fulfilled his promise by hanging him on the *highest* tower in London. We fight not against flesh and blood, but against *"wicked spirits,"* which use flesh and blood as their instruments in seeking to overthrow our faith in God. We are not ignorant of his devices; give no place to the Devil.

JOB'S TRIALS.
JOB 1. 13-22; 2. 1-10.

"Satan desires us, great and small,
    As wheat to sift us, and we all are tempted.
Not one, however, rich or great,
    Is by his station or estate exempted."
                            —LONGFELLOW.

THE very name of Job means persecuted. In his unique trials he is the prototype of Christ. Every perfect man will have his Eden to enjoy, his Isaac to sacrifice, and his wilderness of severe and prolonged testing. It is through much tribulation that we enter into the kingdom of God's greater fullness and power. No affliction for the present is joyous, but grievous, but, nevertheless, *afterward* it yieldeth the peaceable fruits of righteousness to them that are exercised thereby. Was there ever a man more exercised about his troubles than Job? But meanwhile we shall look at—

I. Their Purpose. Two cross-purposes find their centre in Job. The one was Divine, the other was Satanic. Satan said, "Doth Job fear God for nought?...Put forth Thine hand now, and touch all that he hath, and he will curse Thee to Thy face" (vv. 9-11). Satan did not believe that any man would remain true to God if bereft of all material and earthly enjoyment. If Job staggered under such a test, Jesus Christ did not. He had not where to lay His head. He was *"the* Man of Sorrows," yet He always did those things which were pleasing to His Father. Job, being utterly unconscious that he was being used in this fashion as a test case, must have felt it as a severe trial of his *faith*. Well the Devil knows, that if men are going to overcome the world by *faith*, his power is broken, and his kingdom lost. It has been so since the beginning; those who would fear God, and eschew evil, must fight the good fight of faith.

II. Their Nature. The character of Job's troubles was of the worst kind. There were no half measures. Every separate trial was a complete catastrophe. There was the—

1. LOSS OF PROPERTY. His "seven thousand sheep, three thousand camels, five hundred yoke of oxen, and five hundred asses," were all suddenly stolen, or burned up with fire from Heaven. The richest man in the east had in

one day become a bankrupt. That in itself would have
driven many a one into absolute despair.

2. LOSS OF FAMILY. Seven sons and three daughters
all killed by one terrific stroke (v. 19). This judgment
must have been "a great deep" to the upright, sensitive
soul of Job (Psa. 36. 6). There is no natural law by
which such workings of the providence of God can be
understood. The dominion of faith, for the spirit of
man, is beyond nature.

3. LOSS OF HEALTH. "Satan went forth and smote Job
with sore boils from the sole of his foot unto his crown"
(chap. 2. 7). He was covered with a loathsome disease;
there was no soundness in his flesh. Like Lazarus, he was
"full of sores." This bodily affliction, like the others,
came suddenly. He had no premonition of the approach of
this fearful malady—no time to fortify himself even by
prayer against the assault. Satan had permission to touch
his flesh, and he touched every inch of it. With the
exception of the Lord Jesus Christ—for in all things He
has the pre-eminence—it is questionable if ever any other
mortal was so sorely tried. If there was not something
supernatural about faith in God, it could not possibly
survive such a shock.

4. LOSS OF POSITION. The *greatest* man in the east"
has now become the most loathsome object in the east.
He who sat among princes is now sitting "among ashes"
(chap. 2. 8). He has been stripped of everything but
his life.

5. LOSS OF SYMPATHY. "Then said his wife unto
him, Dost thou still retain thine integrity? Curse God
and die" (v. 9). His wife, the only comfort left him,
turns out to be a canker. She cannot understand faith in
God in circumstances like these. Fair-weather Christians
always get ship-wrecked in a storm like this. This taunt

through his wife was the Devil's last weight to break the back of Job's integrity. It was the poisoning of his last earthly spring of consolation. Job has at last sounded the abyss of his sufferings; he has found the bottom of this great deep. His is now "a lifeless life," a finished monument to that great master of the malignant art. And this is the master many take pleasure in serving. To serve sin is to be the slave of the Devil.

III. **Their Effect.** The immediate result of those awful trials which stripped Job naked of every earthly comfort was a clearer revelation of the inward, spiritual man. "He fell upon the ground, and *worshipped*, and said, The Lord gave, and the Lord hath taken away: blessed be the Name of the Lord" (chap. 1. 20, 21). These words, spoken by this pre-eminent sufferer, have come down as a legacy to the bereaved in every generation since then; on many tombstones they may be read as the language of deep, heart-felt sorrow and submission. "The *Lord* hath taken away." Job saw the Lord behind the Sabeans and the Chaldeans who fell upon his flocks. "In all this did not Job sin with his lips" (chap. 2. 10). That no murmur escaped those burning lips in such a furnace proves how completely he had given himself and all that he had to God. "What! shall we receive good at the hand of God, and shall we not receive evil?" Has the Giver of all good not the right to withhold that good or His own pleasure? What have we that we have not received? Job may not be a prophet, but he has "spoken in the Name of the Lord, for an example of suffering affliction, and of patience" (James 5. 10). There is a life that does not consist of the *things* which we possess; it is infinitely superior to them and independent of them. After getting a glimpse behind the scenes of the purpose of Job's trials, let us by faith count it all joy when we fall into divers temptations (trials), knowing that the *testing* of your faith leads to power of endurance (James 1. 2, 3).

JOB'S COMFORTERS—ELIPHAZ.

JOB 4-7.

"How that to comfort those that mourn
          Is a thing for saints to try;
      Yet, haply, God might have done less
          Had a saint been there—not I.

"Alas! we have so little grace,
          With love so little burn,
      That the hardest of our works for God
          Is to comfort those that mourn."—FABER.

THE beauty and meaning of some pictures are best seen and understood at a distance. We can see deeper into the meaning of Job's sufferings than either Job or his comforters could see. From our sun-lit mountain top, we look down upon these friends as all working in the darkness, just as, perhaps, some of the angels of God may look down upon us in pity as they see us vainly striving to find out the reason why God in His providence so deals with us. The great fundamental lesson of the book of Job is "Have faith in God." These comforters cannot be charged with hardness of heart, or of having impure motives. Men that could "lift up their voice and weep" at the sight of Job's condition, and sit in company with him for "seven days and seven nights" were surely not void of real sympathy and compassion. Their weakness and their sin lay in their self-confidence. Each seemed sure that he was laying his finger on the cause of Job's downfall, although his experience was a *new thing* in the providence of God. To us, their eloquent reasonings is a powerful evidence of the utter inability of the "wisdom of this world" to explain or to understand the mysteries of Christian experience.

Job began this great wordy warfare by opening his mouth and "cursing the day wherein he was born" (chap. 3. 1-3). Satan had said, "Touch his bone and his flesh, and he will *curse Thee* to Thy face." Job went perilously near the fulfilling of the Devil's prediction, when he "cursed his day," but yet he did not curse his God. Many a one has been constrained, through sin and suffering, to curse the day of their first birth, but history has never told us of one who had any desire to curse the day of their *second* birth. Man that is born in sin is born to trouble as the sparks fly upward, but the man that is born again is born into the kingdom of peace. During those long, weary, seven days the gold of Job's character seemed to become dim, and the most fine gold changed, for he did speak unadvisedly with his *lips* (chap. 2. 10). In the day of darkness and trial let us beware of that "unruly evil," the tongue. This opening speech of the suffering patriarch betrays a soul overwhelmed with bewilderment. It has many questions. Yet this outburst of agony has taught many to be still under the mighty hand of God. It is no mere hyperbole to say that the sufferings of Job, like the sufferings of Jesus Christ, were for the good of others. The Bible would have been much poorer if there never had been the conflict and the patience of Job. It will be impossible in these brief notes to grasp anything like the full meaning of those great torrent speeches. We shall only attempt to catch a word here and there that might help us to understand the book, and to enter into a deeper experience of the things of God.

I. The Speech of Eliphaz (chaps. 4, 5).

1. "IF WE ASSAY TO COMMUNE WITH THEE, WILT THOU BE GRIEVED" (chap. 4. 2). Eliphaz begins very tenderly; he feels that the wound to be dressed is very deep and painful. One needs the tongue that is learned by experience to speak a word in season to him that is so weary and heavy-laden. It is a solemn and gracious work to commune with the sorrowing, but let such missionaries see that their own hearts are at the same time in communion with God, or they may but aggravate the anguish.

2. "THY WORDS HAVE UPHOLDEN HIM THAT WAS FALLING
...BUT NOW...THOU FAINTEST" (vv. 3-5). This friend
knew Job's past life, and ventures to remind him of how he
had been a means of blessing to others in their time of
need. This was but a small spark of light for Job's great
darkness, but still there was a glimmer in it. To tell a
man that he once was rich will not console him much now
that he is bankrupt. It is easier to speak cheering words
to the tempted than to bear the temptation. The comforters of others need at times to be comforted. "They
that wait on the Lord shall...not *faint.*"

"Remember, I pray thee, who ever perished, being
innocent?" (v. 7). This saying is like a double-edged
sword, it cuts both ways. It may mean, if you were
innocent, as you profess to be, you would not have been
perishing in this fashion; or, because you are innocent, it is
impossible for you to perish. The Lord knoweth them that
are His, and how to deliver them out of temptation
(2 Peter 2. 9). The Lord could do nothing with the guilty
Sodomites until the righteous were taken out (Gen. 19. 22).
The facts of history are well worth *remembering.*

3. "AFFLICTION COMETH NOT FORTH OF THE DUST...AS
FOR ME, I WOULD SEEK UNTO GOD" (chap. 5. 6-8, R.V.).
Affliction doth not spring up by chance; it is not the
sudden outcome of spontaneous generation. The law of
microbes is included here, and if I were you, "I would seek
unto God, and unto Him would I commit my cause."
What could be better than this? But Eliphaz was not in
Job's position, and so it was comparatively easy for him
to say what he would do. Still, it is the best thing to do.
To whom can we go but unto Him. The Lord alone knew
all the reasons why this dark and cloudy day had come.
In the day of adversity consider, yes, consider Him who
endured contradictions for us.

4. "BEHOLD, HAPPY IS THE MAN WHOM GOD CORREC-
TETH" (v. 17). To be reproved of God is a comforting
evidence of His love and carefulness. Every true child of
God desires to have their thoughts, feelings, and ways
corrected by their heavenly Father. We ought to count
it a great privilege to be put right by either His word or
His rod.

5. "HE SHALL DELIVER THEE IN SIX TROUBLES; YEA, IN
SEVEN" (v. 19). "HEAR IT, AND KNOW IT FOR THY GOOD"
(v. 27). Solomon says that "a just man falleth seven
times, and riseth up again" (Prov. 24. 16). Six troubles
had overtaken Job, and he had not yet been delivered out of
any of them; but God is the God of deliverances. Let not
the *number* of our troubles or our difficulties limit the
Holy One. "Hear it." Let not the voices of the world,
or an evil heart, so dull the ear that you cannot hear the
still small voice of promise (Psa. 34. 19).

II. Job's Reply (chaps. 6, 7). The wonderful words
of Eliphaz had little effect. Job begins by saying:

1. "OH, THAT MY GRIEF WERE THOROUGHLY WEIGHED."
What is more heavy and more difficult to weigh than grief?
But what benefit would it bring the distracted sufferer
even could he know the full weight and measure of it. His
grief, like the grief of Him who agonised in Gethsemane,
was both terrible and mysterious.

2. "THE ARROWS OF THE ALMIGHTY ARE WITHIN ME"
(chap. 6. 4). A week ago he said, "The *Lord* gave and the
Lord hath taken away," but now his soul is pierced with
the arrows of the *Almighty*. Still, he does not say with
"the fiery darts of the Devil." The arrows have been many
and sharp, but they have come from the finger of God
(Psa. 38. 2). The arrows of the Almighty never miss the
mark (Lam. 3. 12), and when they are *within* us, only He
who sent them can remove them (2 Cor. 5. 11).

3. "Is my flesh brass?" (chap. 6. 12). God could easily have made our flesh to be as hard, as endurable, and as insensible as brass, and our strength as "the strength of stones," if it had not been good for us to be afflicted. The rod of correction would be useless on a brazen body. He knows the frailty of our frame, and will not lay upon us more than we are able to bear.

4. "Cause me to understand wherein I have erred" (chap. 5. 24). If this calamity has come upon me because of my sin—as Eliphaz seemed to think (chap. 6. 8)—then, show me, says Job, where the sin is. Suffering is not always a chastisement or correction, it may be but a narrow gate or a rough road into a place of larger blessing, the Jordan, through which we go into a new land of promise. Job was not conscious of having sinned. The last thing we see him doing, is offering sacrifices for his sons, lest they may have sinned. If in our affliction there is no consciousness of sin, we may be sure God has something new to reveal to us. Wait patiently on the Lord.

5. "I will speak...I will complain" (chap. 7. 11). This is the language of a spirit in anguish, and a soul in bitterness. We would much rather have heard him say, "I will trust....I will pray." There is a silence and a dimness that savours of unbelief more than submission, but why should a believer in God make up his mind to complain? When the Man Christ Jesus was in an agony He prayed more earnestly. The "perfect man" in the Old Testament comes far short of the perfect Man in the New. *"Call* upon Me in the day of trouble." It is just as easy to call as to complain.

6. "Let me alone" (chap. 7. 16). It may at times be hard to bear the weight of the heavy hand of God, but it is infinitely worse to be let alone. What becomes of the branch that is let alone by the tree? What would happen

to the child that was left alone by its mother? Ephraim
is joined to his idols—let him alone. There is a painless
disease that speaks of certain death. As saints or as sinners we know not what we do when we ask God to let us
alone. It is of the glory of His grace in His kindness
towards us in Christ Jesus that He does not let us alone.
There are prayers God graciously refuses to answer.

JOB'S COMFORTERS—BILDAD.
JOB 8-10.

I. The Speech of Bildad (chap. 8). His manner is
abrupt to begin with, and seems less sympathetic than
Eliphaz. His argument amounts to this, that unless God
sends deliverance speedily we must conclude that both you
and your family have been guilty of sinning against God,
and that this dire calamity is the just reward of your works.
Like Eliphaz, he is in total ignorance of the purpose of
Job's trials, but speaks with all the confidence of an oracle.
Mark some of his key-notes—

1. "DOTH THE ALMIGHTY PERVERT JUSTICE?" (chap.
8. 3). Is it possible for God to be unjust? Can He who
sits upon a Great *White* Throne be unrighteous in His
dealings with any one? No. But what comfort can an
aching, bleeding heart find in this? That the *Law* is holy,
just, and good, is not much of a consolation to a soul
smitten with profoundest anguish. The troubled heart
yearns for love, and grace, and pity.

**2. "IF THOU WERT PURE AND UPRIGHT, SURELY NOW HE
WOULD AWAKE FOR THEE"** (v. 6). If you are all that you
profess to be, surely *now*, when you have got into such a
depth of misery, God would arise to your help. The
glitter of the cold steel is easily seen in this merciless
thrust. How the tender soul of Job must have felt it.
It is the silver not dross that the refiner puts into the fire.

"Every *branch in me* that beareth fruit He purgeth *it.*"
Joseph was fruitful in the land of affliction (Gen. 41. 52).
Yet there is truth in Bildad's statement, for "Whatsoever
we ask, we receive of Him, because we keep His commandments, and do those things that are pleasing in His sight"
(1 John 3. 22).

3. "PREPARE THYSELF TO THE SEARCH" (v. 8). There
is much to be learned from the past, and from God's
dealings with the fathers, but that all things are to continue
as they were is not the teaching of the Holy Ghost (1 Peter
3. 4). Job would "prepare himself" in vain to search for
the cause of his sorrows in the teaching of a "former age."
Man by *searching* cannot find out God; it is by *trusting*
that we learn to know Him. The life of faith is on
altogether a different plane from the life of reason and of
sight. Believe and thou shalt see.

4. "CAN THE RUSH GROW UP WITHOUT MIRE?" (v. 11).
The Shuhite now says some plain things about hypocrisy.
As the rush cannot grow up without mire, neither can a
"hypocrite's hope" flourish without being nourished with
that which is suitable to it. If Job has still hope, it is
because of the mire of his hypocrisy. If "he is still green
before the sun's" withering rays it is because he has within
him the waters of deceit (v. 16). Although "the hope
of the hypocrite shall perish" that does not prove that
because, through excessive trial, a man's hope has fainted
that he is perishing without hope. God pity the man
whose trust is only in "a spider's web" (v. 14). Hope
thou in God.

5. "BEHOLD, GOD WILL NOT CAST AWAY A PERFECT MAN"
(v. 20). This, like many others of their sayings, is capable
of a double interpretation. If you had been a "perfect
man" God would not have cast you away like this; or, if
you are in reality a perfect man, God will not cast you

away although you have been brought so low. It is a mercy to know that when others are misjudging you, that God looketh upon the heart. He knoweth them that are His. "He will not forsake His inheritance" (Psa. 94. 14). To Bildad's credit let us say, that he closes his address with a word of hope (vv. 21, 22). They that sow in tears shall reap in joy.

II. Job's Reply (chaps. 9, 10). Job begins his answer to Bildad by asking a very searching question.

1. "HOW SHALL MAN BE JUST WITH GOD?" (v. 2). It is easy to tell a man what he should be, but how is this thing to be done? A *man* should be just with *God*, but in what way is this to be accomplished? How is man's iniquity to be put away, and the guilt of his sin cleansed? Who shall make the key that shall fit this lock? On what ground shall a sinner stand righteous *before* God (R.V.). There is no use of "contending with Him" (v. 3). It is a question of how shall we escape. But this question has been fully answered by God Himself who doeth wonders without number (v. 10) in the gift and sufferings of Jesus Christ His Son.

2. "HOW SHALL I . . . REASON WITH HIM" (v. 14). He is not a man as I am. What arguments can an unholy man use with a holy God? If it is a question of sin and judgment then there is absolutely no room for man's reasonings. He cannot justify himself (v. 20). Although he should wash himself with snow water, yet will he find himself plunged into a filthy ditch, and his own clothes an abhorrence to him (vv. 30, 31). But God's own backsliding *children* are asked to "Come and reason" with Him, (Isa. 1. 18) and a precious promise is herewith given to such. What God asks for those smarting for their sins is, not to come and reason, but to confess, and forsake their sins.

3. "NEITHER IS THERE ANY DAYSMAN BETWIXT US"

(v. 33). These well-known words truthfully express the deepest need of a sinful suffering spirit. O for one capable to act as umpire between a mighty God and a miserable soul. One who is Divine and human, one able to lay his hand on both and meet the need of each, satisfying the just claims of God and speaking peace to a troubled heart. This great need has been perfectly met in Jesus Christ for, "If any man sin, we have an advocate *with the Father*, Jesus Christ the *righteous*, and He is the *propitiation* for our sins" (1 John 2. 1, 2). "No man cometh unto the Father but by Me" (John 14. 6).

4. "I WILL SAY UNTO GOD . . . IS IT GOOD UNTO THEE?" (chap. 10. 2, 3). Yes, say it unto God. Let the thoughts of the heart come up before Him. There is nothing hid from His eyes, and as a gracious Father He will even listen to our complaints. Many things may seem bad to us which are "good unto Him." If Job could have but known all the meaning of his sufferings, he no doubt would have said, "Good is the will of the Lord." He had said this before (chap. 1. 21).

5. "THOU KNOWEST THAT I AM NOT WICKED" (v. 7). If our hearts condemn us not then have we confidence toward God. Negative purity is not everything, but it is something. This is not the language of the Pharisee, "I thank God that I am not as other men," it is the honest confession of one who is not conscious of having, through sin, merited such terrible judgments. This is not a boast, but a protest against the idea of *punishment*, being an explanation of the mystery of his afflictions. We should surely bow with holy reverence, submission, and faith, when His hand is heavy upon us, if our hearts are clean. "The pure in heart shall see God."

6. "REMEMBER . . . THOU HAST MADE ME AS THE CLAY" (v. 9). Then it is not for the clay to resist the wonder

working hand of the Divine Potter. He will not reduce the clay to dust; the potter cannot fashion dry dust into a useful vessel. When we have been brought low by the weight of affliction, so low that we feel as if we had been brought back to that condition of soul in which we were at first, when God, by His Spirit, began to operate upon us. Let us believe that His purpose is to make us into "another vessel" more meet for His service; or in other words, when God's vessels are reduced again to *clay* it is that they might be refashioned for higher and more honourable work. Job's latter days is an evidence of this.

7. "I AM FULL OF CONFUSION, THEREFORE SEE THOU MINE AFFLICTION" (v. 15). This is an honest confession: he cannot understand the meaning of this terrible tragedy. He is covered with shame, yet his conscience is clear, but he makes his appeal to the eye of the Omniscient, "See Thou mine affliction." My light is turned into darkness, I cannot see, but see Thou. There is no confusion in the mind of God, no matter how perplexing and inexplicable His providence toward us may be. In the realm of spiritual things, human *reasonings* can only end in confession. Saul was full of confusion when he said, "What wilt Thou have me to do?" (Acts 9. 6). So were many on the Day of Pentecost, when they cried, "Men and brethren, what shall we do?" God who commanded light to shine out of darkness, can still bring order out of confusion. Commit thy way unto Him.

JOB'S COMFORTERS—ZOPHAR.
JOB 11-14.

The Speech of Zophar. Like the others, he is fully convinced that Job is suffering because of his sins, and like Bildad, he opens his address with some biting questions. He cannot bear to hear Job justifying his "doctrine as

pure" and his life as being "clean in thine eyes" (chap.
11. 4). So he says, as in an agony of soul, *"Oh that God
would speak!"* He is sure that if God would but speak, he
and his friends would be justified in all that they said, and
Job's secret sins revealed, and all his arguments confounded and put to shame. They found it otherwise
when God did speak (chap. 42. 7). We may know much,
but let us remember that we don't know everything. He
that exalteth himself shall be abased. But Zohpar goes
on to say, "Canst thou by searching find out God? Canst
thou find out the Almighty unto perfection?" A perfection that is "high as Heaven," "deeper than Hell," "longer
than the earth and broader than the sea." The soul makes a
great find when it finds God, although it may never be able
to search out the fathomless depths of His infinite per-
fections. This is eternal life, to know Him and Jesus
Christ whom He hath sent. The closing part of his speech
contains wonderful words and might be called—

A HOMILY ON THE WAY OF LIFE.

I. The Needed Work. He mentions three things that
are essential to salvation:

1. "Prepare thine heart" (v. 13). The heart needs
preparation, for it is deceitful above all things. The one
good thing found in Jehoshaphat was that he "prepared
his heart to seek God" (2 Chron. 19. 3). The best way
to get the heart prepared is to yield it unto the Lord
(Prov. 16. 1).

2. "Stretch out thine hands." Let the hands of
prayer and supplication be stretched toward God. He only
can bring about the great deliverance so much needed.
He is able to save to the uttermost. Stretch out thine
empty, helpless hands to Him, whose mighty hands are
outstretched in mercy for the uplifting of the poor and the
needy.

3. "PUT AWAY INIQUITY" (v. 14). Let the wicked forsake his wicked ways, and his unrighteous thoughts about God, and let him *turn*, and the Lord will have mercy upon him. "He that covereth his sins shall not prosper." Those who would draw nigh to God must confess and forsake their sins. Then, what follows?

II. The Blessed Result. Such heart preparation, and stretching out of hands, will certainly be answered in a copious, soul-satisfying measure. Zophar mentions eight privileges that will be enjoyed.

1. "Thou shalt LIFT UP THY FACE without spot" (v. 15). Thou shalt have *confidence* before God, and a clean countenance. All the boil spots of sin and suffering will be taken away (1 John 3. 19).

2. "Thou shalt be STEDFAST." Established as a house built upon the rock. Taken from the fearful pit, and the feet established in the ways of truth and righteousness.

3. "Thou shalt FORGET THY MISERY" (v. 16). Like Joseph, in the day of his exaltation and glory, thou shalt forget all the toil of the past (Gen. 41. 51). In the joy of the new life in Christ, the wretchedness of the old life of sin is forgotten.

4. "Thou shalt SHINE FORTH...as the morning" (v. 17). Thou shalt not only be illumined, but shall also become a guiding light to others. This new light is not of thine own kindling, but, like the dawning of the day, it is the gift of God—the brightest and the best.

5. "Thou shalt be SECURE, because there is hope" (v. 18). Thou shalt have such a hope as will make you and all your higher interests perfectly secure—a hope that maketh not ashamed.

6. "Thou shalt take thy REST IN SAFETY." Thou shalt have such a rest as cannot be disturbed by the turmoils of earth—a God-given rest (Matt. 11. 28).

7. "Thou shalt lie down, and NONE SHALL MAKE THEE AFRAID" (v. 19). Thy salvation will be so perfect that thou shalt be fearless in the face of men or of devils. This is the blessing wherewith the Lord shall bless all those who put their trust in Him.

8. "MANY WILL ENTREAT THY FACE" (v. 19, *margin*). The face that has been lifted up to God, and cleansed and brightened, is always attractive.

Job's Reply. His answer to Zophar occupies three chapters, and has reference to the unanimity of his three friends in condemning him through a false judgment of his case. "No doubt but ye are the people, and wisdom will die with you" (chap. 12. 2). Perhaps if they had prayed more and argued less, they all would have come sooner to a better understanding of the whole case. As long as they trusted their own wisdom, and depended on the skill and force of their own reasonings, they were all "physicians of no value" (chap. 13. 4). Their prescriptions were worthless, because their diagnosis was wrong. In this world of mysteries we cannot judge moral principles by physical symptoms. Job's well-known saying in chapter 13, verse 15, expresses the true attitude of the soul in the midst of such a storm of bewildered suffering, "Though He slay me—or is slaying me—yet will I trust—or wait for Him." Knowing as we do the Divine purpose in Job's calamities, it makes it much easier for us to say, like the Psalmist, "Yea, though I walk in the shadow of death, I will fear no evil" (Psa. 23. 4), or with the apostle, "I am persuaded that neither death...*nor any other creature* shall be able to separate me from the love of God" (Rom. 8. 38, 39). In the last part of his speech the patriarch deals with *man* in general (chap. 14). This portion might be fitly entitled—

WHAT IS MAN?

It has been said that "man was made to mourn." This

chapter begins with "man" and ends with "mourn." But hear the voice of this man of sorrows.

1. Man! he "is FULL OF TROUBLE" (v. 1). His troubles are so numerous that he is brimful of them. "He is as a rotten thing" (chap. 13. 28). Who can bring a clean thing out of this? (v. 4). Who is able to prescribe for such a complication of troubles as man's? What a bundle of miseries God has to deal with in saving man.

2. Man! HE "FLEETH ALSO LIKE A SHADOW" (v. 2). As the cloud shadows rush along the hillside like breathless spectres, so man hurries on from the mystery of birth to the mystery of death. Here he has no continuing city. He cometh forth like a flower, to be seen and felt by a few, and cut down.

3. Man! HIS DAYS AND MONTHS ARE NUMBERED (v. 5). The limit of his life has been fixed by God. He knoweth not when the end will be. He has not even authority for saying, "I will do so and so *to-morrow*."

4. Man! HE "DIETH AND WASTETH AWAY" (v. 10). He soon becomes insensible to the pains or pleasures of earth, his mental and physical powers speedily waste away. He has scarcely attained maturity when the wasting process begins.

5. Man! HE "GIVETH UP THE GHOST, AND WHERE IS HE?" (v. 10). He yieldeth up his spirit as one who cannot keep it longer, but where has he gone? Where is he? He must be somewhere. The *where* depends on the character of that spirit (see Luke 16. 22, 23).

6. Man! HE "LIETH DOWN, AND RISETH NOT TILL THE HEAVENS BE NO MORE" (v. 12). When he lieth down it is till the dawning of the new heavens (Isa. 65. 17). This seemed a long way off to Job, but it is not so far away now (1 Thess. 4. 14-16).

7. Man! "IF HE DIE, SHALL HE LIVE AGAIN?" (v. 14).

"There is hope of a tree, if it be cut down, that it will sprout again" (v. 7), and how much better is a man than a tree? Job was not without the hope of immortality; he knew that after his body had been destroyed by worms, that he would yet—in another body—see God (chap. 19. 25, 26). This question finds its perfect answer in Rev. 20. 12: "I saw the *dead*, small and great, stand before God."

THE WORK OF THE DEVIL.
JOB 16. 7-14.

IN this book we see much more than "the patience of Job;" we are face to face with the dreadful deeds of the Devil; for just now Job is in the hand of Satan, but with this Divine limitation, "Save his life" (chap. 2. 6). The upright patriarch would fain see the hand of God in it all, and this constrains him to say something about God, that coming from other lips would be sheer blasphemy; but God graciously overlooks it all. He knows that His servant is entirely in the dark as to the purpose and cause of his sufferings. By the Lord's permission, Satan was the cause of all his sorrows. Job, in the midst of his hopeless misery, is a finished specimen of the Devil's workmanship. His purpose and business is to kill and to destroy. It is a terrible thing to fall into the hands of the living Devil. The "god of this world" is also a "consuming fire." Our God consumes the chaff and the dross, but this god would burn up the wheat and the silver. The Lord delights to *give*, but Satan glories in *taking away*. Note here some of his devices—

I. **He Separates from the Best Company.** "Thou hast made desolate all my company" (v. 7). His family was cut off, and even his wife became strange to him. The fellowships in which he formerly delighted had all been broken up by the hand of the enemy, and his new friends were all miserable comforters. This is what happens when any child of God falls into the condemnation of the Devil through yielding to sin. Christian fellowship is made desolate, and the company that he keeps, in his backsliding state, are miserable helpers in his time of need. Satan is a professional schismatic. Beware of him in the church and in the family.

II. He Disfigures the Face. "Thou hast filled me with wrinkles" (v. 8). The joy and peacefulness that used to beam in the countenance of Job has now given place to gloom and discontent. Those who walk in fellowship with the Lord have their faces transfigured with the heavenly light, but those in the power of the Devil have often his own dark image stamped upon their faces. The Devil will so mar and blacken the face that the man is ashamed to lift it up unto God. This satanic change has often been observed in the countenance of backsliders. The wrinkles of sullen despair and God-defiance are easily seen. That face that should be illumined with the glory of God, becomes an index of the darkness of death.

III. He Brings Leanness into the Life. "My leanness beareth witness to my face." No wonder the face gets wrinkled and disfigured when the soul is being starved to death. When the Devil gets a man out of touch with God he will soon get him out of touch with His Word. The Devil's corn is all bran, and his wheat nothing but chaff. His dupes mistake quantity for quality; they may eat much, but still *leanness* "riseth up in them." No servant of sin can know anything of the soul-satisfying fullness of the Lord Jesus Christ.

IV. He Takes Advantage of the Helpless. "He teareth me in his wrath; he hateth me; he gnasheth upon me with his teeth" (v. 9). This language is highly figurative, but most terribly expressive. Satan can show no mercy, the weaker we are the better for him.   Job has been, for the time, handed over to him to be tested, and he makes it his business to pile on sorrow upon sorrow and agony after agony.   If he gets possession of a boy he will tear him and cast him into the fire and into the waters (Mark 9. 22), he hath no compassion on the helpless lad.   If he even gets hold of the helpless swine, he will hurl them out into the sea.   To be without Christ is to be without power and without a defence against the wiles and wrath of the Devil.   Tears have no effect on him (v. 16).

V. He Breaks Asunder, and Shakes to Pieces (v. 12). Job "was at ease" in his prosperity, like a ship at sea with a fair wind, but suddenly the ship was overtaken with a crushing tempest, and driven furiously on the rocks, and broken asunder, and shaken to pieces by the violence of the waves.   Whenever Satan gets hold of the helm of the life he seeks to make a shipwreck of the faith.   He will break the soul asunder, separating all he can get of it from God and spiritual things, and shake in pieces the future prospects of his victims.

VI. He has Many Helpers.   "His archers compass me round about" (v. 13).   The Devil has many angels, or demons, waiting his bidding to surround the soul, guarding every way of escape, and ready to shoot their fiery darts at every attempt made for liberty and salvation.   It is no easy matter for some to escape out of the hands of this Giant Despair.   His archers are sharp-eyed, and have had long practice in dealing with fugitives.   They know when and where to hit to be most effective.   Men and women that are likely to do damage to his kingdom are specially watched. His most zealous servants usually prove, when delivered, his bitterest enemies.   No garrison of demons can hinder a soul for a moment when the overcoming blood of Christ is trusted.

VII. He Uses Powerful Tactics. "He runneth upon me like a giant" (v. 14). He does not trifle with his opportunities. When he sees a chance of overcoming any upright man, he *runneth* like one in haste to catch a felon, and grips at once with a giant hand. He lingers about the gates of the soul, with luring temptation and bewitching enticement, until he gets a gate open, then he rushes in like a giant, to overthrow the citadel. He is a strong one, and seeks to get possession of the goods of man's soul, and then make peace, a peace that means certain death and destruction. But a stronger than he has come to spoil him of his goods, establish a new order of things, making peace and inaugurating the Kingdom of Heaven. "Resist the Devil and he will flee from you." Job longed for "One that might plead for a man with God." To us, Jesus Christ is that One (v. 21).

_____

TERRIBLE PROSPECTS.
Job 18. 5-18.

BILDAD begins his second speech, if anything, more exasperated than the others at the reasonings of Job. His wickedness must be very great he thinks, when he still persists in justifying himself in their eyes, and maintaining his integrity in the sight of God. The Shuhite's description of the dreadful calamities that are sure to come upon the wicked, and those that "knoweth not God" (v. 21), is most graphic and appalling in its fullness and truthfulness, but utterly wasted on the innocent patriarch. Still, we feel thankful to Bildad for these burning words. As a description of the condition and prospects of those who are living in lawlessness toward God, it is one of the most powerful within the compass of the Bible. The key-note of this terrible speech is found in the last sentence of it: "And this is the place (portion) of him that knoweth not God" (v. 21). See what this portion is. It implies—

I. Darkness. "The light of the *lawless* shall be put out, and the spark of his fire shall not shine" (v. 5). The light of the ungodly is of their own making; it is but the sparks of the fire which they themselves have kindled, and which *shall not shine* when abiding light is needed (Isa. 50. 10, 11). This light is in their own eyes, and when their eyes grow dim, and faint, and blind, their candle is put out, and darkness settles down in the tabernacle of the soul. How different it is with the man of faith! He can say, "The Lord my God who hath lit my candle, He will enlighten my darkness" (Psa. 18. 28).

II. Disappointment. "The steps of his *strength* shall be straitened, and his own *counsel* shall cast him down" (v. 7). The confidence of the self-righteous and the ungodly is in their strength and their wisdom, but both shall utterly fail to bring them into their desired haven. The *steps* of *his strength* shall be suddenly shortened and hindered, so that he will be compelled to give up the objects of his pursuit, and sink down like a weary exhausted traveller who has lost his way and finds it impossible for him to reach his home. "His own counsel shall cost him dear." His boasted wisdom shall turn out to be his confusion. The counsel he has given to others shall cover his own face with shame, when he staggers and falls under the burden of his own folly and failure. "He that trusteth in his own heart is a fool." By the wisdom of this world God is not known.

III. Danger. The position of the ungodly is so fraught with dangers that the fowler's vocabulary is exhausted in describing them. "His feet in a *net*...the *gin* shall take him by the heel...the *noose* (R.V.) shall prevail against him...the *snare* is laid for him...a *trap* set for him in the way" (vv. 8-10). Satan uses every possible means to prevent that man who "knoweth not God" from escaping out of his hands. But it is with "his own feet" that a man walks into the Devil's net. It is when he yields to temptation that the noose "prevails against him." He falls into the snare of the Devil, because he walks in the Devil's territory. If he neglects the salvation of Jesus Christ, there is no escape for him; but by trusting Him the snare will be broken, and his soul shall escape like a bird.

IV. **Dread.** "Terrors shall make him afraid on *every side*" (v. 11). He may say peace, peace, but the time will come when terrors shall break in upon him from every side. Terrors behind him, and terrors in front of him; the past, the present, and the future, all full of dread. Terrors crowding in upon him, and "chasing him at his heels," like so many beasts of prey (v. 11, R.V.). What an awful experience, to go into eternity and up to the Judgment Throne of God, chased by the sins and iniquities of a God-neglected life. The terrors of the Lord must follow close upon the "heels" of the sinner. The guilty man's feet are never swift enough to outrun the pursuing justice of God.

V. **Desolation.** "The firstborn of DEATH shall devour his strength, root up his confidence, and bring him to the king of terrors" (vv. 13, 14). What a sorrowful plight to be in: strength devoured, confidence rooted up, and face to face with the king of terrors. The *firstborn* of death is like that disease, or physical disorder, which is the forerunner of death, and is gradually eating up the strength, and tearing the hope of health up by the roots, and bringing the life under the dominion of temporal death. Spiritually the *firstborn* of death is *unbelief*, that forerunner of eternal separation from God and Heaven, which devours all strength for the service of Christ, roots up all real confidence before God, and brings the soul into the bondage and dread of the king of terrors (Mark 16. 16). After death the judgment. The Lord, the righteous Judge, upon the great White Throne will be the King of Terrors to all who have rejected His redeeming grace (Rev. 6. 15-17).

VI. Despair. "His roots shall be dried up:..,his remembrance shall perish:...he shall be driven from light into darkness, and chased out of the world" (vv. 16-18). Could words present a more dismal picture than this? The "place of him that knoweth not God" is indeed the place of dispair. His *roots* shall be dried up, because they are not in God, but in the barren wastes of self and the world (Mal. 4. 1). His *remembrance* shall perish, because his name is not written in the Lamb's book of life. He shall be *driven* from the light of the Gospel into the darkness of hopeless despair. He shall be *chased* out of the world as unworthy to live in it, as one unfit for the Kingdom of Heaven, and as one who is as loath to leave this world as Lot's wife was to leave Sodom.

VII. Destruction. "Destruction shall be ready for his halting" (v. 12, R.V.). All that destruction means is here personified as a powerful enemy. Keeping step with the man that knows not God, watching, and waiting for that moment when death shall cause him to halt, that he might have the opportunity of accomplishing his dreadful work. To the ungodly, death means destruction. It is the destruction of all his coveted fellowships, of all his boasted possessions, of his joy, of that false peace with which he comforted himself, of his hope for time and eternity. It is the destruction of all the faculties of his soul for the seeing or enjoying of those pleasures which are at God's right hand. His god was his belly, his glory was his shame, and his end is destruction.

LIGHT IN DARKNESS.
Job 19. 25-27.

Job's soul was sorely vexed with the words of his would-be comforters. "These ten times have ye reproached me," he says. Anybody with enough hardness of heart can easily reproach another in the day of their downfall. "If ye will magnify yourselves against me," he continues then, "know now that God hath overthrown me" (vv. 5, 6). The overthrowing was the work of the Devil, and it was complete, permitted by God, as was the crucifixion of Christ, yet the work of "wicked hands." It is most interesting to notice that it was after Job had experienced the weakness and deceitfulness of *all earthly kinships*, that the vision of the kinsman-Redeemer came upon his desolate spirit. Surely this is the work of the Spirit of God, it is absolutely true to the manner of the Holy Spirit in New Testament times. The unsatisfactory nature, the insufficiency and inability of all earthly friendship to meet the needs of a sinful, sorrowful soul, must be fully realised, ere the glories of the kinsman-Redeemer can be fully appreciated. "I know that my Redeemer liveth" (v. 25). Who but the Lord Jesus Christ was ever able to record such a melancholy list of broken friendships as Job does in this chapter. Hear what he says about them: "My *brethren* are far from me...mine *acquaintance* are estranged from me...my *kinsfolk* have failed, my *familiar friends* have forgotten me...my *maids* count me a stranger...my *servant* gave me no answer...my breath was strange to my *wife*...all my *inward friends* abhorred me" (vv. 13-19). There was not one arm of flesh left on which he could lean, when this new light dawned upon him constraining him to say, "I know that my *kinsman-Redeemer* liveth," and that apart from my flesh I shall have God on my side (R.V.). We are cautioned by some commentators not to read

too much into these words, but we are bound to take
them as they stand, and believe they mean all that they
say   The teaching of the Spirit of God is not limited to
the conditions and circumstances of men.   The language
of Job here is full of prophetic meaning, and is rich in
spiritual consolation.   *We* can at least easily read into
these words—

I. The Fact of Redemption.   "My Redeemer liveth. "
What a relief for the oppressed and bewildered soul to
turn from the failing kinships of earth to the unfailing
Kinsman above, who ever liveth to make intercession for
us.   Yes, Job, out of all your troubles this Kinsman-
Redeemer will yet deliver you.   He shall redeem thy life
from destruction, and crown thee with lovingkindness and
tender mercies.   He *vindicates* the cause of all who put
their trust in Him.   He who redeems and purchases the
soul by His own blood lives for the salvation and vindi-
cation of His own.   That HE, the eternal Son of God,
should condescend to be our Goel (kinsman) is the mystery
and marvel of infinite grace.

II. The Joy of Personal Assurance.   "I know. "   He
knew that all his earthly friends had forsaken him, but he
also knew that his Kinsman in Heaven, the living One
would ultimately prove Himself to be good and faithful.
There were some things Job did not know.   He knew not
the reason why he had been so suddenly stripped of every
earthly comfort, and crushed down to the dust with a load
of sorrow, but he knew and believed that "*my* Redeemer
liveth, " and liveth to make all things work together for
good to them that love Him.   He could scarcely talk now
of *my* brethren, *my* kinsfolk, *my* friends, *my* servant, for
they had all forsaken him, but he could say "MY
REDEEMER. "   When heart and flesh fail, God will be the
portion of the believing soul.   It will still be sweet to say,

"my Redeemer," when all the joys and friendships of this world have to be left behind.

III. **The Prospect of His Appearing.** "I know... that He shall stand at the latter day upon the earth." All that this meant to Job we cannot say, but he surely believed in the personal appearing of his great Kinsman-Redeemer on the earth. Now we know that this prophecy hath been fulfilled, and that the Redeemer hath come, and by the sacrifice of Himself has put away sin—the seed of the woman hath bruised the serpent's head—and by His own blood hath provided a ransom price for the souls of men. The earth needed Him, and He hath identified Himself with its sins and sorrows by standing on it and dying for it. To us these words are still prophetic, and we look for the appearing of our great God and Saviour Jesus Christ, who shall yet as King of kings stand in the latter day upon the earth.

IV. **The Hope of a Beatific Vision.** "Though worms destroy this body, yet without my flesh shall I see God" (R.V., *margin*). The flesh is the veil that hides the vision of God from the spirit of man. Even the Redeemer's flesh had to be rent asunder as a veil, ere the new way of entrance could be made for us (Heb. 10. 20). Paul's way of putting it is, "*Absent* from the body, *present* with the Lord" (2 Cor. 5. 8). When He shall appear we shall be like Him, for we shall see Him as He is. "The pure in *heart* shall see God." If there be no God to see, why should the purest of hearts have this longing and hope strongest within them? It surely does not follow, that because a man is good and upright, he is in greater danger of being deluded and deceived in the most important of all questions—that of future hope.

V. **The Confidence of Final Satisfaction.** "Whom I shall see on my side...and not as a stranger" (v. 27, R.V.,

margin). God's present dealings with Job are to him full of
mystery and contradictions. All things seem to be against
him, but when apart from his flesh he sees God, he knows
that he will find that God all along has been on His side,
making all things work together for his good. He will not
see Him as a *stranger*, but as a faithful *Kinsman-
Redeemer.* Here "we see through a glass darkly, but then
face to face." What we know not now we shall know
hereafter. Our present circumstances may be as perplexing
to human reason as Job's was to him; but with the vision
of our Divine Kinsman before us, we are assured that in
love He is doing all things well. "I shall be satisfied
when I awake" (Psa. 17. 15) in the presence of His likeness.

THE WICKED MAN'S PORTION.
JOB 20. 29.

ZOPHAR winds up this speech, which is full of the horrors
which belong to a life of ungodliness, with these words:
"This is the portion of a wicked man from God" (v. 29).
It is interesting to find that this is the view of wickedness
held by these wisest of men, away back in times before the
law was given. The word "wicked" here is *lawless*, and
refers to those who are not restrained in any way through
the knowledge or fear of God. The description still holds
good of the man that *obeys not* the Gospel of Jesus Christ.

I. **His Triumph shall be Short** (vv. 5-7). He does
triumph in a way; he has "joy," he has "excellency,"
and his head seems to "reach unto the clouds." His
success is of such a nature that failure and ruin looks
like an impossibility. But his triumph is short, his
joy is but for a moment, his excellency shall perish like
his own dung. Like the Egyptians, these lawless ones say,
"*I will* pursue, *I will* overtake, *I will* divide, *my lust* shall

be satisfied; but God shall blow upon them, and they shall
sink like lead in the mighty waters of death and destruction" (Exod. 15. 9, 10). Permanent victory only belongs
to those who "Overcome by the blood of the Lamb."

II. **His Sin shall Abide with Him.** "His bones are
full of the sin of his youth, which shall lie down with
him in the dust" (v. 11). David dreaded this terrible
experience when he prayed, "Remember not the sins of my
youth" (Psa. 25. 7). SIN is a most uncomfortable bed-
fellow to lie down with in the grave. No human power
can shake it off. It seeks to cling to the soul in death, in
resurrection, in judgment, and in eternity. To die in sin
is to die out of Christ, and to meet Him with a sin-stained
resurrection body.

III. **His Moral Appetite shall be Vitiated.** "Wickedness sweet in his mouth...yet the gall of asps within him"
(vv. 12-14). He finds that sweet to his taste which he
knows shall prove bitter to his conscience. Through
practice and force of habit he now clings to the things
which, in his innermost nature he condemns. His moral
senses are so blunted and perverted that he calls bitter
sweet, and sweet bitter. The lie of Satan is more pleasant
to him than the truth of God. He loves darkness rather
than light, and prefers the broken cisterns to the Fountain
of living water.

IV. **His Precious Things shall all be Disgorged.**
"He hath swallowed down riches, and he shall vomit
them up again" (v. 15). Many a valuable thing he hath
swallowed for the satisfaction of his own lust and passion.
Much goods have been laid up for the future, as a gourmand
would stuff his stomach against coming want, but he shall
vomit them up again, as one who is sickened by them, and
finds himself unable longer to keep them. The things
which formerly delighted him, and in which he trusted

for future strength and succour, will suddenly become
soul-sickening and turned into a vomit.   The riches of
Christ will never be so parted with.

V. His Abundance shall not Satisfy.   "In the
fullness of his sufficiency he shall be in straits" (v. 22). No
matter how much a man may have of the world's riches and
honours, *he* shall still be in straits if the "one thing
needful" is lacking—personal acquaintance with God.
Sufficiency of perishing things cannot meet all the needs of
an imperishable spirit.   The rich man mentioned in Luke
12 was in straits when he said: "What shall I do?"   But
he was in a greater strait when God said unto him: "This
night thy soul shall be required of thee; then whose shall
these things be?"

VI. His Treasures shall be Found to be Darkness.
"All darkness is laid up for his treasures" (v. 26, R.V.).
What an inheritance this is, reserved for those who die
rebels against the grace of God.   Darkness laid up for
him—*all* darkness, nothing but darkness—as the reward of
his earthly life and labours.   Complete disaster is secretly
lurking in the future for him.   His treasures are not in
Heaven, and outside the light of God's presence there is
nothing but the blackness of darkness.   He loved the darkness of a godless life rather than the light of a godly life.
Now all is darkness!   The seed sown has brought forth its
harvest of blackness.

VII. His Iniquity shall be Revealed.   "The Heavens
shall reveal his iniquity" (v. 27).   Even "the earth shall
rise up against him."   The heavens and the earth shall
combine to carry out the unerring word of God.   "The
Lord will bring to light the hidden things of darkness, and
will make manifest the counsels of the hearts" (1 Cor. 4. 5).
"There is nothing *covered* that shall not be revealed" (Luke
12. 2).   Every unforgiven sin and crooked thing shall be

made manifest by the searchlight of Heaven; then who that have died without Christ shall be able to stand when He appeareth as the Judge of the quick and the dead? No Achan will ever be able to bury his sins deep enough that the eye of God will not see them. The portion of the wicked (lawless) is indeed a miserable portion, but, thank God, it may be exchanged for a better portion, if, like Mary, he will choose now the "better part" (Luke 10. 42).

THE PRAYER OF THE WICKED.
JOB 21. 14, 15.

IN Job's reply to Zophar's last speech, he shows that material prosperity is not sufficient evidence that a man is morally righteous, for the wicked "become old and are mighty in power." But in these verses he lays bare the secret thoughts of the ungodly and lawless soul by putting this prayer into their mouth. The godless man of the world would not perhaps audibly dare to use these words, but nevertheless they are practically the sentiments of his every-day life. Look at—

I. **The Meaning of It.** It reveals a—

1. DREAD OF GOD'S PRESENCE. "They say unto God, Depart from us." Their carnal mind is enmity against God. They fear His presence as the owl does the approach of the sun, or as the thief dreads the daylight. As a gracious Saviour, they may say to Him, "Depart," and He may leave their coast, but, as a Judge, they will yet hear Him say, "Depart from Me."

2. DISLIKE AT GOD'S WAYS. "We desire not the knowledge of Thy ways." They are wedded to their own ways, and are not willing to forsake them (Isa. 55. 7). The knowledge of God's ways would make them more miserable in their own sinful ways. They cover their heads with the mantle of ignorance, and say darkness is better than light.

Though His ways are pleasantness and His paths peace, their minds are so blinded by the god of this world, and their spiritual appetite so vitiated, that they have no *desire* for them.

3. DENIAL OF GOD'S CLAIMS. "What is the Almighty, that we should serve Him?" They do not even say, "Who," as Pharaoh did, but "What," as if He were a creation of man, instead of the Creator of all. The Almightiness in their estimation is in the *"we."* What is He that *we* should serve Him. This exalting of self above all that is called God is the essence of Satanic opposition. Those who make it their business to serve themselves are morally unfit for the service of God. "Ye cannot serve two masters."

4. DISBELIEF IN GOD'S LOVE. "What profit shall we have if we pray unto Him?" They have no faith in God as a loving Father ready and willing to answer the cry of the needy. They have no consciousness of real need, and so have no faith in prayer. Like the Laodiceans, they have "need of nothing," not even of Him who stands knocking outside their door. They also said in their own way, "Depart from us, for we desire not the knowledge of Thy ways," by keeping the door closed against His entrance. "Ye have not because ye ask not." Men ought always to pray and not to faint.

II. **The Cause of It.** *"Therefore* they say unto God," etc. The occasion of it is found in the foregoing verses. In their worldly prosperity they had many marks of the goodness of God, *yet* they said unto God, "Depart from us," etc. (R.V.). This lawless spirit manifests itself in the grossest ingratitude and thanklessness. The prosperity of the wicked is a mystery to those who know not that "the wicked have their portion in this life." Observe the nature of that prosperity as it appeared to the afflicted patriarch.

1. THEIR INFLUENCE IS GREAT. "The wicked become old, yea, are mighty in power" (v. 7). Long years after this the Psalmist said the same thing, "I have seen the wicked in great power, and spreading *himself* like a green bay tree" (Psa. 37 35). The godly man seeks to spread the knowledge of God, but the godless, selfish worldling spreads himself. The world loves its own, and admires the man who is able to spread himself like a green bay tree, although he should starve to death all the lesser plants that seek an existence beneath his shade.

2. THEIR AFFLICTIONS ARE FEW. "Their houses are safe from fear, neither is the rod of God upon them" (v. 9). They don't seem to be afflicted as other men. Grey hairs don't seem to come so quickly upon their heads. They are quite unaccustomed to the yoke of discipline. The rod of Divine chastisement does not visit them because they are not harnessed to the will of God, but are, like the wild asses, doing their own pleasure. They have a liberty, but it is the liberty of the *lawless*, the freedom of the rebel. The rod and staff of the Great Shepherd does not guide them, so they rush on comfortably to destruction. "Whom the Lord loveth He chasteneth."

3. THEIR POSSESSIONS ARE MULTIPLIED. "Their bull gendereth, and faileth not; their cow calveth, and casteth not her calf" (v. 10). "Behold the ungodly...they increase in riches" (Psa. 73. 12). They add house to house, and land to land, and offer sacrifices to their own genius (Hab. 1. 16). The rich *fool* had not where to bestow his goods. The meek shall yet *inherit* the earth, but meanwhile it seems to be largely the portion of the godless.

4. THEIR CHILDREN ARE HAPPY. "Their children dance ...and rejoice at the sound of the organ" (vv. 11, 12). Well, God bless the "little ones," why should they not be happy? They have not yet become positively lawless by

actual transgression. They are in ignorance of the enmity that lurks in the heart of that father to the being and grace of God. But they are in great danger of following in the steps of their world-deluded parents, by setting their affections on the things of earth and neglecting the eternal treasure. This picture of the ungodly is very attractive to many. No wonder the Psalmist said, "I was *envious* at the foolish, when I saw the prosperity of the wicked (they are not in trouble as other men...their eyes stand out with fatness; they have more than heart could wish)...UNTIL *I went into the sanctuary of God* and saw them in the light of His presence; then understood I their end" (Psa. 73. 3-17). They who said, "Who is the Almighty, that we should serve Him!" "shall drink of the wrath of the Almighty" (v. 20). What an awful cup awaits those who refuse the cup of salvation. The rich man died, and in Hell he *lifted up* his eyes. Better far to lift them up now.

ACQUAINTANCE WITH GOD.
Job. 22. 21-30.

IN closing his third speech, Eliphaz talks like a New Testament prophet. The phraseology is, of course, old, but the teaching is up-to-date, and the moral order in which the truths are presented are almost apostolic. His words suggest—

I. **A Great Need.** "Acquaint now thyself with Him, and be at peace" (v. 21). Acquaintanceship with God is the first step toward peace. A theoretical knowledge of God cannot satisfy the heart. *Acquaintanceship* implies a personal intimacy. After Adam, through sin, had separated himself from God, a new acquaintanceship had to be formed. Divine friendship had to be set up on a new basis (Gen. 3. 15). Sin implies separation and enmity;

acquaintanceship implies reconciliation and peace. No man now can be said to be acquainted with God who is a stranger to the Lord Jesus Christ, who bore the combined image of God and of man. He who was God manifest in the flesh, hath made peace by the blood of His cross. Kiss the Son lest He be angry with thee, and ye perish in the way. "This is life eternal that they might know Thee, the only true God, and Jesus Christ whom Thou hast sent" (John 17. 3).

II. **A Plain Way.** The way back into the favour and fellowship of God is very simple and easy to the willing heart. It is stated here in two words: "Receive!" "Return!" "Receive the law from His mouth,...and return to the Almighty" (vv. 22, 23). Receive into thine heart the word that has come from His mouth, believe what He hath said about sin and salvation, and return to God by yielding your will to Him, and resting your soul upon His finished redemption. We can now read into the words of Eliphaz a much deeper meaning than he could at that time understand. Receive the word of the Gospel and return, not to a creed or a church, but to the living God.

III. **A Manifold Result.** To be closely acquainted with any great personality will certainly affect our manner of thinking and acting; how much more when we are acquainted with GOD. There will be—

1. A RENEWAL OF THE NATURE. "Thou shalt be built up" (v. 23). The spiritual nature of man has been so broken down by sin that it is a complete ruin. Apart from the knowledge and grace of God, he can never build himself up as a temple of God. It is when we come into the light of His presence that we get rebuilt, and made new creatures. "If any man be in Christ he is a new creature." "We are His workmanship, created (anew) in Christ Jesus." Return unto Him just as you are, and He shall build thee up.

2. GREAT RICHES. "The Almighty shall be thy treasure" (v. 25, R.V.). The gold of Ophir is but the dust of the earth compared with the riches that are in Him. Material things cannot meet the needs of an immaterial spirit. Our eternal spirits need the adorning of the eternal God. Your little life shall be filled up out of His infinite fullness. When you get truly acquainted with Him, you will find that Himself is sufficient for thee. To know God is to be a spiritual millionaire. "My God shall supply all your need," (Phil. 4. 19), not only with His gifts, but with Himself. We have this treasure in the earthen vessel when we are filled with the Holy Spirit.

3. UNFAILING JOY. "Then shalt thou have thy delight in the Almighty" (v. 26). Only the pure in heart who see God can find their delight in Him. The unrenewed in nature will still seek after the world's broken cisterns, which cannot hold water enough to quench the thirst of the soul. Those who find their delight in God have the purest of all pleasures from a source which can never fail. "We joy in God through our Lord Jesus Christ, by whom we have received the reconciliation."

4. BOLDNESS OF ACCESS. "And shalt lift up thy face unto God." When we become the *children* of God through faith in Jesus Christ, it is but natural that we should lift up our faces unto our Father. The consciousness of unforgiven sin hinders many from lifting up their faces unto God (Luke 18. 13). Those who see no beauty in Him who was the Man of Sorrows, hide, as it were, their faces from Him. The open face turned to God is the evidence of a soul at peace with Him. "Our fellowship is with the Father."

5. ANSWERED PRAYER. "Thou shalt make thy prayer unto Him, and He shall hear thee" (v. 27). What a privilege! The ear of the Almighty God always at your

lips to hear thee when thou speakest unto Him. Speak out the desires of thy soul, and wait patiently on Him. "If we know that He hear us, whatsoever we ask, we know that we have the petitions that we desired of Him" (1 John 5. 15).

6. FRUITFUL TESTIMONY. "Thou shalt also decree a thing, and it shall be established unto thee" (v. 28). The word of thy testimony in His Name shall be made to stand firm. His word shall not return unto Him void. New eyes will be given thee to see wondrous things; and thy tongue shall speak forth things which God will make to come to pass (Jer. 23. 28).

7. WALKING IN THE LIGHT. "The light shall shine upon thy ways." Thou shalt not walk in darkness, for the guiding light of His presence shall be with thee. His Holy Spirit will guide thee into the truth, which always illumines the heart and mind. Just now Job was enveloped in thick darkness, but, by yielding Himself unreservedly to God, light would arise, and he would yet walk with a light step in the sunny paths of peace.

8. ABILITY TO HELP OTHERS. "When men are cast down, then *thou* shalt say, There is lifting up" (v. 29). We must be lifted up ourselves before we attempt to lift up others. There be many who are "cast down" through sin and shortcoming, disappointment and failure, many who need this cheering message, "There is lifting up." When crushed and broken spirits are saying, "Who will show us any good?" it is the privilege of those whose faces have been lifted up to God to carry the uplifting Gospel of Jesus Christ, who was "lifted up," that He might draw men to Himself. The man of God is the only man that has the real message of hope for fallen humanity.

THE OUTSKIRTS OF GOD'S WAYS.
Job 26. 6-14.

Job's three comforters said much, and did the best they could, but their remedies never touched the disease. They were as blind men seeking to lead a blind man. In the previous chapter, Bildad, whose great arguments have all been already spent in vain, has his last little say which closes the whole case for him and his friends. Now when they have exhausted themselves, Job begins his great and final oration, which occupies the following six chapters. These wonderful words bear ample proof that although Satan had brought such ruin and desolation upon Job, he had no power to touch his living spirit within. His mind remained clear, which doubtless made his anguish all the more keen. In brief but striking language we have here parts of His ways set before us. If these are but the "outskirts" (R. V.)—the ripple on the shore of the Divine doings, what must it be to get into the centre of the operations of God. What, then, are these merely out-lying acts of the great Creator of all? Here they are—

I. **"Hell is naked before Him"** (v. 6). Sheol, or the shady world of spirits, lies uncovered before His gaze. His eyes pierce the gloom of that awful abyss called "the bottomless pit. " If I make my bed in Hell (Sheol) Thou art there—there in justice and judgment. No darkness, no matter how dense, can cover a human soul from the holy eye of God (Psa. 139. 8-11). If Hell is naked before Him, so is your heart and mine. There is many a human heart that is little else than a miniature Hell, yet it, with all other things, is naked and opened unto the eyes of Him with whom we have to do (Heb. 4. 13).

II. **"He Hangeth the Earth upon Nothing"** (v. 7). Some seem to be afraid lest we should read into these words more than was meant by the afflicted patriarch, lest we

credit Job with knowing more about astronomy than he
really did. He surely meant what he said when he said,
"He hangeth the earth upon *nothing.*" He could not mean
that He hangeth the earth on *something.* The statement is
scientifically accurate, although made thousands of years
before the fact was discovered by science. But the point
is, this wonderful balancing of worlds in space is but one
of the outworks of this wonder-working God. Job may not
know anything about the law of gravitation, but, if moved
by the Spirit of God, he speaks worthy of God. The Spirit
of truth is always in advance of the discoveries of men.

III. **"He Bindeth up the Waters in His Thick Clouds"**
(v. 8). The seemingly fickle clouds are God's. He binds
them together with invisible bands so that they cannot be
rent to pour out their treasures until He unties them.
How often have we seen those great water-carriers rolling
along the heavens, and piled up at times like huge bales
of wool. "Great and marvellous are Thy works, O Lord."

IV. **"He Closeth in the Face of His Throne"** (v. 9.
R.V.). Behind all the laws and forces of nature, Job sees
the throne of God. The whole visible creation is as a veil
spread over the face of His eternal throne, but the glory and
majesty of the Divine Personality, who ruleth over all,
shines through this cloudy covering. The material world is
like the pillar of cloud in the wilderness. God is in the
midst of it. Clouds and darkness are round about Him
(Psa. 97. 2).

V. **"He Describeth a Boundary upon the Face of the
Waters"** (v. 10, R.V.). The waters of the great deep are in
the hollow of His hand, and by His infinite wisdom He has
marked out that line which we call the horizon, where the
sea and sky seem to meet and kiss each other. God sets
His limitations to every earthly thing. So far, but no
farther; but the Spirit-taught soul looks beyond to the

things which are eternal and lie hidden in the depths of eternity.

VI. **"He Stirreth up the Sea with His Power"** (v. 12, R.V.). The same mighty hand that pushed back the rolling flood and made "dry land" that the Israelites might pass over, still controls the restless billows (Psa. 74. 13).

VII. **"He Smiteth through Rahab"** (v. 12, R.V.). Rahab stands for pride and arrogance. By His understanding is human pride smitten through. The wisdom and power of God, even as seen in the visible creation, ought to pierce the arrogance of man. But how much more ought the wisdom and love of God, as seen in the Cross of Christ, stay the enmity of the carnal mind. Rahab is condemned already.

VIII. **"He hath Garnished the Heavens by His Spirit"** (v. 13). The same Spirit who beautified the heavens now beautifies the soul in whom He dwells. "The Spirit of God *moved* upon the face of the waters." His *moving* is always for the glory of God, whether it be in the heart or in the heavens. Bildad said, "Yea, the stars are not pure in His sight." But Job takes a different view of that work which at the beginning was pronounced "good." When the beauty of the Lord our God is put upon us, we are clean and beautiful in His sight. The Spirit of God is a wonderful artist. He who beautified the heavens can beautify thy life.

IX. **He hath Subdued the Swift Serpent** (v. 13, R.V.). Whether this swift fleeing serpent is the Devil, or the forked lightning-flash, it matters not, both are under His control. Neither of them can fly so fast that God cannot at any time pierce them through with His arrow. The forked lightning is an apt emblem of the movements and terrible character of Satan, but he is a conquered foe.

What a mighty God our God is, when THESE are but the

outskirts of His ways, part of the fringe of the great garment of His works. In these parts of His ways, Job adds, we hear but *a small whisper of Him* (v. 14, R.V.). From the visible creation there comes an unmistakable "whisper of Him," which any attentive ear may hear. The voice may be "small," but it is the voice of God. In creation, we hear the small whisper of the goodness of God; but in Christ, the loud cry of an agonising heart of love. This God who in times past whispered into the dull ears of men, through the marvellous works of His hands, now speaks with a loud voice through the death of His Son. "God in these last days hath spoken unto us by His Son" (Heb. 1. 2). "To-day, if ye will hear His voice, harden not your hearts." Consider the two *cries* of Christ: John 7. 37; Matthew 27. 46.

PRICELESS WISDOM.
JOB 28. 12-28.

IN this chapter Job continues his wonderful parable. He has just been showing that there is a *place* where gold and silver and precious stones can be found (vv. 1-6), and how that men by searching and digging and overturning (vv. 9, 10) bring these hidden treasures to light, but as these can never meet all the needs of a human heart, he goes on to ask this great question of world-wide interest, "But where shall WISDOM be found?" (v. 12). A man may be loaded with the treasures of earth and yet be a fool (Luke 12. 19, 20). The soul of man cannot find its perfect satisfaction even in the very best that this world can yield it. Wisdom is the chief thing; with all thy getting, get wisdom.

I. **Its Nature.** Wisdom is not something we can put on like a garment. Wisdom is character; it is the quality of *being wise*; it is a condition of heart, and has to do with our relationship to God. It *begins* with fearing the Lord (v. 28), and grows as the knowledge of God increases. If Job had not "Christ, the wisdom of God" in his mind when he spoke these beautiful and far-reaching words, doubtless the guiding Spirit of God had, for they are brimful of New Testament meaning to all who are wise in Christ. Men have no difficulty in finding the wisdom of this world, which is foolishness with God, but a man is not truly wise until he becomes a partaker of the wisdom of God.

II. **Its Unearthliness.** "Where is wisdom to be found? and where is the place of understanding?" Where is this knowledge of God to be got? this wisdom of heart that enables a man so to act before God and men that it will bring satisfaction to his own soul, good to his fellows, and glory to God. Where? It is not found "in the land of the living" (v. 13). This barren wilderness of human beings cannot produce it. "The depth saith, It is not in me; and the sea saith, It is not with me" (v. 14). No created thing, or one, can offer to a thirsty soul this satisfying gift. Out of the *land*, and the *depths*, and the *sea*, men have brought multitudes of valuable things, but the wisdom that maketh wise unto eternal life has never yet been found there, although generation after generation have followed in diligent search. These are all as broken cisterns which cannot hold this heavenly water. Is there no answer to this cry of Job, "Where is the place?" Yes, that place is called Calvary, where Christ the wisdom of God is offered to a world perishing for lack of knowledge.

III. **Its Preciousness.** The language here concerning wisdom is sublimely graphic, if we read it with our eye on Him who is the wisdom of God.

1. IT CANNOT BE PRICED. "Man knoweth not the price thereof" (v. 13). What man on earth would dare to

attempt to reckon up the value of the Lord Jesus Christ?
"In Him are hid all the treasures of wisdom and knowledge" (Col. 2. 3)—"unsearchable riches."

2. IT CANNOT BE BOUGHT. "It cannot be gotten for
gold" (v. 15). All the wealth of the world could never
purchase the wisdom of God. It would be an insult to
God, even if man had the power, to offer Him a whole
world of gold as a price for His Son. Even the gold of
man's *righteousness* is as filthy rags when offered as a
recompense to God.

3. IT CANNOT BE EQUALLED. "The gold and the crystal
cannot equal it" (v. 17). "The price of wisdom is above
rubies; the topaz of Ethiopia shall not equal it" (vv. 18, 19).
The world's best cannot be compared with this gift of
God. The joy of finding rubies and diamonds cannot
equal the joy of finding the wisdom of God in Christ Jesus.

4. IT CANNOT BE EXCHANGED. "The exchange of it
shall not be for jewels of fine gold" (v. 17). Nothing can
take its place. There is no substitute or equivalent for
heavenly wisdom. Nothing will ever stand in Christ's
stead.

5. ITS POWER CANNOT BE DOUBTED. "Destruction
and death say, We have heard the fame thereof" (v. 22).
We have here the testimony of wisdom's enemies. The
fame of this wisdom is that it saves from "destruction and
death." They have heard the tidings to their cost.

IV. Its Discovery. Another question is asked,
"Whence then cometh wisdom?" (v. 20), and the answer
is, "God understandeth the *way* thereof, and He knoweth
the *place*" (v. 23). The *way* is the way of love and mercy,
the *place* is the place where Christ was crucified. Only
God could understand how the deep eternal need of man
can be fully met. He only could unveil the secret of
everlasting bliss. He alone knew where this soul-satisfying

treasure could be found.   Deliver from going down to the
pit, I have found the Ransom.   It will put a new meaning
into verse 27 if you read "Him" instead of "it." "He
did see *Him,* and declare *Him*; He prepared *Him,* yea, He
searched Him out." Then "unto man He said, Behold, the
fear of the Lord, that is wisdom; and to depart from evil
is understanding" (v. 28).   To be made a recipient of
this wisdom, we must so *fear* the Lord that we shall submit
ourselves entirely to Him, and so hate evil that we shall
depart from it.   Foolishness and evil go together; wisdom
and holiness are twin sisters.   "Whence then cometh
wisdom?"   Christ is made of God unto us wisdom,
which is accompanied with righteousness, sanctification,
and redemption.   "With all thy getting, get wisdom"
(Prov. 4. 7).

THE MAN IN GOD'S STEAD.

JOB 33.

AFTER the words of Job were ended, and the three men
had ceased to answer him, Elihu—God is He—broke forth
in holy wrath at the manner, or spirit, in which the great
controversy had been carried on.   Job had been more
inclined to justify himself than God, and his three friends
had condemned him without discovering a cause (chap. 32.
1-3).   Elihu had evidently been a silent listener during the
whole debate; but now, though young, he would unburden
his soul before them all.   This young man was not one of
the "three friends" who came to comfort Job; he is an
independent witness—an outsider, so to speak—specially
fitted by God to throw fresh light upon the mystery
of the whole case, or, at least, to put a new emphasis into
some of the phrases commonly used.   This is what the
"man of God" always does.   He does not speak a new
language; he does not coin ear-tickling sentences, he speaks

plain words with a new power. Elihu, then, comes before us as a typical Spirit-filled man, and as such we shall look at—

I. His Character. This apostle of the Old Testament will compare favourably in many ways with the great apostle of the New Testament. Of course, in judging Elihu by the light of New Testament teaching, we must never lose sight of the fact that we are putting a meaning into his words that perhaps Job or his friends or himself could not understand. But it is a wonderful evidence of the consistency of the Holy Spirit's work and words all down through the ages. He never contradicts Himself. If the Spirit of God fashioned and taught Elihu, He must, in some measure, reveal the same features of a Spirit-filled life to-day. Light is light, although it is 3000 years old. What are some of these features?

1. HE IS A SPIRIT-MADE MAN. "The Spirit of God hath made me" (v. 4). This may be true, in a general sense, of all men, but it is true, in a very special and unique sense, of the real "man of God." He is born by the Spirit— quickened by the Spirit into a new life. He is a new creation after the image of God by the Holy Ghost. God needs *new* vessels for the new wine of His Gospel.

2. HE IS A SPIRIT-INSPIRED MAN. "The breath of the Almighty hath given me life." This also may be true, in a measure, of every man, but it is a marvellous description of the new life in God. Those dead in sin need the breath of God to put new life into them (Ezek. 37. 9). Those quickened by the Spirit of God are possessed by Him and inspired, as by the very warmth of the breath of the living God dwelling in them. They can say: "I live, yet not I, but Christ, who is the life of God, liveth in me; the breath that I now breathe is the breath of the Almighty; the spirit that I now have is animated by the Spirit of God."

Christ *breathed* on them and said: "Receive ye the Holy Ghost."

II. **His Position**. Job longed for a "Daysman" (9. 33). Elihu is bold enough to say: "I am according to thy wish *in God's stead*" (v. 6). It was a great statement to make, but the man who is appointed by God to stand in His stead ought surely to know it, and should not be ashamed to confess it before men. Did not the Apostle of the Gentiles say: "*We* are ambassadors for Christ, as though God did beseech you *by us*: we pray you *in Christ's stead*, be ye reconciled unto God?" The man in God's stead is "an *interpreter*, one among a thousand, to shew unto man what is right for him" (v. 23 R. v.). He himself is an example and interpretation of the invisible God. His business is to seek first the Kingdom of God and His righteousness, and to exhort others to seek these first. He knows nothing about flattering men with self-pleasing titles (chap. 32. 22), the claims and character of Him whose he is and whom he serves are ever before him. An interpreter of God's mind and will must first be a partaker of that mind and will. We must drink deeply of this water of life, if we would become springs of living water for others. Every spirit-possessed man is an interpreter for God, and such interpreters are needed, for "the things of God knoweth no man, but the Spirit of God" (1 Cor. 2. 11). A man may have all the wisdom of the world, and yet be unable to interpret the things of God. "The natural man receiveth not the things of the Spirit of God" (1 Cor. 2. 14).

III. **His Message**. He it is who can say with the utmost confidence, "God speaketh" (v. 14). He knows in his own soul that God hath spoken to him, and that He can still speak in divers ways to the slumbering spirits of men, that He may draw man away from his evil and delusive purpose (vv. 15-17). This is a comforting truth

to those who seek the salvation of others, that God in
answer to prayer can speak to men "in dreams and visions
of the night." Even then He can open the ear, and seal
instruction in their hearts. So, the man of God is a man
of faith and hope. But he has also a very definite message
to deliver. What is that message? There is in it—

1. REDEMPTION. "Deliver him from going down to the
pit: I have found a ransom" (v. 24). God hath found
the ransom—the atoning sacrifice in the Man Christ Jesus
(1 Tim. 2. 5, 6), so He calls upon all those who stand in His
stead to say to that man going down to the pit of darkness
and death, "There is *deliverance*." He, as it were,
commands His servant and interpreter to "deliver him"
who is on the way to the pit, on the ground that He hath
found and provided the Ransom. Apart from the power
and virtue of the Cross of Christ, there is no message of
salvation from the pit to give. "The Son of Man came...
to give His life a ransom for many" (Matt. 20. 28).

2. REGENERATION. "His flesh shall be fresher than a
child's (v. 25). This may be figurative language, but
it expresses most forcibly the radical change which is
wrought by God's redeeming power. Like Naaman—after
he had dipped himself seven times in Jordan—he was made
a new creature. What the waters did for the famous Syrian
captain, the atoning blood of Christ now does for those who
believe Him—makes *clean*. The redemption that is in
Christ Jesus not only "*satisfies* thy mouth with good," but
also "thy youth is *renewed* like the eagle's" (Psa. 103. 5).

3. FELLOWSHIP. "He shall pray unto God, and He shall
be favourable unto him; and he shall see His face with
joy" (v. 26). After redemption and regeneration comes
the privilege of praying and *rejoicing* in the *favour* of God.
Yes, the pure in heart shall see God's face and rejoice—
that face of love and mercy which has been unveiled to us

in Jesus. "We joy in God through our Lord Jesus
Christ, by whom we have now received the atonement."
"Our fellowship is with the Father and with His Son"
(1 John 1. 3).

4. TESTIMONY. They who would preach redemption to
others should themselves be examples of its regenerating
power. The words here are full of evangelical fervour and
personal experience. "He *singeth* before men, and *saith*,
I have sinned and perverted that which was right, and it
profited me not; He hath redeemed my soul from going
into the pit, and my life shall behold the light" (vv.
27, 28, R.V.). His past life was *profitless*, because it was
one of *perversion*; but now, being *redeemed*, he lives in the
light of the truth. This man who is as one in "God's
stead" was once a sinner like others, but by grace was he
saved. "Such were some of you, but ye are washed." The
personal element must have a place in the preaching of
the Gospel.

THE LORD ANSWERED.
JOB 38. 1; 40. 1-5.

"MAN'S extremity is God's opportunity." It was when
the words of Job and his friends were ended that the Lord
answered Job out of the whirlwind. God's answer is
always final. There is no appeal. The book of Job, like
the books of the Old Testament, closes with the Theophany
—the *appearance* of God. Here, as when He sent His Son,
God's last plea was the manifestation of His own character.
Although God answered Job *out of* the whirlwind, we need
not infer that the *voice* was like a roaring, uprooting
tempest, but that the arguments used had a whirlwind
effect upon the spirit of Job, completely lifting him out of
his present condition of mind into a better way of thinking.

I. **Job's Prayer.** "Answer Thou me. How many are

mine iniquities and sins? Make me to know my transgression" (chap. 13. 22, 23). He was set on maintaining
his own way. He had lived, no doubt, in all good
conscience before God, but there was now a tendency to
boast of his integrity, as if it were something independent
of the grace of God. If I have sinned, he says, make
me to know the number and nature of my transgressions. God's answer to Job reveals the fact that his
iniquities lay in a different direction than what he
supposed. He is not charged with actual transgression,
but he is overwhelmed with a sense of his own ignorance
and impotency. His *self-confidence* has been rebuked
and withered up.

II. God's Answer. "Then the Lord answered Job"
(chap. 38. 1). God's answer comes in the form of an
avalanche of questions. There are fifty-seven in chapters
38 and 39 alone. Every question seems to bring with
it a flash of self-blinding light. Each interrogation is
in itself a revelation and an education to the wavering
patriarch. All His "hast thous" and "canst thous" are
evidences of what HE *has done* and *can do*. These questions
are so many revelations of God's wisdom and power—of
His perfect control of "the ordinances of Heaven" (chap.
38. 33), or of what we call natural phenomena. Those who
would find fault with the providence of God should study
this divine declaration. The Lord's first question is
enough to take Job's breath away: "Where wast *thou* when
I laid the foundations of the earth?" (v. 4). His word is
truly as a "hammer and a fire." Think of these burning
inquiries: "Hast *thou* commanded the morning?" "Hast
thou entered into the springs of the sea?" "Hast *thou*
walked in the secret of the depth?" "Hast *thou* entered
into the treasures of the snow?" "Canst *thou* bind the sweet
influences of Pleiades?" "Knowest *thou* the ordinances of

Heaven?" "Canst *thou* lift up *thy* voice to the clouds?"
"Canst *thou* send lightnings, that they may go and say unto
thee, Here we are?" The wisdom of man is but foolishness
with God, as the brightest of earth's lights is but a black
spot in the face of the sun. So man at his best is but a
vile speck in the presence of the glory of God.

   III. **Job's Confession.** "Behold, I am vile: what
shall I answer Thee? I will lay mine hand upon my mouth
Once have I spoken; yea, twice; but I will proceed no
further" (chap. 40. 4, 5). Job's boasted greatness, like the
tower of Babel, ended in utter confusion when God
appeared. As long as we compare ourselves with men like
ourselves there may be occasion for glorying, but let God
speak, then the hand is laid upon the mouth. "Behold, I
am vile," for this mouth of mine has been speaking the
God-dishonouring thoughts of my mind, but I will "proceed no further" along this way of self-confidence and self-
assertiveness. I will lay mine hand upon my mouth, and
bow in silent submission to the word and will of the Lord
my God. The Lord is in nature as in a holy temple; let all
the earth keep silence before Him. God who at sundry
times, and in divers manners, spake unto the fathers by the
prophets, and to Job through the whirlwind of natural
phenomena, has in these last days spoken unto us by His
Son. The voice is the same, but the revelation is vastly
different. What have we to say for ourselves in the
presence of the Cross of Christ? Here every boastful
mouth must be stopped. Although in self justification,
I have spoken once, yea, fifty times, "but I will proceed
no further" when I see sin in the light of the sufferings and
death of the only begotten Son of God. "Behold, I am
vile;" my righteousness, in the glare of His light, has
turned out to be but "filthy rags." "God be merciful to
me a sinner."

THE BLISSFUL END.

JOB 42.

THE storm-tossed soul of Job has got anchored at last in the harbour of God's manifest goodness. As a traveller he has been passing through a dark and dreary desert, hearing anon the howling of ravenous beasts, but is now entered into the light and joys of home. Through much tribulation he entered into this new kingdom of honour and blessing. All great spiritual attainments are reached through suffering. It was so with Moses, Abraham, Joseph, David, Daniel, and Christ. The disciple is not greater here than his Master. "If we suffer, we shall also reign." Now the great climax of Job's history has been reached, but there is about it more of the quietness of a birth than the shock of a revolution. The storm of words is over; the calm of His "Peace be still" has settled upon the troubled waters. In the closing act of this powerful drama there is—

I. **Confession.** Job began his brief answer to the Divine appeal by saying, "I know that Thou canst do everything, and that no thought can be withholden from Thee." Thou canst *do* everything, and Thou dost *see* everything. Thou art omnipotent and omniscient. The whole universe, visible and invisible, is under Thy control, and naked and bare before the eyes of Him with whom we have to do. As man is to be judged by his works, so may the Lord be judged by His. By *His works* ye shall know Him. "The heavens declare His glory, and the firmament showeth forth His handiwork" (Psa. 19. 1). But what does the Cross of His Christ declare? What handiwork does the firmament of His infinite love and mercy shew forth? In the matter of salvation, as well as creation and government, "I know that Thou canst do everything."

II. **Revelation.** "I have heard of Thee by the hearing of the ear, but now mine eye seeth Thee" (v. 5). It is

one thing to hear another speak about God; it is a very
different thing to see Him by the revelation of His own
word, spoken personally to the heart, as Job had now seen
Him. The sum of the LORD's answer to Job was a *manifestation of Himself* through His word. The voice of
God brought the vision of God to the patriarch's faith.
He saw God by the hearing of faith. "Believe, and thou
shalt see" (John 11. 40). "The Word of God is quick and
powerful,...and is a *discerner* of the thoughts and intents of
the heart" of man, and is also a *revealer* of the thoughts and
intents of the heart of God. This is the mystery of the
incarnation. "The *Word* which was God was made flesh
and dwelt among us,...full of grace and truth." Christ, the
Word of God, was to a suffering world the revelation of
God. You may have often heard of Him, but has your
eye yet seen Him?

III. Humiliation. "Wherefore I abhor myself, and
repent in dust and ashes" (v. 6). Self-abhorrence is the
natural consequence of coming face to face with God.
When Isaiah saw the Lord upon a throne high and lifted
up, he also abhorred himself, saying, "Woe is me!...
because I am a man of unclean lips" (Isa. 6. 5). Oh, these
lips! It was Job's lips that had been acting as traitors in
the cause of God. But the lips are only the instruments of
the heart and will. Where is boasting when the truth of
God comes home to the heart? It is excluded. Saul of
Tarsus found this out when the light of the exalted Son
of God fell upon him on the way to Damascus. Then he
abhorred himself and *repented*.

IV. Intercession. "My servant Job shall pray for
you; for him will I accept" (v. 8). Job's friends did
all that human wisdom and eloquence could do for a man
overwhelmed by the power of the Devil, and that was
nothing. This kind goeth not out but by prayer and

sacrifice. *"My servant,"* sweet words to the perplexed and bruised sufferer. It is easy for us to thrash others with our scourge of words, whose prayers we need to save us from our sins. What a privilege and responsibility rests upon the servant of the Lord: *"Him* will I accept." What an encouragement to those who have found favour with God, to plead for others. This ministry belongs to every one who has been reconciled to God. In this Job is a type of our Lord Jesus Christ, who maketh intercession for us, and whom God heareth always, and in whom we are accepted (Heb. 10. 10-14).

V. Emancipation. "The Lord turned the captivity of Job when he prayed for his friends" (v. 10). To Job's "miserable comforters," and to himself, *praying* was much more effectual than arguing. Is it not always so? His friends had misjudged him, but he had all the more need to pray for them. In so doing, the Lord loosed him from the bondage and power of Satan, and made him once more a free man. The Devil had him chained as with iron bands, but God honoured prayer as the means of deliverance. Praying for his friends implied a willingness to forgive them and a readiness to return blessing for cursing. Such an attitude of soul, and such a work of grace, cannot but bring greater liberty and blessing into the life of the suppliant. "First be reconciled to thy brother, and then come and offer thy gift" (Matt. 5. 24).

VI. Satisfaction. "The Lord gave Job twice as much as he had before...The Lord blessed the latter end of Job more than his beginning" (vv. 10-17). Satan has been defeated, and the mercy and truth of God hath triumphed. James said, "Ye have heard of the patience of Job, and have seen the end of the Lord, that the Lord is very pitiful and of tender mercy" (James 5. 11). Yes, the the *end* of all God's dealings with us is *mercy*. While the

number of Job's sheep, camels, oxen, and asses was
doubled, it was not so with his sons and daughters. He
had but the same number that he had before, perhaps
implying that his former family were not lost, but only
"gone before"—still his, although on the other side of the
Jordan of death. If Job was *seventy* years old when he
lost all, his years were also doubled, for he lived after this
"an hundred and forty years" (v. 16). The Lord's measure is always "heaped up and running over." Those to
whom He shows His salvation will be satisfied with long
life, yea, eternal life (Psa. 91. 16). No one would covet
Job's sufferings. but who would not say, "Let my last
end be like his." Judge not before the time. If God hath
begun a good work in you, He will carry it on till the day
of perfection. Comfort one another with these words.

READY.

1. Some are Ready to Perish (Isa. 27. 13).
2. God is Ready to Pardon (Neh. 9. 17).
3. Be not Ready to Halt (Psa. 38. 17).
4. Be Ready to Speak (Isa. 32. 4).
5. Be Ready to Go (Luke 22. 33).
6. Be Ready to Work (Titus 3. 1).
7. Be Ready to Testify (1 Peter 3. 15).
8. Be Ready to Suffer (Acts 21. 13).
9. Be Ready for His Appearing (Matt. 25. 10).

GREAT NEEDS.
PSALM 80. 18, 19.

1. Life, ... "Quicken us."
2. Faith, ... "We will call upon Thy Name.
3. Consecration, .. "Turn us again, O Lord."
4. Fellowship, .. "Cause Thy face to shine."
5. Full Salvation, "We shall be saved."

STUDIES IN THE PSALMS.

THE HAPPY MAN.

Psalm 1.

THIS First Psalm is a fitting introduction to the sacred Psalter. It constitutes almost a perfect epitome of the whole book. Like the sermon on the mount, it begins with the word "Blessed." The word is in the plural, and has been rendered, "O the happinesses of the man," etc. He is not only blessed, but blessed with all spiritual blessings. This happy man comes before us in a twofold aspect:—

I. **His Negative Character.** There are some things that he will not do; not because law and judgment dares him to do them, but because he has got something better to enjoy, and a positive hatred in his heart for ways and things that are at enmity with the mind and will of God.

1. HE DOES NOT WALK IN THE COUNSEL OF THE UN-GODLY. He knows that "the way of the ungodly shall perish," and he keeps out of it. The *counsel* of the ungodly is to walk in the broad way that leadeth to destruction. His manner of life is not directed by the wisdom of this world, but by that wisdom which cometh from above.

2. HE DOES NOT STAND IN THE WAY OF SINNERS. The *ungodly* may mean those who live in ignorance of God, but *sinners* are those who deliberately transgress against the light. To abide in their way of doing things is to show an attitude that is more at home with the way of sinners than merely walking in the counsel of the ungodly.

3. HE DOES NOT SIT IN THE SEAT OF THE SCORNFUL. Those who begin to walk in the counsel of the ungodly are

in danger of ending in the seat of the scornful. This seat is the chief seat in the kingdom of Satan. There is no promotion beyond this. In a few hours, the Apostle Peter ran through all this experience, from walking in the counsel of the ungodly to the seat of the scornful. He sat by the fire and denied the Lord with oaths and curses, but when he was converted he strengthened his brethren. Those who scorn at the things of God and His Christ walk after *their own lusts* (2 Peter **3**. 3).

.II. His Positive Character. He is—

1. JOYFUL. He has many blessings, but "his *delight* is in the law of the Lord" (v. 2). The Christian life is not one merely of giving up this or that, but it is entering into a new and happy inheritance in the Word of God. True, the prodigal had to give up some things ere he could possess the best robe and enter into the joys of a happy home. But what were they? The swine troughs and his rags. The Word of the Lord is a land flowing with milk and honey. "Here everlasting streams abide, and never withering flowers." It is indeed a *"delightsome* land." All who love the Lord will find delight in His Word.

2. THOUGHTFUL. "In His law doth he meditate day and night." In the day of prosperity, and in the night of adversity, he makes the Word of God the man of his counsel. *Meditation* on the word of truth is as needful to our spiritual health and strength as mastication is for the physical. Like Elijah's servant, we may need to look again and again before we see the cloud like a man's hand. "What *think* ye of Christ?" The Lord expects us to think deeply into these things which He hath caused to be written for our learning. There is no book in all the world that yields such a harvest of blessing to the humble student as the Bible. The testimony of Thomas à Kempis was, "I have no rest, but in a nook, with the *Book.*"

3. HOPEFUL. "He shall be like a tree planted by the streams of water" (v. 3, R.V.). He is full of expectation, because his circumstances are so very favourable. He is "like a tree that spreadeth out her roots by the river." While other trees are being starved and stunted by drought, his roots are being fully satisfied; buried in the streams of God's truth, and mercy, and grace. He has a meat to eat that others know not of. All whose delight is in the law of the Lord are as trees planted by streams of living waters. The roots of faith and love feed in these life-giving streams.

4. FRUITFUL. "That bringeth forth its fruit in its season." The fruit is according to the character of the tree, and is always in season. Men do not gather grapes of thorns. His roots being in the rivers of God, he has abundance of life, so that fruit-bearing is the natural and simple result. Being *filled* with the Spirit, the fruit of the Spirit is manifested (Gal. 5. 22, 23). The man who is ready, as opportunity offers, to bear testimony for Christ, will bring forth fruit in his *season*. Being filled out of the river of life, he will be filled with the fruits of righteousness (Phil. 1. 11).

5. BEAUTIFUL. "Whose leaf also doth not wither." There is a vital connection between the root and the leaf. Dry roots soon bring the dry rot into the leaf. Men cannot see the roots of the Christian character, but they can see the leaf, and the hidden condition of the roots may be judged by the outward appearance of the leaf. The outward life will be fresh and green when the inward life is pure and full. Withered leaves are signs of a withered life. When our testimony for Christ and His truth loses its freshness and power, we may be sure that there is something wrong with the *roots*, for the streams never run dry. It is the Spirit's purpose to put the beauty of the Lord our God upon us.

6. Successful. "Whatsoever he doeth shall prosper;"
or, whatsoever the tree produceth shall come to maturity.
The bud, and the blossom, produced by the Spirit of
life, will come to perfect fruition. "All cry and no
wool," does not belong to the sheep of His pasture. The
purposes of God begotten in the heart of Joseph, ripened
into perfection, for the Lord was with him and made it to
prosper (Gen. 39. 23). Our Lord could say, "I have
finished the work Thou gavest me to do." And He has left
us an example that we should follow His steps. If it be
God who worketh in us both to will and to do, then what
soever we do shall prosper, for He who hath begun the
good work will carry it on, until the day in which it is
perfected.

III. **The Contrast.** "The ungodly are not so" (v. 4).
No, they are far from it. The ungodly are the *lawless ones*
who have no delight, or reverence for the law of the Lord;
They are a law unto themselves, and the fruits of their own
character and deeds shall be reaped by them. They are
not likened to a tree planted, but to chaff driven. They
have neither root, nor life in themselves. Chaff had once
a close connection with the wheat, and may, in its outward
aspect resemble it, but it is a dead worthless thing, to be
burned with unquenchable fire (Matt. 3. 12). "The way of
the ungodly shall perish" (v. 6). The chaff has no power
to resist either the wind or the fire. The lawless, like
chaff, are driven about with every wind of doctrine,
popular opinion, or worldly success; they have no connection with, or capacity for receiving of those streams of life,
that flow so copiously in the hidden Kingdom of God. They
shall not stand accepted in the judgment nor be numbered
with the congregation of the righteous (v. 5). Only "he that
doeth the will of God abideth for ever" (1 John 2. 17).
How helpless the empty chaff is before the driving force of

the wind. There is no refuge for it. "The wicked is driven away in his wickedness; but the righteous hath hope in his death." "Every plant which My heavenly Father hath not planted shall be rooted up" (Matt. 15. 13). The way of the ungodly must perish, because it is the way of pride, pleasure, unbelief, and Christ rejection. It is the way that seemeth right unto a man, but the end is death. "He that believeth not the Son shall not see life, but the wrath of God abideth on him."

THE TRIUNE TESTIMONY.

PSALM 2.

IN the book of the Acts, Peter and Paul both quote this Psalm as having reference to David, and also to the Lord Jesus Christ as the exalted Son of God. Paul refers to it as the *Second* Psalm (Acts 4. 25; 13. 33). Undoubtedly a greater than David is here. This Psalm is separated into three divisions, and these different sections contain the testimony of Father, Son, and Holy Spirit; the declaration of God the Ruler, God the Mediator, and God the Comforter. Let us hear them—

I. **The Voice of God the Sovereign.** In verses 1 to 6 it is God who speaks. His words reveal the attitude of the nations toward Himself, and His attitude toward them as rebels against His law and His Son. These words of the Lord contain an exhibition of—

1 HUMAN ENMITY AND FOLLY. Why do the nations rage, and their representatives—kings and rulers—take counsel together against the Lord and His Anointed? There can be no denial of this, for the charge is made by Jehovah Himself, who judgeth not by the outward appearance, but who looketh upon the heart. Man, in all his madness and folly, never imagined a more "vain thing" than when he thought by breaking the *bands* of His law and

casting away the cords of His love, he could enjoy liberty
and prosperity. To cast off His yoke which is easy, and
His burden which is light, is to put on the iron shackles of
diabolical rule and eternal despair. God anointed Jesus
of Nazareth with the Holy Ghost and with power, that He
might deliver us from all our enemies. Why *rage* against
the Lord and His Anointed? Because the carnal mind is
enmity against God. They will not have this *Anointed*
One to reign over them. These words also reveal—

2. DIVINE DERISION AND DEFIANCE. "He that sitteth
in the Heavens shall laugh: the Lord shall have them in
derision." 'Jehovah, as the Ruler of the world, is at rest
in the highest Heaven. The rage of a tumultuous people
can no more hinder Him in the fulfilment of His purpose
than the howling of dogs can arrest the progress of the
moon. *"Yet,"* despite all their wrath and rebellion, He
has set His King upon His holy hill of Zion. With wicked
hands men crucified the Lord's Anointed, but God raised
Him from the dead and enthroned Him at His own right
hand in the Heavens. The resurrection of Christ is God's
derisive answer to the rage and hatred of men against His
Son. As the waves of the sea put to defiance the silly
mandate of King Canute, so shall the irresistible purposes
of God roll over the proud purposes of men, and "vex them
in His sore displeasure" (v. 5). It is a fearful thing
to fall into the hands of the living God, as Pharaoh's host
fell into the Red Sea. In derision He shall *laugh* at them;
in wrath He shall *speak* to them; and in His sore displeasure
He shall *vex* them. Who shall comfort those whom God
hath purposely vexed? The policy of Mr. Blatchford was
"to fight and defeat the churches," but He that sitteth in
the Heavens shall laugh, and have all such in derision; for
until He is defeated the gates of Hell shall not prevail
against His Church.

II. The Voice of God the Son (vv. 7-9). Hear now the language of the Anointed One who shall reign until all His enemies are put under His feet. In David, these words were not fulfilled in their literal and complete sense, but in David's Lord they shall be perfectly accomplished. This statement from the lips of Him who is the Mediator between God and man is full of deep significance. The meaning may be summed up under these four words.

1. REVELATION. "I will declare the decree." The *decree* may here stand for the covenant, or the purpose of God in His Son, with relation to the ungodly nations. In Christ the Word of God was made flesh and dwelt among us; the Only Begotten of the Father hath declared His mind and will, for the law of God was written in His heart.

2. SONSHIP. "The Lord hath said unto Me, Thou art My Son." Sonship, in a very unique sense, is emphatically taught, but there is no attempt to explain the mystery. Jehovah never said to any of the angels, "Thou art My Son, *this day* have I begotten Thee" (Heb. 1. 5). What "this day" may mean is difficult to understand. But it surely points to the fact that this relationship of Fatherhood and Sonship was entered into for the definite purpose of redemption. These words are referred to by Paul, as being fulfilled when God raised up Jesus from the dead (Acts 13. 33). Spoken as they are in this Psalm by the Son, they may be prophetic of that notable day when He would be begotten from the dead, declaring Him to be the Son of God with power (Rom. 1. 3, 4).

3. TRIUMPH. "I shall give Thee the heathen for Thine inheritance, and the uttermost parts of the earth for Thy possession." The Son of God did not come into this world on a matter of speculation. He had the promise of God the Father that a people would be given Him, and finally, as King of the nations, He would have dominion from sea

to sea, and "from the river unto the ends of the earth"
(Psa. 72. 8). The prophet Daniel saw the ANCIENT of
Days giving Him dominion, and glory, and a kingdom,
that all people, nations, and languages should serve Him.
"The pleasure of the Lord shall prosper in *His hand*."
Surely our interests also are safe enough in His hands.

4. JUDGMENT. "Thou shalt break them—lawless
nations—with a rod of iron; Thou shalt dash them in pieces
like a potter's vessel" (v. 9). When He comes, whose *right*
it is to reign, He shall put down all ungodly rule and
authority. In judgment will He establish righteousness
in the earth. The kings and rulers of the earth take counsel
together against the Lord and against *His Anointed*. But
the Lord shall have them in derision, for "the kingdoms of
this world shall become the Kingdom of our Lord and His
Christ" (Rev. 11. 15). Christ is the Man Child brought
forth to rule all nations with a *rod of iron* (not in grace, but
in unyielding righteousness), and has now been caught up
unto God, and to His throne (Rev. 12. 5). This same
Jesus shall come again.

III. **The Voice of God the Spirit.** In verses 10 to
12 we have a different tone. It is more like the voice of
wounded love and entreaty. It is the Holy Spirit's work
to convince of sin, and to guide into all truth. "To-day, if
ye will hear His voice, harden not your hearts." He says—

1. BE WISE. "Be wise now therefore, O. ye kings"
(v. 10). Seeing that the Son of God will bring you into
judgment, be wise *now*, while the day of your trial lasts.
"Behold, now is the accepted time." Submission to God
and His Son is the highest wisdom. They are wise who
build on this rock.

2. BE INSTRUCTED. "Be instructed, ye judges of the
earth." The wisdom of this world is foolishness with God.
Don't be so puffed up with pride as to refuse Him who

speaketh from Heaven. Be willing as a child to sit at the
feet of the Son of God and learn of Him. Receive the word
at His lips. "Search the Scriptures." Gregory the Great
said, "The Bible is God's heart in God's words."

3. BE RECONCILED. "Kiss the Son, lest He be angry."
To *kiss* the Son is to *lay hold* of Him in an act of love and
devotion. He who so kisses the Son kisses the Father also
(John 5. 23). The Holy Spirit does not speak of Himself,
but pleads with foolish, ignorant men to be reconciled to
God lest they "perish in the way" (R.V.). Be reconciled to
God, for God hath made Him (Christ) to be sin for us...
that we might be made the righteousness of God in Him.

4. BE HUMBLE. "Serve the Lord with fear, and rejoice
with trembling" (v. 11). Having given the Son the kiss
of confession, and received from Him the kiss of forgive-
ness, we should serve the Lord with holy fear all the days
of our life (Heb. 12. 28). Rejoice in His forgiving grace,
but tremble at the thought of falling back into the lawlessness of the self-life. Serve the Lord with that holy
reverence which fears lest it should offend Him in any way.
Be obedient to His word, ready to do whatever your Lord
may appoint. "Grieve not the Holy Spirit" (Eph. 4. 30).

A SONG OF SALVATION.
PSALM 3.

THE historical ground-work of this Psalm is found in the
fifteenth chapter of Second Samuel. David's beloved son,
Absalom, steals the hearts of the men of Israel, and then
rebels against his father. It is a most humbling and
distressing experience to discover that your own flesh,
whom you had nourished and cherished, has become your
most deadly enemy. What Absalom became to David,
self, or the carnal mind, will sooner or later become to us,
if, like him, we fall into temptation and sin. The flesh

warreth against the Spirit. This Psalm may profitably be
read with the Seventh of Romans. The Psalmist here
suffers the agonies and joys of a soul passing from death
into life; or from the power of the enemy into the liberty
and gladness of God's salvation. Several things may be
noted:—

I. **His Enemy.** They were numerous. *"Many* are
they that rise up against me" (v. 1). They were exultant.
They said, "There is no help for him in God" (v. 2).
That soul is in a sad plight indeed, that is shut out from
the "help of God." But sin-blinded men are incapable
of forming a right judgment of such a case as this. They
threw the same taunt in the teeth of our Lord while He
hung helpless upon the Cross. "He trusted in God: let
Him deliver Him now, if He will have Him." What looks
like failure and defeat, in the eyes of our enemies, may be
but God's method of leading us into a larger experience of
the riches of His grace.

II. **His Faith.** "But Thou O Lord art a shield about
me; my glory, and the lifter up of mine head" (v. 3, R.V.).
While the unbelievers are saying, "There is no help for him
in God," the believer is rejoicing in the consciousness that
God is *round about* him as a shield of defence, and that he is
even now *in* God. Being in God, God becomes his glory,
and the *Lifter* up of his head. My Shield, my Glory, my
Lifter. He endures, like Moses, by seeing Him who is
invisible. The heart that trusteth in Him will be *helped*
(Psa. 28. 7).

III. **His Testimony.** "I cried unto the Lord, and He
heard me; I laid me down and slept; the Lord sustained
me" (vv. 4, 5). Selah. This is a comforting word. He
prayed, the Lord heard him, and so delivered him from all
his fears and anxieties, that he was able to lie down and
sleep peacefully, because the Lord sustained him. The

prayer of faith shall save the fearful as well as the sick. The apostle James says, "Is any among you afflicted? let him pray" (5. 13). He shall be kept in perfect peace whose mind is stayed on the Lord (Isa. 26. 3). This "Selah" at the end of verse 4 is most significant, when contrasted with the one at the end of verse 2. The word is supposed to be a musical sign, a *pause*, and used here to arrest attention. The word occurs in the Psalms 73 times. The language of verse 4 contradicts and belies the statement in verse 2. So these "Selahs" should be solemnly emphasised. Christian experience gives the lie to infidelity.

IV. **His Courage.** "I will not be afraid of ten thousands of people that have set themselves against me round about" (v. 6). Why should he fear the forces of evil which surrounded him, while he knew that Jehovah was about him as a *shield*. The man of holy vision is a man of courage. The servant of Elisha was full of fear when he saw the Syrian host encamped round about them, so he cried, "Alas my master, how shall we do?" But confidence and courage came into his heart after his eyes were opened (2 Kings 6). Joshua "feared not" after the "Captain of the Host" revealed Himself to him. As an old writer has said: "It makes no matter what our enemies may be, though for number, legions; for power, principalities; for subtilty, serpents; for cruelty, dragons; for vantage of place, a prince of the air; for maliciousness, spiritual wickedness. In Christ Jesus our Lord, we shall be more than conquerors." "If God be for us, who can be against us?" (Rom. 8. 31).

V. **His Victory.** "Thou hast smitten all mine enemies upon the cheek bone; Thou hast broken the teeth of the ungodly" (v. 7). The Lord never smites a man behind his back. The cheek that was burning with pride and arrogance, will be made to burn with shame and dishonour.

The teeth of the ungodly are often sharp and merciless, seeking to tear the character of the godly man to pieces: but the Lord can break their teeth, so that they become perfectly harmless. The salvation of God's people belongeth unto the Lord (v. 8). We are ready to forget this, and to cease to work out in our daily life, that which God the Spirit hath wrought in us. It is ours to trust, it is His to smite. Vengeance belongeth unto Him. The enemy may count us, as they counted Christ, sheep for their slaughter; and though for His sake we are killed all the day long, yet are we "more than conquerors through Him that loved us" (Rom. 8. 37). Thanks be to God who giveth us the victory through our Lord Jesus Christ

---

WHOLESOME WORDS.

PSALM 4.

THIS psalm is dedicated to the leader of those who use stringed instruments. It is indeed a psalm of life. There are in it notes that speak of sadness, gladness, and madness. The various conditions, or seasons, of the life year are here, in a way, represented. We shall try and gather up the truth taught as having reference to three classes of individuals.

I. **Words of Encouragement to the Believing.** This testimony of the psalmist should be an inspiration to every child of God. What God did for him He can still do for those who put their trust in Him. What was that?

1. HE MADE HIM FREE. "Thou hast set me at large when I was in distress" (v. 1, R.V.). Through fear and distress, he had been like one in a prison, but the Lord set him at liberty. It is when men are at their wit's end, that they are made to see the salvation of God. We are

shut up to *faith* that we might be brought out into a *large* place. To be set at large by the saving grace of God is a great deliverance.

2. HE MADE HIM GLAD. "Thou hast put gladness in my heart" (v. 7). The gladness of a harvest time is not to be compared with the gladness of a great spiritual deliverance. "Corn and wine," the richest of earth's blessings, come far short of the "joy of the Lord." God put gladness in the heart, by the manifestation of His grace and power on our behalf. Although we see Him not, yet believing, we rejoice, with joy unspeakable and full of glory.

3. HE MADE HIM SAFE. "Thou Lord makest me dwell in safety" (v. 8). He could lie down, and sleep the sleep of peace; for the Lord gave him that sweet assurance of His protecting care, that all fear fled. "The beloved of the Lord shall dwell in safety by Him" (Deut. 33. 12). Free, Glad, and Safe, is the condition of all, who by faith have received the Gospel of the Lord Jesus Christ. They are set apart by the Lord as His own peculiar, personal treasure (v. 3).

II. Words of Rebuke to the Unbelieving. There
are three things those "Sons of men" were guilty of, and for which the psalmist rebukes them. Three sins which many of the unbelieving "sons of men" in our own day are guilty of.

1. PRACTISING RIDICULE. "How long will ye turn my glory into dishonour?" (v. 2, R.V.). The glory of David was in that he trusted and hoped in the Lord (Psa. 3. 3). Any fool may mock at faith, as he may mock at sin. The man must be morally mad who would attempt to make confidence in God appear to be a dishonourable thing. Yet some do it.

2. LOVING VANITY. "How long will ye love vanity?"
They love vanity who love that which is worthless to
satisfy, that which is uncertain, that which has the
appearance of being what it is not—the world. The
experience of Solomon stands as a warning and a rebuke
to all who set their hearts on earthly things. Anything
and everything that occupies the place Christ should have,
is vanity (1 John 2. 15).

3. SEEKING FALSEHOOD. "How long will ye...seek
after falsehood" (v. 2, R.V.). One does not need to go
far in search of falsehood. He will find it in his own
heart. To seek falsehood, for its own sake instead of
the truth, is a positive proof of a mind at enmity with
God. The false and deceitful heart seeks food convenient
for it. Christ is the truth; true and honest hearts will
seek Him. "Without are dogs...and every one that loveth
a lie" (Rev. 22. 15, R.V.).

III. **Words of Entreaty to the Anxious.** Let us
now hear as with trumpet tone, a call to—

1. STAND. "Stand in awe, and sin not" (v. 4). Stop,
before you go any further in sinful unbelief, and consider
where, and what you are. Stand in awe at the thought of
disobeying God's Word (Psa. 119. 161). Stand in awe at
the thought of the wages of sin (Rom. 6. 23). Stand in
awe at the thought of opportunities lost, the uncertainty of
life, and the certainty of judgment. Stand in awe as you
think of the infinite love and mercy of God towards sinners,
in the sufferings and death of His Son. Stand in awe, lest
ye should resist the gracious stirrings of His Holy Spirit
and die in your sin.

2. COMMUNE. "Commune with your heart upon your
bed, and be still." Have a quiet time with your own heart.
Examine *yourself*. "If we would judge ourselves, we should

not be judged" (1 Cor. 11. 31). The heart is deceitful. Commune with it, find out its motives, search into its desires, and cross-question its purposes. In the solitude of the bed-chamber, and in the stillness of the night, there is a favourable opportunity of finding out the true character of our own hearts. "Prove your own selves" (2 Cor. 13. 5). The bed and the heart are fields in which many startling discoveries have been made, many great battles fought, and many victories lost and won—bloodless battles, whose issues reach away into the depths of eternity.

3. SACRIFICE. "Offer the sacrifices of righteousness" (v. 5). As the result of standing and communing, there are sure to be revelations. Things to be given up, or offered unto God as sacrifices. Then let the sacrifice be *righteous*. Let there be a willing and whole-hearted surrender to the will of God. There are sacrifices, like Absalom's which are not righteous, but only a hypocritical performance, to blind the eyes of the God-fearing, and secure some personal advantage (2 Sam. 15. 12). Your reasonable service is to present *yourselves* unto God, "for ye are not your own, ye are bought with a price." Let us not forget Him, who did offer unto God the sacrifice of righteousness, when He offered Himself without spot. He hath left us "an example that we should follow His steps."

4. TRUST. "Trust in the Lord." Trust and obey, there is no other way. The standing in awe, and the communing with the heart should lead to *faith* or it will end in failure. *Trust* is a very simple and sweet word, associated as it is with the greatest of all names, JEHOVAH, and the most precious of all privileges and blessings. Any child can understand it, but does any man, or angel in Heaven, understand to the full all the possibilities that lie within it, as the link that binds the soul to the Eternal God?

PRAYERFUL PURPOSES.
PSALM 5. 1-8.

THOSE who believe in set forms of prayer can find no justification for such a practice in the Book of Psalms. There is throughout the whole book a blessed disregard for all such mechanical and stultifying conventionalities, because the prayers of the psalmists are the utterances of burning, agonising hearts. Every variety of form is adopted, according to the varied needs of the soul. We shall note—

I. His Requests. There are four definite petitions. He prays—

1. That his WORDS may be attended to. "Give ear to my words, O Lord." We don't always wish the Lord to mark our words, they are at times such poor vehicles of our soul's desires. But the psalmist *meant* every word that he uttered in the Divine ear. Beware of vain words. We are not heard for our much speaking.

2. That his MEDITATION may be considered. "O Lord, consider my meditation." There may be abundance of eloquent words where there is no real exercise of soul, no true spirit of prayer. The Lord hath said, "Come, let us *reason* together." Surely to reason out a matter implies serious and deliberate thinking. Our prayer-words should be the outcome of solemn meditation on the whole inner condition and circumstances of the soul. God not only heareth the words, but He looketh upon the heart. It has been said that "Prayer without fervency is like hunting with a dead dog."

3. That his CRY may be heard. "Hearken unto the voice of my cry, my King and my God" (v. 2). These are three expressive "Mys." "My Cry, My King, My God." The meditation is the *source*, the words are the *channel*, but the cry is the *force* with which the stream of prayer rushes

on. It is possible to have correct words, and deep thinking, and yet no real intensity of heart, no agony of soul. It was when God heard the *"Cry* of the Israelites" that He sent deliverance (Exod. 3. 7). The cry is unto Jehovah, as his King and God, as his Ruler and Creator. As He who fashioned his being, and governs his life. This consciousness of subjection and ownership gives intensity and hopefulness to the cry of need. It was with kindred, but deeper feelings, that Christ cried on the Cross, "My God, My God."

4. That in RIGHTEOUSNESS he might be *led*. "Lead me, O Lord, in Thy righteousness, because of mine enemies" (v. 8). Newberry reads it, "because of mine *observers*." We need leading into the righteousness of God because of those who are watching our words and our ways, that they, seeing our good works, may glorify our Father in Heaven. This He is willing to do for His Name's sake (Psa. 23. 3). "In all thy ways acknowledge Him, and He shall direct thy paths" (Prov. 3. 6).

II. **His Resolutions.** Earnest praying will lead to earnest acting. Our Lord said, "He that heareth and *doeth* these sayings of Mine, I will liken him unto a wise man" (Matt. 7. 24).

The psalmist resolves that—

1. IN THE MORNING HE WOULD PRAY. "My voice shalt Thou hear in the morning" (v. 3). Let each opening day be met with an open heart. God hears the voice of the bird in the morning, why not thine? Morning by morning let the keys of your life be put into the hands of your Lord and Master. The morning voice must be specially sweet to Him, who, "in the morning, rising up a great while before day, went into a solitary place, and there prayed."

2. IN EXPECTATION HE WOULD LOOK. "In the morning

will I order my prayer unto Thee, and will keep watch"
(v. 3, R.V.). Like Daniel, he would open his window and
look toward the Holy City. He would order his prayer, as
Elijah ordered the sacrifice upon the altar on Carmel, and
kept watch for the coming fire; or as when he prayed
for the rain, and told his servant to go again and watch
for the cloud like a "man's hand." We direct our letters
to our friends at a distance, and "keep watch" for the
postman. In the well-doing of praying and watching be
not weary, "for in due season ye shall reap if you
faint not."

3. IN GRACE HE WOULD COME. "But as for me, in the
multitude of Thy lovingkindness I will come into Thy
house" (v. 7, R.V.). The praying spirit longs for closer
fellowship with God. He believes, that through the great
lovingkindness of God, he would yet have the joy of
fellowship and service in His house. He does not look upon
this privilege as being the result of any merit of his own,
but all according to the goodness of God. The house of
God not made with hands, can only be entered through the
mercy and grace of Him who is the Way, the Truth, and
the Life (John 14. 1-6).

4. IN FEAR HE WOULD WORSHIP. "In Thy fear will I
worship toward Thy holy temple." The earthly temple
had not yet been built, but David would worship toward
the throne of His Holiness. *Worship* is the highest
possible form of service. Praying, serving, worshipping.
We first pray in the outer court, at the altar of sacrifice.
We serve in the holy place, but in the holiest of all we
worship. The voice of testimony should frequently give
place for the silence of adoration. In His strength we
serve, in His fear we worship. What Satan asked of
Christ, Christ expects from us. "Worship Him" (Matt.
4. 9) and the Kingdom shall be thine.

POWERFUL PLEAS.
PSALM 6.

THE chief reason why the Psalms are so full of praise is because they are so full of prayers. In this Psalm we have a troubled soul using some powerful arguments with God, giving us an example of prevailing importunity. He mentions—

I. The Anger of the Lord. "O Lord, rebuke me not in Thine anger." His sensitive soul is deeply alarmed at the thought of the awfulness of God's anger, and the hotness of His displeasure (v. 1). He is terrified at the possibility of deserving his chastening in wrath. Serve the Lord with fear.

II. His Own Weakness. "Have mercy upon me, O Lord, for I am weak" (v. 2). A real consciousness of our own impotency will give urgency and point to our pleadings.

III. His Own Sorrowfulness. "My soul is sore vexed, but Thou, O Lord, how long?" (v. 3). His was no mere lip-praying; the depths of his soul were stirred up; there was agony in his cry.

IV. The Mercies of God. "Oh save me for Thy mercies' sake" (v. 4). This is a mighty plea in the eyes of Him whose Name is the Lord God "Merciful." He who "delighteth in mercy" will not be deaf to this cry.

V. The Profitlessness of Death. "In death there is no remembrance of Thee," etc. (v. 5). This is true of those spiritually dead. Plead for quickening that ye might be saved from a God-forgetting state of soul.

VI. The Significance of Tears. "I water my couch with my tears" (v. 6). Jesus also wept, and God can never forget the value of such pure heart-drops of grief and silent witnesses of love.

VII. His Own Hatred of Iniquity. "Depart from me all ye workers of iniquity" (v. 8). He further pleads his

separateness in spirit from the ways and methods of the
ungodly.

VIII. **His Own Faith in God.** "The Lord hath heard...
the Lord will receive my prayer" (vv. 8-10). The answer
had come into his heart; he believed the message, and
rested on the faithfulness of God. "Go thou and do
likewise."

———

IN THE FACE OF THE FOE.
PSALM 7.

LEARN from this Psalm how to behave when face to face
with wicked men, and the principles and forces of
unrighteousness.

I. **Trust.** "O Lord my God, in Thee do I put my trust"
(v. 1). Keep the shield of faith ever bright with constant
use. "Happy is He who hath the God of (wayward) Jacob
for his help" (Psa. 146. 5).

II. **Pray.** "Save me from all them that persecute me"
(v. 1). Call upon God to arise, and to lift Himself up
for your defence (v. 6). It is His prerogative to execute
righteousness and judgment for the oppressed (Psa. 103. 6).

III. **Search.** Search yourself and your ways, lest this
trial may have come upon you because of iniquity (vv. 3, 4)
Let God also search your heart and your hands, lest there
may be some hidden hindrance to His help (Psa. 66. 18).

IV. **Testify.** "The Lord shall judge the people" (v. 8).
Don't be afraid to speak out and declare His righteousness,
even when His providence seems most against thee, for the
Lord doth reward us according to the cleanness of our
hands (Psa. 18. 20).

V. **Confess.** "My defence is of God, which saveth the
upright in heart" (v. 10). Although the enemy may say,
"There is no help for Him in God," make full confession
of Him as your present and all-sufficient Saviour.

VI. **Warn.** "God is angry with the wicked every day, if he turn not He will whet His sword" (vv. 11, 12). Don't be intimidated by their threatenings or scorn. Warn them that the axe is laid at the root of all fruitless trees (Matt. 3. 10). The sword of the Lord is never sharpened in vain.

VII. **Praise.** "I will praise the Lord according to His righteousness, and will sing praise to the Name of the Lord Most High" (v. 17). Fearless trust is sure to end in fullness of praise. "Blessed are all they that put their trust in Him."

THE EXCELLENT NAME.
PSALM 8.

"How excellent is Thy Name in all the earth." These are the first and last words of this Psalm, and may be taken as the keynote. His NAME stands for all the riches and glory of His character. The glory of it is "above the Heavens," although the Heavens are a reflection of it (Psa. 19. 1). This wondrous glory, the glory of infinite grace, can also manifest itself through such weak things as "babes and sucklings" (v. 2; Matt. 11. 25). God hath been pleased so to choose weak things that the might of the worldling might be confounded (1 Cor. 1. 27). But the glory of this Name, which is seen in the "moon and the stars"—the work of His fingers (v. 3)—finds its chief manifestation in "man," insignificant as he is, when contrasted with the greatness of the material heavens. "What is man that Thou art mindful of him?" (v. 4). See how the excellency of His Name is revealed in His dealings with man. It is seen—

I. **In the Character of Man.** "Thou hast made him a little lower than God" (v. 5, R.V.). Made after His image, but a "little lower." How near God has come to man in imprinting His own likeness in Him. What ravages sin hath wrought that this holy temple should become the workshop of the Devil. Grace restores to sonship.

II. **In His Mindfulness of Him.** "What is man that Thou art mindful of Him?" The mindfulness of God is another manifestation of the excellency of His character. He is mindful of man in all the arrangements of His material creation and providence. This gracious mindfulness began before the foundation of the world, when in His purpose the Lamb was slain. What is man that his highest interests are for ever in the mind of God?

III. **In the Honour given Him.** "Thou hast crowned him with glory and honour; Thou madest him to have dominion over the works of Thy hands" (vv. 5, 6). All things were put under him, till sin entered, then the crown fell from his head, and had to be given to another, even Jesus, who was made for a little while lower than the angels; who, after the sufferings of a substitutionary death, was crowned with glory and honour (Heb. 2. 8, 9). How excellent is the Name of Him who sought to put such glory on the head of man!

> "How poor, how rich, how abject, how august,
> How complicate, how wonderful is man."

IV. **In His Sacrifice for Man** "What is man...that Thou visitest him?" In a very deep and real sense, God hath visited man in the Person of His only beloved Son. Man, in his sin and shame, could not visit God in peace, but in the excellency of His Name, and at an awful cost, He hath visited man. Visited him in his hopeless distress, bringing with Him and offering to him a perfect remedy for all his sins and sorrows. "Lord, what is man that Thou shouldest *set Thine heart upon Him?*" (Job 7. 17).

"WHAT IS MAN?" (vv. 4, 5).

1. "That Thou art *mindful of him?*" Merciful CONSIDERATION.

2. "That Thou *visitest* him?" INCARNATION.

3. "That Thou hast *made him* a little lower than God?" REGENERATION.

4. "That Thou hast *crowned him with glory*?" GLORIFI- CATION.

I WILL, FOR THOU HAST.
PSALM 9. 1-10.

IT is good when *our* "I wills" find their motive power in the "Thou hasts" of God.   In this Psalm there is—

I. **A Joyful Purpose,** This purpose was—

1. To PRAISE GOD.   "I will praise Thee, O Lord" (v. 1). Praise is surely the expression of a full and satisfied heart. The salvation accomplished for us by Jesus Christ is such as demands continual praise (Heb. 13. 15).

2. To TESTIFY FOR GOD.   "I will shew forth all Thy marvellous works." His wonderful works of grace are well worthy of being shown forth by the lips and lives of all who have experienced the power and riches of them.

3. To REJOICE IN GOD.   "I will be glad and rejoice in Thee" (v. 2).   This gladness is something deeper than that produced by the mere increase of corn and wine (Psa. 4. 7). It is the joy of the Lord, because it is joy in God (Phil 4. 4).

II. **A Powerful Reason.** This reason, like the purpose, is threefold.

1. Because of His FAITHFULNESS.   "Thou hast main- tained my cause" (v. 4).   It is His to maintain the cause of the afflicted and the poor in spirit (Psa. 140. 12).   When our cause is the cause of God, it will be stoutly maintained by Him.

2. Because of His POWER.   "Thou hast rebuked the heathen" (v. 5).   All the pride and possessions of the un- godly "shall flow away in the day of His wrath" (Job. 20. 28).

Heathenish thoughts and practices are rebuked in the presence of the Lord.

3. Because of His MERCY. "Thou Lord hast not forsaken them that seek Thee" (v. 10). God, in all the riches of His grace and power is ever within the reach of the whole-hearted seeker (Jer. 29. 13). The great Deliverer of the past, is the same Deliverer for the present and the future.

III. **An Inspiring Hope.** This is—

1. The Hope of ENDURANCE. "The Lord shall endure for ever" (v. 7). The blessings of God's grace are as lasting as God Himself. As long as HE endures, His redeemed ones will be enriched with the Divine life and fullness. "Ye are Christ's, and Christ is God's."

2. The Hope of RIGHTEOUSNESS. "He shall judge the world in righteousness" (v. 8). Unrighteousness, the fruit of the mystery of sin, is ever with us, but "He hath appointed a day, in the which He will judge the *world* in righteousness, by that Man whom He hath ordained" for this purpose (Acts 17. 31). "Shall not the Judge of all the earth do right?"

3. The Hope of SALVATION. "The Lord shall be a refuge for the oppressed" (v. 9). For those oppressed with inward sin or outward trouble. "God is our refuge and strength, a *very present* help in time of trouble." They are safely kept whose life is hid with Christ in God.

CHARACTERISTICS OF THE WICKED.
PSALM 10.

WHEN God, as the light ot His people, hides Himself (v. 1), the ungodly owls of darkness are sure to manifest themselves. They are—

I. **Boastful.** "The wicked boasteth of his heart's

desire" (v. 3) ; although that desire is for things forbidden
of God and destructive to his own soul.   Even the man that
boasted in his lawful riches was branded by God as a fool
(Luke 12. 20).   "The desire of the wicked shall perish"
(Psa. 112. 10).

II. **Perverse.**   "He blesseth the covetous, whom the
Lord abhorreth" (v. 3).   They honour men according to the
amount of their possessions, instead of the pureness of their
lives.   They call light darkness, and darkness light.   Like
Balaam, they love the wages of unrighteousness.

III. **Proud.**   "The wicked, through the pride of his
countenance, will not seek after God"—will not require it
(R.V., v. 4).   In his pride and self-confidence, he has no
sense of his need of God.   The natural man receiveth not
the things of the Spirit of God.

IV. **Godless.**   "God is not in all his thoughts" (v. 4).
Every day he plays the fool, by practically saying, "There
is no God."   No matter how much God in His providence
may be doing for him, in his own soul and character he is
utterly godless, guilty, and hopeless.

V. **Blind.**   "Thy judgments are far above out of his
sight" (v. 5).   He is so short sighted, that he cannot
see the marvellous workings of God in nature or in
grace.   Like the man with the muck rake, the crown
of glory is out of his sight, because he is blinded by the
love of this world.

VI. **Self-confident.**   "He saith in his heart, I shall not
be moved" (v. 6).   Because sentence against unbelief and
evil workers is not executed speedily, they imagine themselves secure.   But while they say, Peace and safety,
sudden destruction cometh upon them.   In wrath God shall
move them—move them out of their very graves, into a
hopeless eternity (Rev. 20. 12, 13).

VII. Deceitful. "Under his tongue is mischief...he lieth in wait as a lion to catch the poor...he humbleth himself that the helpless may fall" (vv. 7-10, R.V.). The principle of righteousness is not in him. His smooth words have under them the poison of sinful lust. If he croucheth in lowliness, it is that he might devour as a lion. His *heart* is deceitful, and his life can be nothing else.

VIII. Deceived. "He hath said in his heart, God hath forgotten; He will never see it" (v. 11). But "God hath seen it, for He beholdeth mischief and spite, to requite it with His hand" (v. 14). In deceiving others, he deceives himself. "Be not deceived, God is not mocked, whatsoever a man soweth, that shall he also reap" (Gal. 6. 7). ————

A BLESSED AND SORROWFUL CONDITION.
PSALM 11.

THE state of the righteous and the wicked are set before us here in striking contrast.

I. The Condition of the Righteous. They are—

1. TRUSTFUL. "In the Lord put I my trust" (v. 1). Their confidence is not in themselves, but in the Lord, and, though He slay them, yet will they trust in Him. They knew the NAME of the Lord as a strong tower, they ran into it, and are safe (Prov. 18. 10).

2. DESPISED. The ungodly deride them, saying, "Flee as a bird to your mountain" (v. 1, Psa. 9. 9). Yes, thank God, they have a mountain to flee to; but where will *they* flee to when the wrath of God is revealed from Heaven against all ungodliness? They may bend their bow now and "shoot at the upright in heart" (v. 2), but where shall they flee when God whets His sword and bends His bow? (Psa. 7. 12).

3. TRIED. "The Lord trieth the righteous" (v. 5). It is because that He is righteous that He trieth the hearts of men (Psa. 7. 9). He tried Abraham, and the blessedness of the man that endureth temptation came upon him (James 1. 12). Wood, hay, and stubble are never put into the fiery furnace of trial (Dan. 6. 23).

4. LOVED. "The righteous Lord loveth the righteous" (v. 7). The compassionate eyes of the Lord are ever over the righteous, and His ears open unto their prayers (1 Peter 3. 12). Loved with an everlasting love, a love that is stronger than death, and that the many waters of this world's sins and sorrows cannot quench.

II. The Condition of the Wicked.

1. THEY SECRETLY OPPOSE THE RIGHTEOUS. "They make ready their arrow upon the string, that they may *privily* shoot at the upright in heart" (v. 2). "They shoot their arrows, even bitter words, that they may shoot in secret at the perfect" (Psa. 64. 3, 4). Their carnal minds are at enmity against God, and all that is Godlike in His people. But every hidden thing shall be revealed.

2. THEIR ACTS ARE SEEN BY THE LORD. "His eyes behold, His eyelids try the children of men" (v. 4). Their secret purposes are naked before Him with whom they *have to do*. Even now they suffer for their evil-doing, for "the face of the Lord is against them" (Psa. 34. 16). All that the "face of the Lord" stands for is set against their principles of life.

3. THEIR MANNER OF LIFE IS HATED BY THE LORD. "The wicked and him that loveth violence, His soul hateth" (v. 5). God loved a world of sinners, but the Cross of Christ is the expression of His infinite hatred of sin. To love wickedness and hate righteousness is to be in league with the Devil, and become a fit subject

for the wrath of God.   God is angry with the wicked
every day.

4. THEIR FINAL PORTION IS FEARFUL.   "Upon the
wicked He shall rain snares, fire and brimstone, and an
horrible tempest: this shall be the portion of their cup"
(v. 6).   The wider the cup of iniquity, the greater the
portion of curse.   This rain of *snares* will entrap every
guilty foot, and this fire and tempest will search out
every hidden thing (Psa. 75. 8).

HELP, LORD.
PSALM 12.

IN this psalm we have a loud cry to the Lord for help in
backsliding times.   To whom can we go, when the tongues
of pride and vanity are clamouring so loudly that the testimony of God's people can scarcely be heard.   Our help
cometh from the Lord, He giveth power to the faint.   The
psalmist gives us many reasons for thus calling upon the
help of the Lord.   "Help, Lord—

I. **For the Godly Man Ceaseth"** (v. 1).   Godliness
has never been popular amongst men.   In proportion to
the fewness of their number, and the weakness of their
character, will wicked men and the powers of darkness
prosper.   "Ye are the salt of the earth; if the salt lose His
savour, wherewith shall it be salted?"

II. **"For the Faithful Fail."**   In such times of testing
and general backsliding, the faithful are in great danger
of letting go their grip of God and drifting down with the
polluting stream.   To fail in our faithfulness to God and
men, in such adverse circumstances, is always a great
temptation.   Then is the time to cry "Help, Lord."

III. **For Vanity, Flattery, and Deceit are Pre-
valent** (v. 2).   This is a threefold cord that can only be

broken by the help of God. In the absence of godliness, vanity, flattery, and deceit, are the natural outcome of the unrenewed heart (Rom. 5. 9).

IV. For Men's Confidence is in Themselves. They say, "With our tongue we will prevail; our lips are our own; who is lord over us?" (v. 4). *Confidence*, was never put to a baser use than this. The tongue is a mighty weapon, but when ungodly men hope to *prevail* by it, it is but an "unruly evil, full of deadly poison." "He that trusteth in his own heart is a fool." Such self-confidence is sure to lead to the denial of the Lordship of Christ.

V. For Thou hast Promised. "For the sighing of the needy, now will I arise, saith the Lord" (v. 5). The promises of God are always a powerful plea for help. The ungodly are "strangers to the covenant of promise," but let us see that we don't act as if we were strangers to them. His promises are given that they might be claimed.

VI. For Thy Words are Pure (v. 6). There is no possibility of corruption and deceit in them. His words are "as silver tried in a furnace *on the earth*, purified seven times" (R.V.). The words of the Lord are pure, *enlightening* the eyes (Psa. 19. 8). The eye-sparkling power of the Word of God is being constantly proven. Every answered prayer, every promise received, has an eye-enlightening effect. "He is faithful that has promised."

VII. For without Thy Help, Wickedness shall Prevail. "The wicked walk on every side, when vileness is exalted among the sons of men" (v. 8, R.V.). The world loves its own. The power of the presence of God, in His people, and with them, is a standing rebuke to all vileness. All our efforts, apart from this, will be utterly useless. "Not by might nor by power, but by My Spirit, saith the Lord." "Help, Lord!"

HOW LONG, LORD?
PSALM 13.

THE preceding psalm is a cry for help: to the psalmist this help seems long in coming. One has to learn to wait as well as pray. Such varied experiences are needed for the discipline of the soul. The language of this psalm is—

I. The Language of Anxiety. He is concerned about—

1. THE DIVINE FORGETFULNESS. "How long wilt Thou forget me, O Lord?" (v. 1). God is mindful of His people, but sometimes His dealings with us may seem as if He had forgotten. Prayers are long in being answered, and the supernatural may for a time have disappeared from our lives.

2. THE FELT WANT OF HIS PRESENCE. "How long wilt Thou hide Thy face from me?" Those who *never* miss the absence of the face of God are more to be pitied. It may be our own iniquities and sins that hide him from us (Isa. 59. 2); but, if not, though He hide His face for a moment, we are still assured of His everlasting kindness (Isa. 54. 7, 8).

3. HIS OWN IMPOTENCY. "How long shall I take counsel in my soul?" (v. 2). Cast upon his own resources, he finds them altogether unavailing. Even the best and wisest of men, when left to themselves, are poor indeed. He longs to get out of himself into the wisdom and strength of God. To be fruitful, we must abide in Him.

4. THE POWER OF HIS ENEMY. "How long shall mine enemy be exalted over me?" The absence of the power of God, implies the presence of the power of the enemy. How long shall mine enemy triumph? Just so long as the

face of God is unseen. Thy face Lord will we seek; that face revealed to us, in the face of Jesus Christ.

II. **The Language of Intercession.** He now pleads for—

1. THE CONSIDERATION OF HIS CASE. "Consider and hear me, O Lord my God" (v. 3). There is a holy familiarity about this request. He who said, "Come, let us reason together," condescends to deal with us as a man. The case that is stated *fully* will by Him be considered carefully.

2. ENLIGHTENED EYES. "Lighten mine eyes, lest I sleep the sleep of death" (v. 3). The influence of Divine light is to awaken from death (Eph. 5. 14). The absence of spiritual light, like the natural, means barrenness and death. The eyes of our understanding need to be enlightened ere we can know what is the *hope* of His calling, the *riches* of His inheritance, or the exceeding greatness of His *power* (Eph. 1. 18, 19).

III. **The Language of Confession.** He makes confession of his—

1. FAITH. "I have trusted in Thy mercy" (v. 5). What else can any needy soul trust. Having trusted *His* mercy in the past, we will trust it still. It is a mercy that *His* mercy is available.

2. HOPE. "My heart shall rejoice in Thy salvation." "Weeping may endure for a night, but joy cometh in the morning." He rejoices in hope, at the remembrance of His past mercies, saying, "I will sing unto the Lord, *because He hath* dealt bountifully with me" (v. 6). The God who hath delivered will yet deliver, so faith may sing, even while it seems, in the providence of God, as if He had forgotten. Yet, how long, Lord?

GENERAL CORRUPTION.
Psalm 14.

ALTHOUGH this Psalm is by no means the most popular, it has the unique honour of appearing twice in this book (Compare Psa. 53). The utter failure of man, in the sight of God, needs to be emphasised. See here—

I. **Human Folly.** "The fool hath said in his heart, there is no God." Humanity as a whole is that fool; it is practically atheistic. The word "fool," it is said, comes from a term which means the act of *withering*. The sin-withered deceitful heart of unbelief departs from a living God, and would seek to justify self by saying, "No God."

II. **Divine Scrutiny.** "The Lord looked down from Heaven," etc. What for? To see if there were any seeking the advancement of science, art, or philosophy? No, to see if there were any that did understand their true condition, and *seek God* (v. 2). The chief concern of God about man is, that he seeks not Himself. "Seek ye the Lord while He may be found."

III. **Universal Failure.** "They are all gone aside (all grown sour), all together become filthy: none that doeth good, no, not one" (v. 3). Sour and filthy; like savourless salt, good for nothing. This is a terribly sweeping indictment, but it is a Divine one. God here speaks of what He saw; we may pretend to see something different, but His judgment will stand (Rom. 3. 10-12).

IV. **Practical Ungodliness.** "Have all the workers of iniquity no knowledge? who eat of My people, and call not upon the Lord" (v. 4). Even in the midst of general, moral corruption, God has never been without a witness. The characteristics of the workers of iniquity are the same to-day as of old: ignorance of God; hatred of His people; unbelief—"they call not upon the Lord." To reject the knowledge of God is to be rejected by Him (Hosea 4. 6).

V. Salvation Needed. "O that the salvation of Israel were come out of Zion," etc. (v. 7). Backsliding Israel, like the sinners of to-day, needed to be *redeemed* out of all his troubles" (Psa. 25. 22). The Deliverer, who is able to turn away ungodliness, must come out of Zion (Rom. 11. 26)—out from the presence of God, and the place where His eternal honour dwelleth. "God so loved the world that He gave His only begotten Son." "Grace and truth *came* by Jesus Christ."

THE HEAVENLY CITIZEN.

PSALM 15.

THIS Psalm might be called "The Song of the Sojourner." A question is asked, "Lord, who shall sojourn in Thy tent? Who shall dwell in the hill of Thy holiness?" In the answer given we have the characteristics mentioned which must belong to the spiritual pilgrim, who would abide in the fellowship of God (Rev. 7. 14, 15). He must be—

I. **Upright in his Walk.** "He that walketh uprightly." "He that saith he abideth in Him ought himself also so to walk, even as He walked" (1 John 2. 6). They must walk by faith who would walk uprightly in the midst of a wicked and perverse generation. God can have no fellowship with unrighteousness.

II. **Truthful in his Heart.** "Speaketh the truth in his heart" (v. 2). Their hearts must be clean who would abide in the tabernacle of Him who "looketh upon the heart." "The pure in heart shall see God." When the truth is not in the heart, the lips are prone to be deceitful.

III. **Charitable to his Neighbour.** "He backbiteth not with his tongue...nor taketh up a reproach against his neighbour" (v. 3). A truth-loving heart never uses a backbiting tongue. He cannot help *hearing* reproaches against his neighbour, but he does refrain from "taking

them up. " If evil reproaches were but let alone by God's
people they would soon rot.

IV. **Careful of his Company.** "In his eyes a vile
person is contemned, but he honoureth them that fear the
Lord" (v. 4). Like Mordecai, he can offer no respect to the
vile and haughty Haman. He is a companion of all them
that fear the Lord. He who walks with God, as Noah and
Enoch did, will be separate from sinners.

V. **Faithful to his Promise.** If he swears or gives his
solemn promise to do a thing, he will do it, even to his own
hurt, and change not (Judges 11. 35). This faithfulness
is but a faint imitation of the faithfulness of Him, "who,
for the joy that was set before Him, *endured the Cross*"
(Heb. 12. 2). "Having loved His own, He loved them unto
the end. "

VI. **Merciful in his Dealings.** "He taketh no reward
against the innocent" (v. 5). He will not seek to take
advantage of the ignorant or the poor; he will not be
guilty, as some lawyers are, of taking a reward against the
innocent. To him bribery is robbery. He will not wear
Christ's livery and deny Him honest service (Num. 22. 18).

VII. **Stablished in his Character.** "He that doeth
these things shall never be moved. " The storms and floods
of earth cannot move him out of his place, because his life
is rooted in the will of God. He is like a tree planted by
rivers of water; ye shall not know when drought cometh.
This is the man who abides in the tabernacle of God's
service, and who dwells in the holy hill of His presence.

A GOODLY HERITAGE.
PSALM 16. 5-11.

"THE Lord is the portion of mine inheritance, and of my
cup...yea, I have a goodly heritage. "

I. **The Nature of It.** It is—

1. LARGE. "The Lord is the portion of mine inheritance." The infinite wealth of the character of God Himself is the portion of the believer's cup. No wonder that he has to say, "My cup runneth over." "The Lord is my portion, saith my soul" (Lam. 3. 24); "I know *whom* I have believed," saith the apostle (2 Tim. 1. 12).

2. PLEASANT. "The lines are fallen unto me in pleasant places" (v. 6). Experiences that would otherwise have been desert wastes, have, by the presence and goodness of God become "pleasant places." In this portion we are made partakers of the inheritance of the saints in light. These are the ways of pleasantness and the paths of peace.

3. ETERNAL. "The LORD is the portion of my cup" (v. 5). It will take all eternity to dip up this river of pleasure with the little cup of our life. The portion is divinely suited to the needs of the eternal spirit of man. God's gift of eternal life is the gift of Himself.

II. **The Effect of It.** The conscious possession of such a goodly heritage must powerfully influence the life. There will be—

1. PRAISE. "I will bless the Lord who hath given me counsel" (v. 7). All who have been counselled by His Holy Spirit, and constrained to believe in, and yield themselves to God, have very much to bless Him for. "Ye have not chosen Me, but I have chosen you" (John 15. 16).

2. FELLOWSHIP. "I have set the Lord always before me ...He is at my right hand." "Always before me." What an inspiration and comfort in the midst of all the trials and turmoils of life! What a source of restfulness of spirit, with regard to all that was before him! If the miser, or prosperous man of the world, loves to set his possessions before him, so does the man of God; but how different their nature and results.

3. **Stability.** "Because He is at my right hand, I shall

not be moved. " The man who always sets the Lord before him is little likely to be moved away from the hope of the Gospel. All the popular winds of adverse doctrine cannot move him. His heart is fixed, trusting in the Lord.

4. Gladness. "Therefore my heart is glad, and my glory rejoiceth" (v. 9). His *heart* is glad, because it is healed and satisfied. This is not an attempt at rejoicing, like many of the world's "get-ups"; it is the natural or inevitable consequence of a certain condition or attitude of soul. "We joy in God through our Lord Jesus Christ" (Rom. 5. 11).

5. GUIDANCE. "Thou wilt shew me the path of life" (v. 11). Though this holy path of life may be narrow, the trusting soul is confident that He will reveal it moment by moment, and step by step. The path of the high Christian life is the path of continual faith and continual obedience. Day by day we need to be shown the path He would have us follow

6. HOPE. "In Thy presence is fullness of joy; in Thy right hand are pleasures for evermore" (R.V.). Although now the sons of God, "it doth not yet appear what we shall be, but we know that when He shall appear, we shall be *like Him.* " Although His presence is *with us* now, we have not yet passed into the fullness of the blessing of His presence in the glory-land. He holds in His right hand, reserved for us, "pleasures for evermore. " "Blessed Hope!" (Titus 2. 13).

PRAYER AND TESTIMONY.
PSALM 17. 1-8, 15.

THERE must always be a vital relationship between prayer and testimony. Those who are most powerful in prayer are most likely to give the most powerful testimony. The songs of David are just about equalled with his prayers,

Influence for God springs out of influence with God. Observe here—

I. **The Things Asked from God.** David prays for—

1. DIVINE ATTENTION. "Hear the right, O Lord, attend unto my cry" (v. 1). It is for the glory of His Name that He attends to the *righteous* cry of His children. God has a quick ear to "hear the right." No mother or physician can give such close attention to our need as our heavenly Father.

2. DIVINE UPHOLDING. "Hold up my goings in Thy paths" (v. 5). He knows that it is not in man to direct his steps (Jer. 10. 23). By the help of His gracious hand we are kept from stumbling. Our footsteps will slip when we cease to lean upon His strength. He is able to keep the feet of His holy ones (1 Sam. 2. 9, R.V.).

3. DIVINE MANIFESTATION. "Shew Thy marvellous lovingkindness" (v. 7). He pleads for a further revelation of God's character in His kindness, loving-kindness, marvellous lovingkindness. It is so excellent that it constrains men to put their trust under the shadow of His wings (Psa. 36. 7). This marvellous lovingkindness finds its perfect manifestation in and through Jesus Christ.

4. DIVINE PROTECTION. "Keep me as the apple of the eye; hide me under the shadow of Thy wings" (v. 8). They will surely be securely kept who are hidden beneath His wings, and guarded as the apple of the eye. His pinions are long and powerful, and one is more jealous of the eye than any other part of the body. The *strength* and the *carefulness* of God are more than enough to save from our "deadly enemies!"

II. **The Testimony Given for God.** We are assured by the Psalmist that God had—

1. PROVED HIM. "Thou has proved mine heart" (v. 3).

The *heart*, that is so prone to be deceitful, must first be dealt with. The good seed is only fruitful in a "good and *honest* heart" (Luke 8. 15).

2. VISITED HIM. "Thou hast visited me in the night" (v. 3). The heart is proven that it might be visited in mercy and grace. He visits in the night of quiet restfulness, in the night of darkness and sorrow. He knows when to visit, and what to bring. "Behold, I stand at the door" (Rev. 3. 20).

3. TRIED HIM. "Thou hast tried me, and findeth no evil purpose in me" (R.V., *margin*). The trial of your faith is precious; when perfectly sincere, it will be to His praise and glory (1 Peter 1. 7). When our hearts or secret purposes condemn us not, then have we confidence towards God.

4. SUSTAINED HIM. "By the word of Thy lips, I have kept me from the ways of the violent" (v. 4, R.V.). By taking heed to His Word, any young man may cleanse his way (Psa. 119. 9). We are kept by the power of God through *faith*—faith in His word. Man shall not live by bread alone, but by every word of God. The prayer of our Great High Priest was, "Sanctify them through Thy truth: Thy word is truth" (John 17. 17).

5. ANSWERED HIM. "I have called upon Thee, for Thou wilt answer me, O God" (v. 6, R.V.). He testifies that the reason why he prays is because God answers Him. "Let your requests be made known unto Him" (Phil. 4. 6).

6. SATISFIED HIM. "I will behold Thy face...I shall be satisfied when I awake with Thy likeness" (v. 15). Such a glorious prospect is enough to make the heart sing for joy, even now, when we but see through a glass darkly. God's *likeness* is His best and greatest gift. The more like Him we become now, the deeper will our soul satisfaction be.

THE GOD OF SALVATION.
PSALM 18. 1-3.

FROM the heading of this Psalm we learn that it was written as a song of DELIVERANCE. The first three verses contain a manifold revelation and a manifold obligation.

I. The Revelation. This is a revelation of the character of Jehovah as a Saviour. In verse 2 eight terms are used that are suggestive of so many aspects of His saving grace—

1. For REFUGE, He is *My Rock.* The unchangeable Rock of Ages.

2. For PROTECTION, He is *My Fortress.* "His Name is a strong tower; the righteous runneth into it and is safe." "The Lord encampeth *round about* them that fear Him" (Psa. 24. 7).

3. For OPPRESSION, He is *My Deliverer.* "Deliver us from evil, for Thine is the Kingdom, and the power" (Matt. 6. 13).

4. For WORSHIP, He is *My God.* It is written, "Him only shalt thou worship."

5. For WEAKNESS, He is *My Strength.* They that wait upon the Lord shall exchange strength. "My strength is made perfect in weakness."

6. For DEFENCE, He is *My Buckler.* Put on the whole armour of God, and over all the buckler, or shield of faith.

7. For POWER, He is *My Horn.* "All power is given unto Me; go ye therefore." Who shall resist Him?

8. For PROSPECT, He is *My High Tower.* Those seated in heavenly places have got a delightful view. From their high tower they can see the land that is "fairer than day."

II. The Obligations. Such marvellous privileges of grace have also gracious responsibilities. What are they? To—

1. LOVE HIM. "I will love Thee, O Lord" (v. 1). The

first and great commandment was: "Thou shalt love the
Lord thy God." Surely such manifestation of His love
should constrain us. Let it be also a thing of the *will*
(1 Cor. 13. 13).

2. TRUST HIM. "In Him I will trust" (v. 2). God
has done everything for us, and is willing to be everything
to us, but when there is no heart trust, the door of the soul
is barred against Him.

3. PRAISE HIM. "Who is worthy to be praised" (v. 3).
Those who "call upon the Lord" are most likely to praise
Him. He is worthy. Think of all He hath done, and of
His long-suffering mercy. "Worthy is the Lamb, to
receive glory and honour."

THE GREAT DELIVERANCE.
PSALM 18. 4-20.

THIS most majestic Psalm was sung by David, not as a
king, but as "the *servant* of the Lord." The key-note is
struck loudly at the beginning. "I will love the Lord...I
will trust the Lord...I will call upon the Lord...so shall
I be saved." Love, trust, prayer, assurance. If there are
great heights here, there are also terrible depths. To lift
from the deepest depth, up to the highest height, is the
glory of the grace of this Deliverer. While this Psalm
records the experiences of a soul passing from death unto
life, it is also prophetic of the sufferings, the death, and
resurrection of the Lord Jesus Christ.

I. **The Need.** His need was great for He was compassed about with the—

1. "SORROWS OF DEATH" (v. 4). To a soul without hope
these sorrows are most pungent. It is the sorrow of losing
every earthly blessing, of entering into the darkness of
despair. The Philippian jailer felt the pangs of them.
(Acts 16. 30).

2. SORROWS OF MEN. "Floods of ungodly men made me afraid." In times of soul conviction, the enemy is sure to come in like a flood. The world's mind and ways are against the purpose of his heart.

3. "SORROWS OF HELL" (v. 5). "The cords of Sheol were round about me" (R.V.). Fearful cords that would drag the soul down to eternal death. The joys of Heaven are best known by those who have felt the "sorrows of Hell."

II. **The Confession.** "In my distress I called upon the Lord, and cried unto my God" (v. 6). He was in real distress, and so his prayer was unfeigned, and his confession wholehearted. When a man's distress is as keenly felt as this, he has no hope of saving himself by any work he can do, or by anything he can give. The sorrows of Hell make sin-convicted souls feel that only the power and grace of almighty God can meet their need.

III. **The Deliverance.** In answer to this cry of distress he says that—

1. "HE CAME DOWN" (v. 9). To do this, He had to bow the Heavens. The language here is prophetic of the coming and sufferings of Christ. There are always signs and wonders wrought when He comes down in answer to the agonising cry of human need (vv. 7, 8).

2. "HE TOOK ME, He drew me out of many waters" (v. 16). If we are to be *drawn out* of the many waters of our sins and sorrows, He must take hold of us, and we must be perfectly submissive to His drawing power. Resist not the grace of God. When He does take hold, it is unto a perfect salvation.

3. "HE DELIVERED ME from my strong enemy" (v. 17). Your adversary, the Devil, is a strong enemy, but a stronger than he has come to seek and to save (Heb. 2. 14, 15).

4. "He Brought Me forth also into a large place" (v. 19). Whom the Lord sets free are free indeed. Out from the power of Satan, into the *Kingdom* of our Lord Jesus Christ. This is indeed "a large place," for it stretches into the ages of eternity. It takes a large place to meet all the aspirations of an immortal spirit. Resurrection ground.

5. "He Delighted in Me" (v. 19). He delivers because He delights in saving the objects of His love. "He loved me and gave Himself for me." His is no mechanical, or perfunctory salvation. He "*delighteth* in mercy." Our trust in Him delights His soul.

6. "He Rewarded Me" (v. 20). "He is a Rewarder of them that diligently seek Him." He never said to any, "Seek My face in vain." A clean heart, and clean hands, the Lord will recompense (v. 24). "O taste and see that the Lord is good" (Psa. 34. 8).

THE GOD OF DELIVERANCES.
Psalm 18. 25-39.

I. **His Manner of Working.** He reveals His—

1. Mercifulness to the Merciful (v. 25). "With the merciful Thou wilt shew Thyself merciful." The mercifulness of men can never rise to the mercifulness of God. Human mercy is to be measured by the Divine.

2. Perfection to the Perfect. "With the perfect *man*, Thou wilt shew *Thyself* perfect" (R. V.). The perfection of men is to be seen in the light of the perfection of God. The man with the "upright heart" desires this, "Shew me Thy glory."

3. Purity to the Pure. "With the pure Thou wilt shew Thyself pure" (v. 26). The pure in heart shall see a God that is infinitely purer. The desire after holiness is thus encouraged by this promise.

4. Frowardness to the Froward. "With the froward

Thou wilt shew Thyself froward. " The *frowardness* (lit.) of man, turning away from God, will be met with the frowardness of God. If man chooses to be perverse toward God, then they have the perversity of God to deal with.

5. PURPOSE IN SO DEALING WITH MEN. "For Thou wilt save the afflicted, but the haughty Thou wilt bring down" (v. 27, R.V.). If there is in us a mercifulness, a perfection, or a purity that is unreal, then the manifestation of His character is to rebuke pride and lead to repentance. His purpose is to save honest seekers, and to bring down the proud boasters.

II. **His Manifold Mercies.** All God's gifts are deliverances.

1. He gives LIGHT. "Thou wilt light my lamp...My God will lighten my darkness" (v. 28). In Him was life, and the life was the light of men.

2. He gives COURAGE. "By Thee I have ran through a troop; and by my God have I leaped over a wall" (v. 29). Troops of troubles and walls of difficulties need not hinder the man of faith.

3. He gives STRENGTH. "It is God that girdeth me with strength" (v. 32). Loins girded with the Word of God will be strong to do exploits.

4. He gives STABILITY. "He maketh my feet like hinds' feet" (v. 33). The hind is sure-footed, and can walk and leap with safety in slippery places.

5. He gives WISDOM. "He teacheth my hands to war" (v. 34). We war not with flesh and blood, but with principalities...and wicked spirits. For this battle Divine wisdom is needed.

6. He gives PROTECTION. "Thou hast given me the *shield* of Thy salvation" (v. 35). The salvation of God is a shield as long as our life, and as broad as our need.

7. He gives HONOUR. "Thy gentleness has made me great." The gentleness of almighty grace brings wonderful promotion to the whole nature of the spiritual man.

8. He gives VICTORY. "Thou hast girded me with strength; Thou hast subdued under me those that rose up against me" (v. 39). "Thanks be unto God who giveth us the victory, through our Lord Jesus Christ." "Great deliverance giveth He" (v. 50).

THE WORD OF GOD.
PSALM 19.

WHILE the Heavens declare the glory of God, the Bible declares His will. The speech of the Heavens is silent, "their voice is not heard" (R.V.). But even His eternal power and Godhead can be understood by the things that are made (Rom. 1. 19, 20). We have to come to the written and Incarnate Word for the *doctrine* of God. In verses 7-9 six different terms are used to express the fullness and preciousness of *His word*.

I. **It Converts the Soul**, because it is *perfect* (v. 7). It takes a perfect instrument to accomplish such delicate and powerful work as this. The soul needs conversion: the sword of the Spirit can do it (James 1. 18).

II. **It Makes Wise the Simple**, because it is *sure* (v. 7). It is sure because it is given by inspiration of God (2 Tim. 3. 15). It makes wise unto salvation all who are simple enough to believe it.

III. **It Rejoiceth the Heart**, because it is *right* (v. 8). It is the right thing for all the needs of the heart, so the heart rejoices in the receiving of it. The poor, hungry soul that finds great spoil (Psa. 119. 16). "Thy Word was the joy of my heart" (Jer. 15. 16).

IV. **It Enlightens the Eyes**, because it is *pure* (v. 8).

As the weary Jonathan had his eyes enlightened by partaking of the honey, so doth new light and vigour possess us when we taste the pure honey of His Word. The eyes are opened to see wondrous things. "Every word of God is pure." "Thy Word is a lamp" (Psa. 119. 105).

V. It Endureth for Ever, because it is *clean* (v. 9). It is the very thing a young man needs to cleanse his way (Psa. 119. 9). It is uncorruptible, and so endureth for ever. It does, and can, offer everlasting life, because the word itself is everlasting.

VI. It is Altogether Righteous, because it is *truth* (v. 9, *margin*). It is altogether right—right in its every warning and demand, counsel and promise. It is not only true, it is the TRUTH, and, therefore, cannot possibly be wrong on any point.

VII. It is Most Desirable, because it is better than *gold*, and sweeter than *honey* (v. 10). It is better than the best, and sweeter than the sweetest of all earthly things.

VIII. It is Most Needful, because it both *warns* and *rewards* (v. 11). It warns both servants and sinners of the danger and doom of unbelief. It assures the obedient of a glorious reward. It is both a law and a Gospel, a hammer and a fire, a beacon light, and bread from Heaven.

INTERCESSION AND CONFIDENCE.
PSALM 20.

WHILE it is good to pray for ourselves, it is gracious to pray for others. A powerful incentive to intercessory prayer is a satisfied and thankful heart.

I. An Example of Intercession. Here are seven requests that the Psalmist would put into prayerful lips. A sevenfold blessing which God is able to bestow.

1. "The Lord HEAR thee" (v. 1). It is a wonderful

privilege to have the God of Heaven bending His ear like a fond mother to the confidential whisperings of a child.

2. The Lord DEFEND thee (v. 1). To be defended by "the NAME of the God of Jacob," is to have power with God, and to prevail (Gen. 32. 28).

3. The Lord HELP thee. "Send thee help from the sanctuary" (v. 2). Help from the place of His holiness is sanctifying help. Provision was made for this (1 Kings 8. 44, 45).

4. The Lord STRENGTHEN thee. "Strengthen thee out of Zion," by the supplications of the people of God. Perhaps the *oneness* of the body of Christ may be suggested here.

5. The Lord REMEMBER thee (v. 3). "Remember all thy offerings," all thy gifts, and sacrifice for Him. May He have thee in everlasting remembrance. "I know thy works and labour of love."

6. The Lord SUPPLY thee. "Grant thee thy heart's desire" (v. 4, R.V.). To obtain this, there must be a delighting in the Lord (Psa. 37. 4). "The desire of the righteous is only good" (Prov. 11. 23).

7. The Lord FILL thee (v. 5). They are truly filled who have all their petitions fulfilled. "He filleth the hungry with good."

II. **An Example of Confidence.** A confidence—

1. In the SALVATION of God. "We will rejoice in Thy salvation" (v. 5). It is a salvation worth rejoicing in, because of its greatness, its costliness, and its fullness.

2. In the CAUSE of God. "In the Name of our God we will set up our banners." The banner of truth (Psa. 60. 4), of victory, of progress. His Kingdom cannot be moved.

3. In the FAITHFULNESS of God. "Now know I that the Lord saveth His anointed" (v. 6). Blessed are they that

know this joyful sound. This is experimental knowledge of Divine faithfulness.

4. In the NAME of God. "Some trust in chariots, but we will remember the Name of the Lord" (v. 7). To remember His Name is to remember His revealed character, and this is all sufficient to faith (2 Chron. 32. 8).

5. In the POWER of God. "They are brought down... but we are risen" (v. 8). He casteth down the proud, but the lowly in heart He lifteth up. Hold fast the confidence which you had at the beginning. Pray and trust.

THE JOY OF SALVATION.
PSALM 21

THE prayers in the preceding Psalm seem to find their fulfilment in the first nine verses of this Psalm. The one appears to be the perfect complement of the other, when compared verse by verse. "In Thy salvation," he says, "how greatly shall he rejoice" (v. 1). Note then—

I. **The Joys of the Saved.** In this state of blessedness there is the joy of—

1. HEART SATISFACTION. "Thou hast given him his *heart's* desire" (v. 2). God's great salvation is for the heart. He only knows to the full its nature and its need.

2. ANSWERED PRAYER. "Thou hast not withholden the request of his lips." What a privilege to ask and receive of Him who is the Creator of the universe, and the Father of our spirits.

3. PROVIDENTIAL GOODNESS. "Thou preventest (goeth before) him with the blessings of goodness" (v. 3). The God of goodness goeth before him with his blessing, and goodness, and mercy followeth after him (Psa. 23).

4. CROWNED WITH HONOUR. "Thou settest a crown of pure gold upon his head." All the glory of this world

cannot be compared with the pure gold of Divine favour (Matt. 4. 8).

5. ETERNAL LIFE. "He asked life of Thee; Thou gavest him length of days for ever and ever" (v. 4). "The *gift* of God is eternal life." His gift, like Himself, belongs to the eternal ages.

6. DIVINE FELLOWSHIP. "Thou hast made him exceeding glad with Thy countenance" (v. 6). This is the presence that brings fullness of joy (Psa. 16. 11). The reconciled countenance of God is the most soul-gladdening vision that man can ever have. Our fellowship is with the Father, etc.

7. PERFECT ASSURANCE. "Through the mercy of the Most High, he shall not be moved" (v. 7). He knows in whom he has believed, and is persuaded that He will keep.

8. SONGS OF PRAISES. "So will we sing and praise Thy power" (v. 13). His saving and satisfying power is worthy of our loudest song, for it will be our longest, for as the God of salvation we shall praise Him for ever.

II. **How this Salvation is Received.**

1. BY ASKING. "He asked life of Thee, and Thou gavest it" (v. 4). "If thou knewest the gift of God, ye would ask of Him" (John 4. 10). "Ask and ye shall receive."

2. BY TRUSTING. "The king trusted in the Lord" (v. 7). Without *faith* it is impossible to please Him (John 3. 36).

III. **The Miseries of the Unsaved.** They shall be—

1. FOUND OUT. "Thine hand shall find out all Thine enemies" (v. 8). Those who reject His *Word* of mercy will be apprehended by the *hand* of justice.

2. SORELY TROUBLED. "Thou shalt make them as a fiery oven in the time of Thine anger" (v. 9). Despised

and rejected love must be met with fury and indignation. The "wrath of the Lamb" awaits those who tread under foot the "blood of the Lamb."

3. MISERABLY DISAPPOINTED. "They intended evil... they imagined...which they are not able to perform" (v. 11). In different ways, men still command that the sepulchre of Christ be made sure, but all such devices result in wretched failure. No matter how often men, by their wicked works and ways, crucify and bury Christ God will raise Him from the dead. No wisdom or counsel can stand that is against the Lord (Prov. 21. 30). "The wages of sin is death" (Rom. 6. 23).

HIS SUFFERINGS AND GLORY.
PSALM 22.

THIS is a prophetic declaration of "The sufferings of Christ and the glory that should follow." It is not only "The Psalm of the Cross," but also of the Crown and the King- dom. These sufferings cannot be David's. Who "pierced his hands and feet?" Who "parted His garments, and cast lots upon His vesture?" (v. 18). These words are the tender breathings of the Holy Spirit, through this holy man of old. Here the Spirit testifies beforehand the sufferings of Christ.

I. The Nature of His Sufferings. He was—

1. DESERTED. "My God, My God, WHY hast Thou forsaken Me?" (vv. 1, 2). This is a mysterious and awful *why*. The question of sin and judgment is in it. He was forsaken of God because "He was made a *curse* for us."

2. REPROACHED. "A reproach of men, and despised of the people" (v. 6). Although God hid His face from Him, there was no reproach on His part. The reproach and the scorn came from wicked men, for whom He suffered.

3. DERIDED.   "Commit thyself unto the Lord... let
Him deliver Him, seeing He delighteth in Him" (v. 8, R.V.).
They mocked at His faith in God as a vain thing.   They
laughed at His weakness, as an evidence of failure and
presumption.

4. EMPTIED.   "I am poured out like water" (v. 14)
He emptied Himself and became of no reputation.   He
poured out His soul unto death.   He gave all that He had.

5. HUMBLED.   "Thou hast brought Me into the dust of
death" (v. 15).   He was brought to the dust, through
His own voluntary humility.   "He humbled Himself, and
became *obedient* unto death."

6. PIERCED.   "They pierced My hands and My feet"
(v. 16).   They nailed Him to a Cross.   They crucified
the Lord of Glory.

7. SHAMED.   "I may tell all my bones... They part My
garments among them."   The death of the Cross was the
most painful and shameful of all deaths (John 19. 23, 24).
They put Him to an open shame.   "He suffered for us, the
Just for the unjust, that He might bring us to God"
(1 Peter 3. 18).

II. The Glory that was to Follow.

1. THE DECLARATION OF HIS NAME.   "I will declare
Thy Name" (v. 22; see Heb. 2. 12).   "Wherefore,"
because of His sufferings and death, "God hath highly
exalted Him, and given Him a Name that is above every
other name."   The preaching of His *Name* is the preaching
of His holy and wondrous saving characters.

2. THE ASSURANCE OF HIS GRACE.   "He hath not
despised nor abhorred the affliction of the afflicted" (v. 24).
"The meek shall eat and be satisfied" (v. 26).   Grace
and truth came by Jesus Christ.   "My grace is sufficient for
thee."   "Hearken diligently unto me, and eat ye that which
is good, and let your soul delight in fatness" (Isa. 55. 1, 2).

3. THE TRIUMPH OF HIS CAUSE. "All the ends of the world shall remember and turn to the Lord...for the Kingdom is the Lord's, and He is the Ruler over the nations" (vv. 27, 28, R.V.). The rejected King shall yet rule over the earth (Zech. 14. 9). "The kingdoms of this world shall become the Kingdom of our Lord and of His Christ" (Rev. 11. 15). He died for us, that He might be Lord both of the living and the dead. "Thine is the Kingdom, and the power, and the glory, for ever" (Matt. 6. 13).

THE ALMIGHTY SHEPHERD.
PSALM 23.

AMONG all the Psalms, the twenty-third is the "pet lamb" of the flock to many. Beecher called it the "Nightingale Psalm, small, and of a homely feather, singing shyly out of obscurity; but, oh! it has filled the air of the whole world with melodious joy." After the Psalm of the Cross comes the Psalm of Life, and *fullness of blessing*. The path of this pilgrim is like the shining light that shineth more and more till the day of perfection. Let us follow him step by step. There was—

I. Decision. "The Lord is my Shepherd." His personal choice was made as to whom he would follow. He would not follow his own heart nor the blind reasonings of men; he would claim Jehovah as his Saviour and Guide and not be ashamed to say so.

II. Assurance. "I shall not want." The godless, although strong as young lions, do lack and suffer hunger, but they that seek the Lord shall not want any good. "My God shall supply all your need." He has his Shepherd's promise, and he believes it.

III. Rest. "He maketh me to lie down in green pastures, and beside the waters of rest" (*margin*). The rest of faith in the Lord is a rest that is calm and refreshing. He does not say "rest," without leading into the best place where it can be found—in His love—green pastures.

IV. **Restoration**. "He restoreth my soul." If through self-confidence, or discontent, we should stray from His paths of greenness, He is gracious enough to forgive and restore. He, only, can restore the backsliding soul (1 John 1. 1).

V. **Guidance**. "He leadeth me in the paths of righteousness." The paths that are *right* may not always be the paths that seem easiest. Bunyan's pilgrims found it "easy going" over the stile which led to the castle of Giant Despair. His leading is for His own *Name's sake*.

VI. **Courage**. "Though I walk through the valley of the shadow of death, I will fear no evil." The shadow of death is a dreadful thing to the man whose portion is in this life. But there is no evil to fear when the Shepherd is near (Isa. 43. 2).

VII. **Fellowship**. "Thou art with me." The heavenly pilgrim is always in good company. The Lord stands by when all men forsakes (2 Tim. 4. 16, 17). His presence is always sufficient at all times.

VIII. **Comfort**. "Thy rod and Thy staff they comfort me." The club and the crook of the shepherd were the instruments of defence and deliverance. What they were to the sheep, the Word of the Lord is to us. It is a club to beat off our enemies, and a crook to guide or lift those who have fallen into a pit or ditch. The sword of the Spirit doth comfort me.

IX. **Provision**. "Thou preparest a table before me in the presence of mine enemies." He knows when and how to feed His flock. We have a meat to eat that they know not of.

X. **Enduement**. "Thou anointest my head." This

anointing, or unction from the Holy One, is significant of authority and power. Kings and priests were anointed. Ye are a kingdom of priests unto God (Acts 1. 8).

XI. Satisfaction. "My cup runneth over." The God of grace gives good measure, pressed down, shaken together, heaped up, running over. The holy anointing must go before the overflowing (see John 7. 37, 38).

XII. Prospect. "Surely goodness and mercy shall follow me...and I will dwell in the house of the Lord for ever." Goodness to supply, and mercy to forgive, all the days of this life; and a mansion is prepared beyond this life, where we shall be for ever with the Lord (John 14. 1-3).

PSALM 23 (again).

1. **Beneath me**, "green pastures." 2, **Beside me**, "still waters." 3, **With me**, "my Shepherd." 4, **Before me**, "a table." 5, **Around me**, "mine enemies." 6, **Upon me**, "anointing." 7, **After me**, "goodness and mercy." 8, **Beyond me**, "The house of the Lord."— *Selected.*

THE ASCENT OF MAN.
PSALM 24. 3-6.

IN the twenty-second Psalm we have the Lord's sorrowful descent to man. Here is the way of man's ascent to the Lord.

I. The Goal. "The hill of the Lord...His holy place." The hill of the Lord is the holy place of His presence. Mount Zion stands for the tabernacle or habitation of God (Psa. 55. 1). The highest ambition of the soul should be the fellowship of God—the fellowship of Him to whom the earth belongs, and the fullness thereof (v. 1).

II. The Way. "Who shall *ascend*?" The way of sin and impurity is downward, but the way of holiness is ever *upward.* The ascent of this mount is the ascent of every faculty in man. No one can climb this hill without having their own moral, spiritual, and intellectual being invigorated.

III. **The Pilgrim.** The characteristic features of this hill-climber are given:—

1. His HANDS must be *clean.* "He that hath clean hands." Not hands washed in water, like Pilate's, but washed in innocency, like David's (Psa. 26. 6). We cannot ascend to Him with the lie of a deceitful motive in our right hand. Let the wicked forsake his ways, and let him return to the Lord. The laver stood outside the door of the tabernacle, at which the approaching priest must wash his hands.

2. His HEART must be *pure* (v. 4). Holiness is something that has to do with the heart, and without holiness no man shall see the Lord. "The pure in heart shall see God." It is with the heart that man believeth *unto righteousness.* It is when the seed of the Kingdom falls into an "honest heart" that it brings forth fruit.

3. His SOUL must be *humble.* "Who hath not lifted up his soul unto *vanity.*" When vanity, or spiritual pride, gets into the soul, then there is an end to growth in grace. If we would ascend into the holy hill of the Divine likeness, there must be no vain lifting up of ourselves.

IV. **The Attainment.** "He shall receive the blessing from the Lord, and righteousness from the God of his salvation." The blessing of perfect rightness with God is a crown of life within the reach of every spiritual pilgrim. *The blessing* of the Lord embodies every needful and desirable thing.

V. **The Application.** "This is the generation of them that seek Him" (v. 6). This is the character and attitude of the true seed of Abraham—the father of the faithful. This is the generation that belongs to the *re*-generation. These are the marks of the children of God, who climb the hill of holiness into the Father's house.

ELEMENTS OF SUCCESSFUL PRAYER.
PSALM 25. 1-11.

THE Psalms have been called by Dr. A. Murray "The prayer book of God's saints." In this book, the spirit of prayer, and the spirit of praise are twin spirits; they are indivisible. This psalm would teach us how to pray.

I. Elements of Prayer.

1. WHOLEHEARTEDNESS. "Unto Thee, O Lord, do I *lift up my soul*" (v. 1). What is the use of lifting up our voice, or our eyes, unto God, if the *soul* is not in them. God's ear is not to be charmed by such soulless music. We find Him when we seek Him with the whole heart.

2. FAITH. "O my God, I trust in Thee." We cannot *taste* the goodness of the Lord by mere talk; the tongue of the soul must touch Him. Faith is the hand that lays hold of His promise.

3. DESIRE FOR HIS WAYS. "Shew me Thy ways, O Lord; teach me Thy paths" (v. 4). This implies a forsaking of our own ways (Isa. 58. 6), and a readiness to follow His footsteps. "Yield yourselves unto God."

4. DESIRE FOR HIS TRUTH. "Lead me in Thy truth, and teach me" (v. 5). This must be the longing of that heart in which the Holy Ghost is, for "when He, the Spirit of truth, is come, He will guide into all truth" (John 16. 13). A craving after the mind and will of God, is a powerful factor in prevailing prayer.

5. DESIRE FOR HIS HONOUR. "For Thy goodness' sake, O Lord" (v. 7). "For Thy Name's sake, O Lord" (v. 11). To plead His Name is to plead His nature. His

goodness stands for His character (see Exod. **33. 18, 19**;
34. 5, 6). When He "sanctifies His great Name among the
heathen" (Ezek. **36. 23**), He makes *Himself* known as
the Lord God, merciful and gracious. "If ye ask anything
in My Name I will give it. "

6. PATIENCE. "On Thee do I wait all the day" (v. 5).
Let your requests be made known unto God, but let patience
also have her perfect work. There is no virtue in waiting,
unless we are waiting *on* HIM. "They that wait upon the
Lord shall renew strength. "

7. CONFESSION. "Remember not the sins of my youth,
nor my transgressions" (v. 7). There must be no hiding of
sin; no glossing over the trangressions of earlier days.
Those who would deal with a holy and righteous God must
be perfectly honest in the purposes of their heart. "God is
not mocked. "

II. **Encouragements to Prayer.** "Let your requests
be made known unto God. "

1. Because He is GOOD AND UPRIGHT (v. 8). God is
love, and God is light. The goodness of a Father is here
associated with the uprightness of a righteous sovereign.

2. Because He TEACHES SINNERS (v. 8). What conde-
scension: the Almighty God willing to become the sinner's
teacher. His desire is to lead us in His way. He teacheth
savingly and to eternal profit.

3. Because He GUIDES THE MEEK (v. 9). He does not
guide a man because he is rich, or learned, for all cannot
attain to these, but any man may be *meek*, and learn
heavenly wisdom.

4. Because "ALL THE PATHS OF THE LORD ARE MERCY
AND TRUTH unto such as keep His Word" (v. 10). Mercy
and truth, constitute the daily need of the heavenly
pilgrim. Mercy, to forgive, and to cleanse; truth, to
guide, to strengthen, and to satisfy. To get out of the
Lord's paths, is to get out of the channel of supply.

FEATURES OF A WHOLE-HEARTED CHRISTIAN
PSALM 26.

I. He Desires to be Tested by God. "Judge me, O Lord...Examine me, O Lord" (vv. 1, 2). It is a small matter to him, to be judged of men, who seeks the judgment of God. He who can pray, "Search me, O God, and know my heart; try me, and know my thoughts," lives above the fear of man (Acts 23. 1).

II. He has Faith in God. "I have trusted also in the Lord, therefore I shall not slide" (v. 1). God has become the greatest reality in the world to his soul, and in Him he hath put his trust. His heart condemns him not, because he has confidence toward God (1 John 3. 21).

III. He Adheres to the Word of God. "I have walked in Thy truth" (v. 3). To walk in His truth is to walk in His way, and so walk in the light. He chooses the will of God as revealed in His Word, rather than the imaginations of his own heart.

IV. He Separates Himself from the Enemies of God. "I have not sat with vain persons, neither will I go in with dissemblers" (v. 4). The evil communications of the worldling corrupt the good manners of the child of God. "Wherefore come out from among them and be ye separate."

V. He Offers Sacrifices unto God. "I will wash mine hands in innocency: so will I compass Thine altar, O Lord" (v. 6). The sons of Aaron washed their hands at the laver ere they compassed the altar of incense (Exod. 30). The man that had to leave his gift at the altar and be reconciled to his brother was taught to first wash his hands (Matt. 5. 23). "The sacrifices of God are a broken spirit."

VI. He Testifies for God. "That I may publish with the voice of thanksgiving, and *tell* of all Thy wondrous works" (v. 7). He is most thankful and willing to tell of that most wonderful work of God in his own heart and experience. "Great and marvellous are Thy works, O Lord;" Thy works of mercy and grace in the sinful souls of men; Thy work of redemption by the Cross of Thy beloved Son.

VII. He Loves the House of God. "I have loved the habitation of Thy house, and the place where Thy glory dwelleth" (v. 8, R.V.). He loved the house because of Him who dwelt therein. When his soul thirsts for the "courts of the Lord" it is because he was thirsting for the "living God" (Psa. 84. 1, 2). They are idolaters who love the *habitation* of God rather than God HIMSELF.

VIII. He Praises God. "In the congregation will I bless the Lord" (v. 12). He is not ashamed to praise the Lord with his *whole heart* (Psa. 3. 1). He has often asked the Lord to bless him, but he does not forget to "bless the Lord." "Whoso offereth praise glorifieth Me" (Psa. 50. 23).

_____

THREEFOLD CORDS.
PSALM 27.

THE thoughts in this most precious Psalm seem to run in triplets.

I. A Threefold Need (v. 1).

1. LIGHT. "The Lord is my light." The world needs light. Christ is the light of the world. Satan hath blinded the minds of men.

2. SALVATION. "The Lord is...my salvation." He took me from a fearful pit.

3. STRENGTH. "The Lord is the strength of my life." He established my goings. This threefold need is met only *in the Lord* (Phil. 4. 19).

II. A Threefold Desire (v. 4).

1. To "DWELL in the house of the Lord." To dwell in

His house is to "Abide in Him." It is an expression of holy affection for the Lord Himself.

2. To "BEHOLD the beauty of the Lord." This was the good part that Mary chose, when she sat at the feet of Jesus. To learn of Him is to behold His glory.

3. To "INQUIRE in His temple." If any man lack wisdom, let him ask of God. The temple door of the Holy Scriptures is always open to inquirers. Counsel not with the ungodly (Psa. 1. 1)

III. A Threefold Privilege (v. 5).

1. HIDDEN IN HIS PAVILION. In the time of trouble, sheltered in the great pavilion of His special providence (Rom. 8. 28).

2. SECRETED IN HIS TABERNACLE. In the secret of His *presence*, as well as His power, doth He hide from the pride of man. The life that is hid in God can never be found out by His enemies.

3. SET UPON A ROCK. His feet, or ways, are established on a sure foundation. His life is not built up on the shifting sands of human theories.

IV. A Threefold Assurance (vv. 8-10).

1. OF HIS FACE. "When Thou saidst, Seek ye My face; my *heart* said unto Thee, Thy face, Lord, will I seek." The pure in heart shall see the face of God in His Son, in His Word, and in His Providence.

2. OF HIS FELLOWSHIP. "Thou hast been my help; leave me not." He hath said, "I will never leave thee," so that we may boldly say, "The Lord is my Helper" (Heb. 13. 5, 6).

3. OF HIS FAVOUR. "When my father and mother forsake me, then the Lord will take me up." The Good Shepherd carries the weary, or forsaken lambs in His arms. Those who forsake their father, the Devil, will find favour with the Lord (Hos. 14. 3).

V. A Threefold Prayer (vv. 11, 12).

1. For Teaching. "Teach me Thy ways." His ways are ways of pleasantness. He teacheth *savingly*.

2. For Guidance. "Lead me in a plain path, because of mine enemies." We are best able to use "plainness of speech" when our feet are walking in a plain path. We walk by faith, and not by sight.

3. For Deliverance. From "The will of mine enemies." As David has his Doig, and Christ His Judas, and Paul his Coppersmith, so every true servant of God may have those from whom he needs deliverance.

VI. A Threefold Encouragement (vv. 13, 14).

1. To Believe. "I had fainted unless I had believed." Troubled on every side, yet not distressed (2 Cor. 4. 8-10), because our faith is in God. Peter fainted while on the water because he doubted.

2. To Wait. "Wait on the Lord." Wait on Him because the expectation of faith is from Him (Psa. 62. 1-5). All who truly wait on Him will yet be able to say, "Lo, this is our God" (Isa. 25. 9).

3. To Work. "He shall strengthen thine heart, be of good courage." "Whatsoever thy hand findeth to do, do it" (Eccles. 9. 10), for His strength is made perfect in weakness.

———

A STRIKING CONTRAST.
Psalm 28.

This Psalm opens with a strange request, "Be not silent to me: *lest*" (vv. 1, 2). It is not every one who dreads the miseries of a *silent* God. They must have had deep experiences of God who get so alarmed at His silence. Alas, for those who interpret His silence as meaning peace. Note the contrast here—

I. The Character of the Wicked. They are—

1. Mischievous in their Nature. "They speak peace

to their neighbours, but mischief is in their hearts"
(v. 3). They may have fair lips, but the poison of asps
is under their tongues. Their hearts are deceitful. "Full
of wounds... and putrifying sores."

2. FOOLISH IN THEIR ACTIONS. "They regard not the
works of the Lord, nor the operation of His hands" (v. 5).
They are indifferent to their highest and best interests.
They heed not the voice of God in creation and in grace.
The operation of His hand in providence, and in their
own individual lives is systematically disregarded. "A
brutish man knoweth not" (Psa. 92. 5, 6).

II. **The Character of the Godly.** They are—

1. PRAYERFUL. "He hath heard the voice of my
supplications" (v. 6). God is not silent for ever to the cry
of His people. Although at times He may answer "never
a word," yet the pleading saint knows that He hears every
word. "Pray without ceasing."

2. BOASTFUL. "The Lord *is* my strength and my shield...
and I *am* helped" (v. 7). He is full of boasting, but not
in himself, his boast is in God. He will glory in the
Lord, because He hath done great things for him.

3. TRUSTFUL. "My heart trusted in Him." The heart
of man finds its true refuge and source of supply in the heart
of God. It is the sum of all blessedness when our hearts
answer to the heart of our Heavenly Father. With the
heart man believeth unto righteousness.

4. JOYFUL. "My heart greatly rejoiceth." The
trusting heart is sure to be a joyful heart. Faith in God
produces joy in God. A happy heart is a continual feast.

5. PRAISEFUL. "With my song will I praise Him."
The Christian's hero is Christ. His song shall be
of Jesus. This is the "new song" put into the heart and
lips of those redeemed by grace.

6. HUMBLE. "He is the saving strength of His anointed"

(v. 8). HE is. What have we that we have not received? It is because of what *He is*, not because of what *we are*, that we glory in the Lord. All is yours, for ye are Christ's and Christ is God's.

7. HOPEFUL. "Save Thy people, and bless Thine inheritance, feed them, and lift them up" (v. 9). They confidently expect that all God's people will be saved, blessed, fed, and lifted. What an encouragement this is for others to trust in Him. There will be a great lifting up when the Redeemer and Bridegroom appears (1 Thess. 4. 17).

————

THE POWERFUL VOICE.
PSALM 29.

In the preceding Psalm David speaks of the "operation of His *hands*;" here, amidst the terrors of a thunderstorm, he sings of the *voice* of the Lord. The Psalmist does not confound nature with the personality of God. He "gives unto the Lord the glory due unto His Name" (v. 2). The voice of the Lord is not a mere noise, it is a message. This voice we hear in all the riches of its majesty and glory in the person of His Son. "God hath in these last days spoken unto us by His Son." This voice of the Lord, in its "breaking," "making," "dividing," "shaking," and "discovering" power may prefigure the influence and effects of the voice or Word of Jesus Christ. It is a—

I. **Universal Power.** "The voice of the Lord is upon the waters" (v. 3). Metaphorically, these waters may represent the nations of the earth. The voice of God's word is for every people, tribe, and tongue. "Go ye into all the world and preach the Gospel to every creature."

II. **Majestic Power.** "The voice of the Lord is full of majesty" (v. 4). There is a God-like dignity about the Bible which belongs to no other book, it is full of majesty. The Gospel of Christ is the *power of God* to every one that believeth. The word of God asserts its own majestic character by being "quick and powerful." It has all the nobility of "Spirit and life."

III. **Breaking Power.** "The voice of the Lord breaketh the cedars" (v. 5). The strongest of *nature's* growths are bowed and broken by its pressure. "Is not My Word a hammer?" Saul in Jerusalem, was like a cedar in Lebanon, but on the way to Damascus he was broken down.

IV. **Separating Power.** "He maketh them (cedar branches) to skip like a calf" (v. 6, R.V.). His Word can not only break down, but can also break into pieces; separating branch from branch, tearing them away from their roots. A storm of Divine truth makes havoc with old associations and conservative habits and manners.

V. **Dividing Power.** "The voice of the Lord divideth the flames of fire" (v. 7). Every word of God is a flame of fire, and He can divide them as the lightning flashes are divided. He can make His tongue of flame to rest upon every holy head (Acts 2. 3). God's Word makes great distinctions. It is a divider of soul and spirit, of sinners and saints. The voice of the Lord is a terror to some, it is heavenly music to others.

VI. **Shaking Power.** "The voice of the Lord shaketh the wilderness" (v. 8). Yes, the *wilderness*, in all its desolation, barrenness and hopelessness; whether that wilderness is your heart, your home, or your city, the power of the Word of God can shake it, and make it to tremble into a transformation (Isa. 35. 1-7).

VII. **A Life-giving Power.** "The voice of the Lord maketh the hinds to calve" (v. 9). Because of the awfulness of God's thunderings, the hinds, through terror, were made to calve. It is when God's Word thunders and lightens most, that Zion's travail for the birth of souls becomes greatest. It is by His mighty Word of truth that souls are still being "born again."

VIII. **Stripping Power.** "The voice of the Lord... strippeth the forest bare" (v. 9, R.V.). The hidden depths of the heart of the forest are laid bare by His discovering voice. The Word of God is a *discerner* of the thoughts and intents of the heart. The fig-leaves of man's covering cannot stand this storm.

IX. **God-glorifying Power.** "In His temple everything saith glory" (v. 9, R.V.). Every iota in the great temple of nature saith "glory." So doth every thing in the temple of His revealed Word—Jesus Christ. So ought every thing in the temple of these bodies, which are His. "The Word was made flesh, and dwelt among us, and we beheld His glory." Not one thing of all that He hath spoken shall fail, everything shall say "glory."

A SONG OF SALVATION.

PSALM 30.

"THOU hast lifted me up" (v. 1). This may be regarded as the key note of this Psalm, sung at the dedication of the house of David. The salvation of God is fitly expressed by a lifting up? He was lifted up—

I. **From the Power of his Enemies.** "Thou hast raised me up, and hast not made my foes to rejoice over me" (v. 1, R.V.). The grace of God that bringeth salvation to all men, lifts up the believing soul out of the kingdom of darkness and tyranny, into the Kingdom of light and liberty. More than conquerors, over self and sin through Him who loved us.

II. **From all his Diseases.** "Thou hast healed me" (v. 2). Only He who forgiveth all our iniquities, can heal our diseases (Psa. 103. 3). A nature that is morally unsound can only be cured by moral and regenerative influences. "The Blood of Christ cleanseth from all sin."

III. **From the Place of Death.** "Thou hast brought my soul from the grave" (v. 3). Sheol was the abode of the dead. Speaking figuratively, he had by the grace of God been delivered from a state of spiritual death. There are many souls that are as dead to the things of God as if they were in their graves. It is the Spirit that quickeneth.

IV. **From Going Down to the Pit.** "Thou hast kept me alive, that I should not go down to the pit" (v. 3). Or, "Thou hast separated me from among them that go down to the pit" (see R.V., *margin*). He was saved from the company and influence of them that were perishing in their sins. Deliver from going down to the pit, for I have found the ransom.

V. **From Weakness and Failure.** "Lord, by Thy favour Thou hast made my mountain to stand strong" (v. 7). By God's *grace* the mountain of his faith had been made to stand strong. His strength had been made perfect in weakness. Unbelief says, "I shall die in my nest" (Job. 29. 18), but faith says, "My mountain is strong."

VI. **From Sorrow and Sadness.** "Thou hast turned my mourning into dancing. Thou hast loosed my sackcloth, and girded me with gladness" (v. 11, R.V.). Our God transforms the inner life of Zion's mourners, by giving them beauty for ashes, the oil of joy for mourning, and the garment of praise for the spirit of heaviness (Isa. 63. 1).

VII. **From Praiseless Silence.** "To the end that my glory may sing praise to Thee, and not be silent" (v. 12). There are those who profess to know God, but they glorify Him not as God, neither are they thankful (Rom. 1. 21). He hath saved us with a great salvation that our praises may abound unto Him, and not be silent (Eph. 5. 19, 20).

THE BLESSED LIFE.

Psalm 31.

There are bright rays of light, and dark gloomy shadows
here. But the blessed life can be lived in the midst
of "nets," "lying vanities," and "lying lips." It is
in circumstances like these that we can best prove
the saving grace of God. Let us try and catch some of
the features of the life of faith as revealed in this song.
There was—

I. **Confidence.** "In Thee, O Lord, do I put my trust"
(v. 1). The blessed life must have its source in God, who
is blessed for evermore. We do not begin to live till
we trust in Him (John 3. 36). To receive by faith the
life-giving One is to receive the right of Sonship (John
1. 12).

II. **Committal.** "Into Thine hand I commit my spirit.
Thou hast redeemed me, O Lord God of truth" (v. 5).
The *redeemed* spirit must be entirely committed to the
Redeemer. "Ye are not your own, for ye are bought with
a price." The life of faith is a life of continual and unre-
served surrender to the will of God. Self-sacrifice in the
will of God is a very different thing from self-sacrifice
outside that will.

III. **Confession.** "Have mercy upon me, O Lord, for
I am in trouble,...my strength faileth...I am forgotten
as a dead man, I am like a broken vessel" (vv. 9-12). It
is no new thing for a man to feel nothing but weakness,
and worthlessness, after he has solemnly and heartily given
himself to God. It may be very painful to discover that,
instead of strength and fullness, there has come the consciousness that we are but as *dead* men, and *broken* vessels!
But these are the first evidences that the consecration has

been real and effectual. Crucified with Christ, having the broken and contrite heart.

IV. Petition. "My times are in Thy hands, deliver me ...make Thy face shine upon Thy servant" (vv. 15, 16). Having committed his spirit and his "times" into the hand of God, he now pleads for the shining of His face. God requires perfect honesty of heart, in confession and in prayer. The shining of HIS FACE is the perfect remedy for those who are "forgotten as a dead man." The longing of every holy heart is for the "light of His countenance" (Psa. 4. 6).

V. Adoration. "Oh, how great is Thy goodness" (v. 19). Those who are wholly yielded to God will find their soul's satisfaction in the goodness of God. The ripest fruit of faith is adoration. The goodness of God in His Son Jesus Christ is so great that we must admire and adore.

VI. Praise. "Blessed be the Lord: for He hath shewed me His marvellous kindness" (v. 21). Although the tongue can never express the overwhelming sense of God's goodness, that at times fill the soul, yet it cannot remain silent. Bless the Lord, O my soul, Praise Him, praise Him for His marvellous works of love and mercy. Join now in the new and everlasting song, "Worthy is the Lamb that was slain."

VII. Exhortation. "O love the Lord, all ye His saints. ...Be of good courage" (vv. 23, 24). The heart that is full of the goodness of God will eagerly long for others to *love* Him, *trust* Him, *serve* Him, and to *hope* in Him. O ye separated ones, love the Lord, and let love lead to courage in His service, and He shall strengthen your heart. The blessed life is a life of faith in God for ourselves, and of faith in His Gospel for others.

SAVED AND KEPT.

Psalm 32.

THIS well-known Psalm might be studied in the light of the ninth chapter of the Acts. It describes the experiences of a soul passing from the sorrows of conviction into the joys of salvation. There is—

I. The Need of Salvation.

1. SIN IMPLIED. "Transgression...sin...iniquity" (vv. 1, 2). Three words that describe three different phases of guilt. Those who would reckon with God must face the question of *sin*. All have sinned. All have gone astray (Isa. 53. 6).

2. SIN DISCOVERED. "Day and night Thy hand was heavy upon me; my moisture was changed as with the drought of summer" (v. 4, R.V.). He tried to keep silence, but the heavy hand of God made him "roar all the day long." It is hard to kick against the pricks of God's goading truth. The moisture of the natural man quickly dries up when the convicting breath of God's Spirit comes.

3. SIN CONFESSED. "I acknowledged my sin unto Thee" (v. 5). As long as the prodigal son tried to cover his sin, he did not prosper, but when he cried, "Father, I have sinned," he found mercy. "If we confess our sins, He is faithful and just to forgive us" (1 John 1. 9).

4. SIN FORGIVEN. "Thou forgavest the iniquity of my sin" (v. 5). Now he has entered into the "blessedness of the man whose transgression is forgiven, whose sin is *covered.*" God's forgiving grace goes deep down, taking all guile out of the spirit (v. 2). Not only forgiven, but *renewed* in the inner man.

II. The Blessedness of the Saved. They are—

1. HIDDEN. "Thou art my hiding place" (v 7). God Himself becomes their refuge and hiding place. Hidden from the strife of the foolish and poisonous tongues of men, and from the day of His wrath, against all ungodliness, your life is hid with Christ in God.

2. TAUGHT. "I will instruct thee and teach thee in the way which thou shalt go" (v. 8). The forgiven ones are to be all taught of God, who teacheth *saving*, from the ways of error, and to *profit*, both for this life, and that which is to come. Ye have the anointing of the Holy One, and need not that any man teach you (1 John 2. 27).

3. GUIDED. "I will guide thee with Mine eye." Sweet promise, as it implies that His eye is to be always upon us for good, so that we may see His face and enjoy His fellowship. We are not to be guided like the ignorant horse, or stubborn mule, with bit and bridle, but like obedient children, who can read the *mind* of God, in the eye of His Word.

4. GUARDED. "He that trusteth in the Lord, mercy shall *compass* him about" (v. 10). "Thou shalt *compass* me about with songs of deliverance" (v. 7). Compassed about with *mercy* and *songs* of deliverance; what a blessed environment. The heart garrisoned with forgiving mercy and songs of triumph. What a contrast to the "tribulation and anguish" that surrounds the soul of the evil doer (Rom. 2. 9).

5. GLADDENED. "Be glad in the Lord, and rejoice... and shout for joy" (v. 11). Not unto us, but unto THY Name, be all the glory. He begins by taking us up out of the fearful pit of sin, then puts the new song in our mouth. Praise to our God! "Rejoice in the Lord alway, for He changeth not."

REJOICE IN THE LORD.

PSALM 33. 1-12.

THERE are abundant reasons here why God's people should
"Shout for joy in the Lord" (Newberry). It is a blessed
choice to leave the doubters and join such shouters. The
source of the believer's joy is not in the world, nor in
themselves, but in the Lord. They sing unto Him a "new
song" (v. 3), because they have been made new creatures,
who enjoy new delights. They rejoice in the Lord because
of—

I. **His Word.** "The Word of the Lord is right" (v. 4).
It is the right thing for the souls and lives of men, because
of its converting and enlightening power (Psa. 19. 7, 8).
The Word of God is powerful, for by it the Heavens were
made (v. 6). It is the incorruptible *seed* that endureth
for ever.

II. **His Works.** "All His works are done in truth"
(v. 4). Every stone built by Him is perfectly plumb.
All His works are perfect. All His works in grace, as well
as in creation, are done in truth. He is a *just* God, and a
Saviour. If Christ is the way and the life, He is also the
truth. To be saved by grace is not to be saved at the
expense of truth, for "grace *and* truth came by Jesus
Christ" (John 1).

III. **His Lovingkindness.** "The earth is full of the
lovingkindness of the Lord" (v. 5, R.V.). Everywhere, to
those who have eyes to see, the tokens of His goodness may
be seen. But it is in Christ Jesus that His marvellous
lovingkindness finds its fullest manifestation. Yet in the
earth, the outer court of His temple, "He maketh the sun
to rise on the evil and on the good, and sendeth rain on the
just and on the unjust" (Matt. 5. 45). "God loved the
world" (John 3. 16).

IV. His Power. "Let all the earth fear the Lord...for He spake, and it was done, He commanded and it stood fast" (vv. 8, 9). Man may make void God's word, but He never speaks in vain. What He hath promised, He is able also to perform. Power belongeth unto God, and He giveth power to the faint, therefore, rejoice in the Lord.

V. His Knowledge. "The Lord bringeth the counsel of the nations to naught. He maketh the thoughts of the people to be of none effect" (v. 10, R.V.). It is a joy of God's children, that He knows all about the secret desires of the ungodly, and that He taketh the wise in their own craftiness (1 Cor. 3. 19). "Ye thought evil against me, but God meant it for good" (Gen. 50. 20). He can sanctify adverse things to the furtherance of the Gospel (Phil. 1. 12, 13).

VI. His Faithfulness. "The counsel of the Lord standeth for ever, the thoughts of His heart to all genera-tions" (v. 11). The *thoughts of His heart*, revealed in His Word, shall stand for ever. Man is famous for his "vain thoughts," but precious are Thy thoughts, O Lord, because they are infinitely great, and good, and true, and faithful.

VII. His Grace. "Blessed is...the people whom *He hath chosen* for His own inheritance" (v. 12). Grace is not an after-thought with God, it belongs to His eternal character, it is an essential attribute of His nature, for we are chosen in Him, before the foundation of the world, and now blessed with all spiritual blessing in Christ (Eph. 1. 3, 4). The grace that hath chosen us is to be made sufficient for us, therefore rejoice in the Lord, and again I say, rejoice.

JUBILIATION.

PSALM 34. 1-10.

IN the original, the verses of this Psalm begin with the letters of the Hebrew alphabet, indicating, perhaps, that special care has been bestowed on its composition. The occasion of it—when David played the fool before Abimelech—was anything but creditable to the king. Nevertheless he would joyfully praise the Lord for His great deliverance. These words seem to be the expression of a soul in an ecstasy of delight. The more keenly we feel our own foolishness and guilt, the more loudly shall we praise the God of our salvation. About this exuberant joy, note—

I. **The Nature of It**. It is—

1. SPIRITUAL. "I will bless the Lord" (v. 1). God is a spirit, and the spirit that finds its highest and deepest delight in "blessing the Lord," has something infinitely better than natural riches.

2. CONTINUAL. "I will bless the Lord *at all times*, His praise shall *continually* be in my mouth." At all times and in all circumstances He is ever the same, so that our praises should never cease. Even the *earth* yields its increase to a praising people (Psa. 67. 5-7).

3. UNSELFISH. "O magnify the Lord *with me*, and let us exalt His Name *together*" (v. 3). The praiseful heart longs for others to join in, and share the happy service.

II. **The Causes of It**. He had experienced Divine—

1. INTERPOSITION. "I sought the Lord and He heard me" (v. 4). Another testimony to the power of prayer. The God of law is also the God of grace.

2. SALVATION. "Delivered me from all my fears... saved out of all his troubles" (vv. 4-6). We must needs be saved from all our sins to be saved from all our fears.

The salvation of God goes down to the "uttermost" of human need, and lifts to the "uttermost" of Divine grace.

3. PROTECTION. "The angel of the Lord encampeth round about them that fear Him" (v. 7). As the mountain was full of horses and chariots to the opened eyes of Elisha, so doth the power of God encompass His people as with a tabernacle (Psa. 27. 5).

III. **The Influence of It.** This holy joy constrains—

1. To INVITE. "O taste and see that the Lord is good" (v. 8). The sweetness of the Gospel of God, like the sweetness of honey, is best explained by tasting it. Those who have proved its preciousness, long for others to share its blessedness.

2. To AFFIRM. "Blessed is the man that trusteth in Him ...They that seek the Lord shall not want any good thing" (vv. 8-10). They confidently testify to the goodness and faithfulness of God, because of their own experience.

3. To EXHORT. "O fear the Lord, ye His saints... Come ye children hearken unto Me" (vv. 9-11). The note of warning must be sounded, as well as the notes of invitation and personal testimony. It is as needful for *saints* to fear the Lord as for *children* to hearken to the voice of those who know Him and can teach the way of life (v. 12).

AN EXPERIENCED TEACHER.
PSALM 34. 11-22.

"COME, ye children, hearken unto Me; *I will teach you* the fear of the Lord" (v. 11). To teach the fear of the Lord is to teach how to know the Lord, and live in the enjoyment of His favour and presence. As *children* then, let us sit down at the feet of this great teacher and learn what he has to say about the way of life and blessedness.

As a man of experience, he sets forth the truth in order. He speaks—

I. **About Desire.** "What man is he that *desireth* LIFE" (v. 12). The anxiety of the soul must be after the right and proper object to begin with. The heart that longs to "see good" has come to the gate of the narrow way.

II. **About Evil.** "Keep thy tongue from evil...depart from evil" (vv. 13, 14). Those who would seek life must be ready to be separated from all their sins. To run this race every weight and sin must be laid aside (Heb. 12. 1). Let the wicked forsake his way, etc.

III. **About Peace.** "Seek peace" (v. 14). He does not teach us that we should *make* peace, but *seek* it. Christ hath made peace by the Blood of His Cross. Seek the peace of God, and follow peace with all men (Heb. 12. 14).

IV. **About Prayer.** "The eyes of the Lord are upon the righteous, and His ears are open to their cry,...the righteous cry and the Lord heareth" (vv. 15-17). Apart from the Lord Jesus Christ no man is better able to instruct in the art of prayer than David. God and prayers were tremendous realities to him. "Ask and ye shall receive."

V. **About Nearness.** "The Lord is nigh unto them that are of a broken heart" (v. 18). Let us give special heed to this teaching. Broken-heartedness is a condition of true fellowship with God. He knoweth the proud afar off. "The sacrifices of God are a broken spirit" (Psa. 51. 17). The Holy One that inhabiteth eternity dwells with him that is of a contrite and humble spirit (Isa. 57. 15).

VI. **About Affliction.** "Many are the afflictions of the righteous; but the Lord delivereth him out of them all" (v. 19). The Lord's people are not saved from afflictions, but saved in them, as Daniel was in the den of lions, and the Hebrews in the furnace of fire. "In the world ye shall

have tribulation, but be of good cheer, I have overcome the
world." Troubled on every side, but not distressed
(2 Cor. 4. 8).

VII. **About Perseverance.** "None of them that trust
in Him shall be condemned" (v. 22, R.V.). None shall
pluck them out of My hand, He is able to keep from
stumbling all those that trust in Him. By faith we are
saved from guilt and sin, by faith are we kept day by day
from the condemning influences that are ever about us and
within us. "I am the Way, the Truth, and the Life"
(John 14. 6).

FALSE WITNESSES.
PSALM 35.
IF any man would live godly, he must suffer persecution.

I. **His Cowardly Enemies.** "False witnesses did
rise up; they laid to my charge that I knew not; they
rewarded me evil for good (vv. 11, 12). In mine adversity
they rejoiced" (v. 15). In this he became a partaker
of the sufferings of his Lord (Matt. 26. 59-61). Even
because of *love*, some will become our adversaries (Psa.
109. 4). Those who are out of sympathy with Jesus Christ
will be out of sympathy with His faithful followers.

II. **His Attitude Towards Them.** "But as for me,
when *they were sick*, my clothing was sackcloth...and
my prayer returned into mine own bosom" (v. 13). All
those, so called, imprecations in this Psalm should be read
in the light of this statement. He who fasted and prayed
for his enemies, when they were in trouble, was not likely
to pronounce curses upon them. As Newberry points out,
these "texts" should be read in the future tense. "They
shall." Well David knew what the future would be of
those who raised false charges against God's people, and

who rejoiced at their halting (v. 15, R.V.). Our Lord's command is, "Love your enemies, bless them that curse you,...and pray for them that despitefully use you," even although your prayer should "return into your own bosom," as it sometimes does.

III. **His Petitions to God.** "Strive Thou, O Lord, with them that strive with me...and stand up for mine help" (vv. 1, 2, R.V.). He pleads for—

1. DIVINE ADVOCACY. "Strive *thou* with them." The servant of Christ must not strive, seeing that he has an advocate with the Father who is Jesus Christ the *Righteous*. Vengeance belongeth unto the Lord; commit thy ways unto Him. GOD is our refuge.

2. DIVINE DELIVERANCE. "Lord, how long...rescue my soul from their destructions" (v. 17). He who is our Redeemer and Lord will not fail to rescue the souls of His trusting ones from all the destructive plans and purposes of His and our enemies. His Name was called Jesus because He shall save.

3. DIVINE JUSTICE. "Judge me, O Lord my God, according to Thy righteousness" (v. 24). Those who have found refuge in His mercy will find strength in His righteousness. "It *is* a righteous thing with God to recompense tribulation to them that trouble you" (2 Thess. 1. 6).

IV. **His Joyful Resolution.** "My soul shall be joyful in the Lord...All my bones shall say, Lord, who is like unto Thee" (vv. 9, 10). "My tongue shall speak of Thy righteousness, and of Thy praise all the day long" (v. 28). When we make our appeal to God, we must in confidence leave the matter in His hands, *rejoicing* that He is able, and *praising* because He will. Those who are joyful in the Lord are best able to speak of His righteousness.

UNDER HIS WINGS.

PSALM 36. 5-9.

THE Psalmist begins here by laying bare the secret thoughts and intents of the wicked man's heart. "There is no fear of God before his eyes; he flattereth himself in his own eyes" (vv. 1, 2). Does the denial of *God* not always spring from the desire for *self*-flattery? How different it is with those who are joyfully resting beneath the shadow of His wings. Note the—

I. Attitude Mentioned. "Under the shadow of Thy wings" (v. 7). They are there because they have "put their trust" in the Lord their God. There is no other way of getting under the saving, protecting power of God but by faith. It was because Ruth *believed* that she found refuge under the wings of the Lord God of Israel (Ruth 2. 12). The feathers of God's wings are the words of His Gospel. "His truth shall be thy shield" (Psa. 91. 4; Matt. 23. 37).

II. Reasons Given. "Therefore" (v. 7). This word suggests the wherefore—

1. "Thy MERCY is in the Heavens" (v. 5). Being in the Heavens, it is high enough to overtop all the altitudes of human guilt. "As far as the Heavens is high above the earth, so great is His mercy toward them that fear Him" (Psa. 103. 11).

2. "Thy FAITHFULNESS reacheth unto the skies" (v. 5, R.V.). The clouds may come and go, but the sky, in all its purity, remains eternally the same, so with the faithfulness of God. He is faithful that hath promised, and that faithfulness will not fail till the objects of it reacheth the skies (1 Cor. 1. 9).

3. "Thy RIGHTEOUSNESS is like the mountains of God" (v. 6, R.V.). The righteousness of God! Who

can rise up to it? It is like the great mountain top
that pierces the clouds, where no human foot has ever
trod. Who can by searching find out God? But He
hath made Christ to be unto us Righteousness, even
the righteousness of God, which is unto all and upon
all them that believe.

4. "Thy JUDGMENTS are a great deep" (v. 6). If His
righteousness is as high as Heaven, His judgments are as
deep as Hell. "O the *depth* of the riches both of the
wisdom and knowledge of God!" There is no escape from
His justice but under the wings of His mercy.

5. "Thy LOVINGKINDNESS is precious" (v. 7, R.V.).
Precious indeed is the lovingkindness of God, who in the
Person of His Son hath spread the wings of His proffered
grace over a perishing world. "Herein is love."

III. Blessings Enjoyed. All those who are under
His wings are in the place of—

1. ABUNDANT SATISFACTION. "They shall be abundantly satisfied" (v. 8). The Hebrew word is "watered"
(R.V., *margin*). The provision of His grace will be found
amply sufficient for those who hide in Him. He shall make
them to drink of the *river* of His own pleasure (v. 8, l.c.).
"At His right hand there are pleasures for evermore."
Jesus cried, "If any man thirst let him come unto Me and
drink." To come to Him is to come to the *"fountain* of
life" (v. 9; John 4. 14).

2. CLEARNESS OF VISION. "In Thy light shall we see
light" (v. 9). In the light of His presence we see clearly
the light of His truth. To trust in Him is to pass out of
darkness into His marvellous light. In His marvellous
light, we see light, on sin, on self, on death, on
immortality, and eternal life (John 8. 12).

COUNSELS FOR CHRISTIANS.

PSALM 37. 1-9.

IN Newberry's "Englishman's Bible" there are seven words in these verses printed in heavy letters, indicating that they are emphasised in the Hebrew. Those words stand out as stepping stones into the blessed life of faith and fullness. Here they are—

I. **Fret Not.** "Fret not thyself because of evil-doers" (v. 1). Be not envious at the foolish, when you see the prosperity of the wicked (Psa. 73. 3). Be content with such things as ye have. Knowing that "all things work together for good to them that love God." All things are yours, for ye are Christ's.

II. **Trust.** "Trust in the Lord, and do good" (v. 3). To be content, without trusting in the Lord, is no virtue, it is imbecility or madness. God's *amen* is given to our faith, "*Verily* thou shalt be fed." Faith is an active grace, therefore be not slothful, but followers of them who through faith and patience inherit the promises (Heb. 6. 12).

III. **Delight.** "Delight thyself also in the Lord: and He shall give thee the desires of thine heart" (v. 4). We may well question our *trust*, if it does not lead to "*delight* in the Lord*." We cannot delight in Him, unless we believe that He is the chief and perfect good of the soul.

IV. **Commit.** "Commit thy way unto the Lord...and He shall bring it to pass" (v. 5). Where there is perfect trust and delight in the Lord, there will surely be a perfect committal of ourselves, and all our ways and purposes unto Him. The life that is wholly committed will be free of all anxious thoughts (Matt. 6. 25). We are encouraged to cast *all* our care upon Him, for He careth for us (1 Peter 5. 8).

V. Rest. "Rest in the Lord" (v. 7). This rest is the result of a whole-hearted committal. In this quietness and confidence ye shall find your strength (Isa. 13. 15). Rest in the Lord, for the battle is not your's, but His.

VI. Cease. "Cease from anger and forsake wrath" (v. 8). If your trust is in the Lord, cease from self and from man. Wrath and strife are the works of the flesh (Gal. 3. 19, 20). "He that hath no rule over his own spirit is like a city that is broken down, and without walls" (Prov. 25. 28).

VII. Wait. "Wait upon the Lord" (v. 9). "Wait patiently for Him" (v. 7).. This word is most needful. After having committed all to Him, and ceased from our will and way, there is a danger of growing weary in well-doing. Wait, "Ye have need of patience, that *after* ye have done the will of God, ye might receive the promise" (Heb. 10. 36). They that wait upon the Lord shall have such manifestations of Himself as shall renew their strength.

———

SEVEN CHARACTERS, AND THEIR PORTION.
Psalm 37. 10-37.

It is what men *are*, not so much what they think, say, or do that determines their character, relationship, and portion in the sight of God.

I. The Evildoer: he shall be cut off (v. 9). "Bloody and deceitful men shall not live out half their days" (Psa. 55. 23). Like chaff, the wind shall drive them away.

II. The Meek: he shall inherit the earth; and delight himself in the abundance of peace (v. 11). The meekest Man the world ever saw "had not where to lay His head," but He and His followers shall yet judge the world.

III. The Lawless: the Lord shall laugh at him (vv. 12, 13). Those who refuse to obey the call of God's grace, and cast away the cords of His commandments from them, shall be rewarded with the laugh of His derision (Psa. 2).

IV. **The Righteous**: the Lord shall uphold him (v. 17). Those who bear the image of the Heavenly Father shall be upheld with His everlasting arms.

V. **The Good**: the Lord shall order his steps, and delight in his way (v. 23). The walk that is ordered by the Lord will be a delight to His heart. The "good man" seeks to get the highest good, and to do the greatest good.

VI. **The Saint**: he shall not be forsaken; he shall be preserved for ever (v. 28). God can never forsake His holy ones, since the Holiest One of all was forsaken on their behalf. They shall be preserved for ever, for they are the heirs of eternal life (1 Peter 1. 5).

VII. **The Perfect**: his end is peace (v. 37). His end shall be perfect peace, because the peace of God already rules in his heart. The peace of God which passeth all understanding can never pass away. In these leading words we may easily trace a gradation of experience in the Godly life. The *meekness* of contrition, the *righteousness* of faith, the *goodness* of grace, the *saintship* of holiness, and the *perfection* of glory.

THE RIGHTEOUS MAN.
PSALM 37. 10-34.

As compared with the "righteousness of God," by nature "there is none righteous." The truly righteous man is the man whose *iniquities* are forgiven, whose moral nature has been "made straight" and who now lives the *upright* life. The blessedness of such a man is here beautifully portrayed.

I. **His Little is Blessed.** "A little that a righteous man hath is better than the riches of many wicked" (v. 16). Although there is but little meal in his barrel, it never

goes done. With his little, he has always the blessing
of the Lord which maketh rich, and addeth no sorrow
(Prov. 10. 22).

II. He is Upheld by the Lord. "The Lord upholdeth
the righteous" (v. 17). His strength is not in himself, but
in the faithful and strong hand of his God (Isa. 41. 10).
He is upheld upon the sinking billows, like Peter, where no
faithless feet can ever go. "I have prayed for thee that
thy faith fail not" (Luke 22. 32). He maketh my feet like
hinds' feet, to stand in slippery places.

III. His Inheritance is Everlasting. "The Lord
knoweth...the upright; and their inheritance shall be for
ever" (v. 18). If he has *little* on the earth, he has "an
inheritance incorruptible, and undefiled, and that fadeth
not away, reserved in Heaven" (1 Peter 1. 4). Being an
heir of God, he is an heir of the eternal joys and glories that
belong to Him; pleasures that are at God's right hand for
evermore.

IV. He is Merciful and Gracious. "The righteous
sheweth mercy, and giveth" (v. 21). He has learned by
the example and Spirit of his Lord, that "it is more blessed
to give than to receive." He has had mercy and grace
shewed him, and as he has *freely* received, he freely gives.

V. He is Never Forsaken. "I am old, yet have I not
seen the righteous forsaken, nor his seed begging bread"
(v. 25). This *old* man's testimony is most precious and
encouraging; he had never seen the righteous forsaken nor
his seed in destitution. "Believe on the Lord Jesus Christ
and *thou* shalt be saved *and thy house*" (Acts 16. 31).

VI. He is Endowed with Heavenly Wisdom. "The
mouth of the righteous speaketh wisdom...the law of his
God is in his heart" (vv. 30-32). When the *Word of God*
is hid in the heart, then out of the *good treasure* of the heart

he can bring forth good things (Matt. 12. 35). "It is not ye
that speak, but the Spirit of your Father which is in you."

VII. **The End is Peace.** "Behold the upright, for the
end of that man is peace" (v. 37). He does not need to
pray, like Balaam, "Let me die the death of the righteous,"
for he has already peace—the peace of God—and the
blessedness of the peacemaker is now his; he is a child of
God (Matt. 5. 9). "My peace I give unto you" (John
14. 27).

VIII. **His Salvation is All of God.** "The salvation of
the righteous is of the Lord...because he trusts in Him"
(vv. 39, 40). He is saved by grace, through faith. There
is nothing in himself to boast of; his life-long salvation is
the result of his life-long trust in the mercy and power of
his God and Saviour. As Daniel was "taken out of the
den, with no manner of hurt found upon him, *because he
believed in his God*" (Dan. 6. 23) so will He save us from
this present evil world, because we trust in Him.

SIN'S MISERIES, AND THE WAY OF ESCAPE.
PSALM 38.

THIS Psalm of "Remembrance" which reminds us of a
boiling pot, in which there are many unsavoury ingredients,
is in marked contrast to the preceding Psalm. We may
partly misunderstand David, if we forget that he acted not
only as king of Israel, but also as Israel's national poet.
This is the language of one who remembers the horrors of
the pit out of which he has been dug. It fitly describes—

I. **The Miseries of Sin.** Sin, when it is finished
bringeth forth death. See here how it operates in the
awakened sinner. There is—

1. CONVICTION. "Thine arrows stick fast in me" (v. 2).
It is not at the sinner God shoots at so much as at his sins

His arrows are sharp and pierce to the core of the evil.
The Word of God is a discerner of the heart.

2. DISORDER. "There is no soundness in my flesh"
(v. 3). His whole moral nature was discovered to be
diseased, and out of order. This is a most humbling
revelation. The heart has been found out as a deceitful
traitor, and all its actions discovered to be polluting
and disorderly.

3. UNREST. "Neither is there any rest in my bones
because of my sin" (v. 3). The strongest features in
his character were shaken and troubled at the thought of
sin. The whole fabric of his moral nature was disturbed.
Real conviction of sin is as an earthquake in the soul—
universal disturbance.

4. OPPRESSION. "Mine iniquities are...as an heavy
burden they are too heavy for me" (v. 4). Too heavy
for *me*? yes, but not too heavy for Him, who bore our sins
on His own body to the tree. What can a man do with a
burden that is too heavy for him, and who cannot cast it
off? O wretched man! who shall deliver?

5. CORRUPTION. "My wounds stink and corrupt
because of my foolishness" (v. 5). This is no exaggerated
figure of speech; it is the sober statement of one who has
seen and felt sin in its true character and effects. There
is no balm in Gilead, no physician on earth that can heal
those deep-seated festering wounds.

6. HELPLESS. "I am feeble and sore broken" (v. 8).
His whole nature was completely *benumbed*, and powerless
to throw off the foul malady. "Without strength" is the
condition of all under the torpid blight of sin.

7. DARKNESS. "As for the light of mine eyes, it has
gone from me" (v. 10). All the light of hope he had
before has died out. Darkness covers the face of his deep.

II. The Way of Escape.

1. CONFESSION.   "I will declare my iniquity" (v. 18).
A full declaration is needed.   He that covereth his sin
shall not prosper, but "if we confess our sins, He is faithful
and just to forgive."

2. CONTRITION.   "I will be sorry for my sin" (v. 18).
This is the godly sorrow that worketh repentance to
salvation.   The confession that does not spring from
contrition of heart is mockery.   It is he that confesseth
and *forsaketh* his sin that finds mercy.

3. FAITH.   "In Thee O Lord do I hope: Thou wilt hear,
O Lord my God" (v. 15).   "Believe on the Lord Jesus
Christ and thou shalt be saved" (Rom. 10. 9, 10).

TAKE HEED.
PSALM 39.

THIS resolution of the psalmist to "take heed to his ways"
is a note of reminder to us.   Let him that thinketh he
standeth take heed lest he fall.   Mark those things which,
like David, we should give special attention to.   I will take
heed to—

I. My Ways (v. 1).   I will scrutinise my motives, my
habits and manners.   I will not think them right because
they are *my* ways.   I will search out whether they are in
harmony with God's word and ways.

II. My Mouth.   "I will keep my mouth with a bridle
(muzzle) while the wicked is before me" (v. 1).   God
is often judged by the ways and mouths of His people,
therefore there is need at times for the muzzle.   The man
that offends not in word is a perfect man (James 3. 2).
Walk in wisdom toward them that are without (Psa.
141. 3).

III. My Heart.   "My heart was hot within me" (v. 3).

Blessed are the hot in heart where the holy fire burns while they muse on the things of God, for their tongues shall speak of His praise. Take heed lest there be in any of you an evil heart of unbelief, or a lukewarm heart of indifference.

IV. **My End.** "Lord make me to know mine end" (v. 4). What shall my end be? is a most important inquiry. Balaam desired that his last end may be like the righteous, but he did not take heed to his end, so he fell numbered with the enemies of God.

V. **My Days.** "Behold Thou hast made my days (lifetime) as hand-breadths" (v. 5, R.V.). As our lifetime is made up of a few hand-breadths, we have need to take heed to each one of them; to "number them that we may apply our hearts unto wisdom" (Psa. 90. 12).

VI. **My Hope.** "My hope is in Thee" (v. 7). **Take** heed that your hope is in the Lord, and not in yourself or your circumstances. We are saved by hope, but hope that is seen is not hope (Rome. 8. 24). Those whose hope is in God will be filled with all joy and peace in believing, for He is the God of hope (Rom. 15. 13).

VII. **My Transgressions.** "Deliver me from all my transgressions" (v. 8). To transgress is to backslide; to fail to *take heed* to it is to fall from grace, and allow sin to have dominion over us (Rom. 6. 14). Although we may fall, we may rise again for the Lord is the Deliverer of His people.

VIII. **My Prayer.** "Hear my prayer, O Lord, and give ear to my cry; hold not Thy peace at my tears" (v. 12). Take heed to your prayers, see that they are the *sincere* expression of your inmost heart, and that they are offered in no cold and formal manner. They are all the better of being soaked with tears.

SAVED AND SATISFIED.
PSALM 40. 1-5.

THE first few verses of this favourite Psalm give us the experiences of a soul passing from darkness into light—from the miseries of a lost condition into the joys of a full salvation. He was—

I. **Distressed.** In "an horrible pit" and "miry clay" (v. 2). Our sins are the cords by which we are let down into the dismal darkness to sink in the mire. It is an horrible awakening when one makes the discovery that this is their condition. The pains of Hell get hold of such.

II. **Heard.** "He inclined unto me, and heard my cry" (v. 1). What a mercy that this pit is not bottomless, and that the gracious ear of God is still within reach. Jonah cried out of the belly of Hell and was heard.

III. **Saved.** "He brought me up" (v. 2). His arm is not shortened that it cannot save, it is long enough and strong enough to lift the penitent sinner, "up out of" the pit of horrors and the treacherous mire. Others may divert and amuse the imprisoned soul, God only can bring him *out*.

IV. **Established.** "He set my feet upon a rock, and established my goings" (v. 2). It is a mighty deliverance, from the sinking miry clay of our own thoughts to the rock of God's eternal truth, and to have our ways so established that we are *kept* from falling back into our former condition. The Lord thy keeper.

V. **Gladdened.** "He put a new song in my mouth, even praise unto our God" (v. 3). This new song belongs to the new life of faith. It is a song of praise unto the Lamb who is worthy, for He was slain and has *redeemed* us to God by His blood (Rev. 5. 9). He puts this song only into the mouths of those whose feet *He* has set upon the rock.

VI. Used. "Many shall see it, and fear, and shall trust in the Lord" (v. 3). The change is so great that many can't help *seeing* it; it is so manifestly of God, that they will be led to *fear* and to *trust* in the Lord. The testimony of a sound, happy, consistent life, must be fruitful.

VII. Satisfied. "Blessed is the man that trusteth in the Lord...Thy wonderful works...Thy thoughts to usward... if I would declare and speak of them, they are more than can be numbered" (vv. 4, 5). He is satisfied that the man who trusts in the Lord has entered into the *blessed* life. He finds that the works, and thoughts of God, on his behalf, are so wonderful and numerous, that they are unspeakable. When the eyes of our understanding have been enlightened, then we may know what is the hope of His calling, and the exceeding greatness of His power to usward who believe (Eph. 1. 18-20).

MESSIANIC FEATURES.
PSALM 40. 6-10.

THERE is much in this Psalm that might have been fitly spoken by the Lord Jesus Christ. Some of these statements can hardly be applied to David (vv. 6-8). Surely the Holy Spirit, the Revealer of Christ, rested upon the Psalmist when he uttered these prophetic words. There are here some—

I. Features of His Character. In him there was the—

1. OPENED EAR. "Mine ears hast Thou opened" (v. 6). When the slave had his ear bored it was a token of entire *submission* to his master's will (Exod. 21. 6). The Lord God bored the ear of His Son, and He was not rebellious, neither turned He back (Isa. 50. 4, 5). This figure is used to denote the entire devotion of the Son to the Father's will.

2. SURRENDERED LIFE.   "Burnt offering and sin offering hast Thou not required; then said I, Lo, I come" (vv. 6, 7).   When there were no more sacrifices required at the hands of the Jewish priesthood, then Christ came.   He came, not to offer sacrifices for sin, but to *give Himself*, an offering unto God.   His life was yielded to God for the purpose of redemption.   He is "the end of the law for righteousness" (Rom. 10. 4).

3. FULFILLED WORD.   "In the volume of *the book* it is written of me" (v. 7).   All that was written in the law of Moses, and in the Prophets and in the Psalms concerning the Messiah, found their perfect fulfilment in Him (Luke 24. 44).   So ought His Word to be fulfilled in us.

4. EMBODIED LAW.   "Thy law is within my heart" (v. 8).   He not only obeyed the law, but the law of His God was so deeply engraven in his heart as to constitute His very nature.   His meat was to do the will of Him that sent Him (John 4. 34).   This is what the Holy Ghost seeks to do in us, by making us partakers of the Divine nature.

5. JOYFUL SERVANT.   "I delight to do Thy will, O my God" (v. 8).   It is a delight to do His will, when His Word is hid in the surrendered heart (Rom. 7. 22).   This is the secret and character of the "holy life," when the self-will is lost in the delightsomeness of the will of God.

6. FAITHFUL PREACHER.   "I have preached righteousness: I have not refrained: I have not hid: I have declared: I have not concealed" (vv. 9, 10).   As a faithful witness, He kept back nothing that was profitable.   Having the Spirit of the Lord upon Him, He preached the Gospel to the poor (Luke 4. 18, 19).   He was manifestly declared to be an epistle of God.

II. Aspects of His Ministry. Christ's life and teaching was a revelation of the—

1. RIGHTEOUSNESS OF GOD. "I have published righteousness" (v. 9, R.V.). The law and the prophets *witnessed* to the righteousness of God, but Jesus Christ alone can *impart* it to all them that believe (Rom. 3, 21, 22).

2. FAITHFULNESS OF GOD. "I have declared Thy faithfulness" (v. 10). Every miracle that Christ performed, every prayer that He uttered, was a declaration of the faithfulness of His Father to His Son, and to His Word. He walked by faith, and received from God all that He needed, thereby proving His faithfulness.

3. SALVATION OF GOD. "I have declared...Thy salvation" (v. 10). Salvation through the grace of God was the *central* theme of our Lord's ministry. This salvation which *began* to be spoken by the Lord: how shall we escape if we neglect it? (Heb. 2. 3).

4. LOVINGKINDNESS OF GOD. "I have not concealed Thy lovingkindness" (v. 10). God is love, and His love and kindness had a new *unveiling* in the gift of His Son. Jesus Christ never concealed the fact that *Himself* was the expression of the lovingkindness of the Father to a perishing world. "Last of all He sent His Son." Herein is love.

5. TRUTH OF GOD. "I have not concealed...Thy truth" (v. 10). The truth as it is in the character of the Father has been manifested to us in the character of the Son. No essential feature belonging to the nature of God was concealed by Him. He is *the Truth*; neither more nor less can be said of Him than what is said of God: "I and My Father are one." Let us thank God that He who is the *Truth*, is also the *Way* and the *Life*.

THE BLESSEDNESS OF CONSIDERING THE POOR.

PSALM 41. 1-3 (*see next Psalm*).

THE word "blessed" here is in the plural, "Oh, the blessednesses" of such.

I. He will be **Delivered** in time of trouble (v. 1).

II. He will be **Preserved** and *kept* in life (v. 2).

III. He will be **Blessed** upon the earth (v. 2).

IV. He will be **Saved** from his enemies (v. 2).

V. He will be **Strengthened** in time of weariness (v. 3).

VI. He will be **Comforted** in time of sickness (v. 3).

THE SUFFERINGS AND CONSOLATIONS OF THE SAINT.

PSALM 41. 4-13.

According to the Hebrew divisions, this Psalm ends the first Book.

I. His Sufferings. He suffers from—

1. EVIL SPEAKING. "Mine enemies speak evil of me" (v. 5).

2. EVIL THINKING. "When shall he perish?"

3. EVIL WHISPERING. "They whisper together against me" (v. 7).

4. EVIL PLOTTING. "They devised my hurt."

5. EVIL WORKING. "Lifted up his heel against me" (v. 9).

II. His Consolations. He is comforted with the—

1. KNOWLEDGE OF GOD. "But Thou, O Lord" (v. 10).

2. FAVOUR OF GOD. "I know that Thou favourest me" (v. 11).

3. FAITHFULNESS OF GOD. "Mine enemy doth not triumph over me."

4. POWER OF GOD. "Thou upholdest me" (v. 12).

5. PRESENCE OF GOD. "Thou settest me before Thy face" (v. 12).

SIN.

THE juice of the manchineel tree is said to be so poisonous that when it touches the blood it works death with awful rapidity. Yet its appearance and fruit look most beautiful. Outwardly, it is very attractive; inwardly, it is a deadly poison. How like sin this is! Its very attractiveness is its greatest danger. It beguiles by promising much; it ends in destruction. "Sin, when it is finished, bringeth forth death."

FALSE AND REAL.

PROFESSOR Robinson once found a plant growing most luxuriantly in a coal-mine. Its form and qualities being quite new to him, he had it removed to his garden and carefully attended. But the plant soon languished and died, but from its roots there sprang up a new, fresh form of life, which he easily distinguished as the common tansy. The pit-life of the tansy was unreal and deceptive, as the lives of all are who are living in the pit of spiritual darkness. Not until we get transplanted into the light of the Kingdom of God do we become really true to the deeper instincts of our nature. "*He* took me from the fearful pit."

EXPOSITORY OUTLINES.

New Testament.

THE SHEPHERD.
JOHN 10. 1-10.

"Now, the training strange and lowly,
Unexplained and tedious now:
Afterward—the service holy
And the Master's "Enter thou."
—F. R. HAVERGAL.

THESE "Verily, verily's" of our Lord, which might be rendered, "In most solemn truth," never seem to be used at the beginning of a discourse, but always to illustrate, or emphasise some preceding statement; so that the last part of chapter 9 is closely connected with the opening verses of chapter 10. Those hirelings, who cast the man out because he said that Christ opened his eyes, are here contrasted with the true shepherd, who cares for the sheep. The allegory of this chapter, like the parable in the fifteenth of Luke, is given to us in three different sections. We have (1) the sheepfold and the (under) shepherd (vv. 1-10); (2) the Good Shepherd giving His life for the sheep (vv. 11-18); (3) the safety of the sheep (vv. 25-30).

I. **The Sheepfold.** This was an enclosure, into which the sheep were put for safety during the night (v. 1). This may have reference to the old theocracy, that position of privilege, which belonged to the Jews as God's chosen and protected people, and into which no man could honourably enter, but by the door of birth—the seed of Abraham; or it may represent that new provision of security which Christ Himself was about to establish for His sheep, through the giving of His life for them.   It is a *sheep*fold, there is no mention of goats here.

II. The Entrance.   There is an entrance, but only *one*. "I am the Door of the sheep" (v. 7).   It is through Him who died for them that they enter into the safety and quiet of this spiritual and heavenly fold.   "He that entereth in by the door is a shepherd of the sheep."   The sheep and the true shepherds all enter in by the same door.   There is none other Name whereby we can be saved (Acts 4. 12). He is no shepherd of the sheep who has not, first of all, appropriated Christ for himself, as the Way, the Truth, and the Life.   If he enters not by this door into the sheep-fold ministry, "the same is a thief and a robber," and those sheep which have entered by the door will not follow him. Christ is the only open door into the salvation of God, and, praise Him, it is open for all   "I am the Door: by Me if *any man* enter in, he shall be saved" (v. 9).

III. The Porter.   "He that entereth by the door... to him the porter openeth" (v. 3).   It is a marvel to us how commentators should ignore or belittle the porter, lest they should press the allegory too far.   In point of fact, the porter is second in importance to Him who is the Door, and undoubtedly represents the ministry of the Holy Spirit. Who abode with the sheep, and was their only comforter during the weary hours of night?   The porter.   Who could take the Door (Christ) and open it and close it at His will? The porter.   Who alone had the power to admit a shepherd into the fold?   The porter (Acts 13. 2).   All who would enter in by the door shall have the porter's help and encouragement.   It is the Spirit who takes the things of Christ and shows them to the seeking soul.

IV. The Shepherd.   "He that entereth in by the door is a shepherd of the sheep" (v. 2, R.V., *margin*).   The reference here is to the under shepherd, who has the liberty of the porter (Spirit) to go in and out, and to lead, and feed the sheep. The hirelings in chapter 9. 34, cast out the true sheep of Christ's flock. They know not the voice of strangers. It is important to note the nature of the shepherd's work and influence as stated here. It is—

1. PERSONAL. "He calleth his own sheep *by name.*" There is no mistaking the purpose of a true shepherd when he comes into the sheepfold. He has not thought of thrashing or amusing the sheep, his chief object is to call them out into a larger place of blessing. To this end he deals with them definitely and personally. All the faithful under-shepherds of Christ's flock rightly divide the Word: they call the sheep by their proper names, and seek their individual good.

2. PROGRESSIVE. "He leadeth them out." It is not enough that the sheep are safe and at rest in the fold, they have to be lead out into fresh healthy pastures. The fields at the disposal of the shepherds are as broad, far reaching, and as rich as the whole Revelation of God. But those who have not examined those rich pasture lands will not be likely to lead the sheep into them.

3. EXEMPLARY. "He goeth before them." The true shepherd *leads* by example, as well as by precept. He does not say, "Go," but *"Come."* He goeth before them in doctrine and in practice (Titus 2. 7). Not as lords over God's heritage, but as examples of the flock (1 Peter 5. 3). Paul wrote to Timothy: "Be thou an example of the believers in *Word,* in *conversation,* in *charity,* in *spirit,* in *faith,* in *purity.*" To the Corinthians he said: "Be ye followers of me, even as I also am of Christ." The *shepherd* leads into green pastures, and by the still waters, not into the howling wilderness of that "higher criticism," which offers only doubt and perplexity to a hungry soul.

3. PROTECTIVE. "A stranger will they not follow...for

they know not the voice of strangers" (v. 5). The true sheep know the voice of a true shepherd, and will not be led away by the call of a stranger, who has climbed up by some other way. Some religious teachers have the form of godliness, but deny the *power* thereof (Holy Spirit); from such turn away. The sheep that have a faithful shepherd are too well taught to become the followers of any hireling, or thief, who may don the shepherd's attire.

V. The Intruders. "He that entereth not by the door, but *climbeth up some other way*, the same is a thief and a robber." It does not matter much what that "other way" is, so long as it is *another way*, it is an ignoring and a denial of Him who is the Door—and of Him who is the Porter—a denial of Christ, and of the Holy Spirit. Those who will not enter by the door of grace into this Kingdom will have some *climbing* to do, and in the end rewarded only as thieves and robbers. The "other way" that some prefer is the way of legalism, or learning, human *works*, or human *wisdom*. They will climb away for years to get into the fold, rather than submit to enter by the door. But all such climbers are, in their hearts, at enmity with the Shepherd and the sheep, and seek only their own base and selfish ends. "The same is a thief." There is no other way for a sheep, or a shepherd, for salvation or service, but by the Lord Jesus Christ, who is the Door. "I am the Door: by Me if any man enter in, he shall be saved."

THE GOOD SHEPHERD.
JOHN 10. 11-18.

THE Lord Jesus Christ is the good or perfect Shepherd. All that ever came before Him—*in His stead*—or that shall yet so come, are thieves and robbers. There is only one Good Shepherd who can lay down His life for the sheep *and take it again* (v. 18). There is perhaps no image of

Christ that has so powerfully appealed to the imaginations of men in all ages as the "Good Shepherd." Let not the familiarity of the term rob us of the great sweetness and depth of precious teaching that it reveals.

I. **"He Giveth His Life for the Sheep"** (v. 11). This is the outstanding characteristic of the Good Shepherd. He is not only ready to sacrifice His life in defence of the sheep, but has a *command* from the Father to *lay down* His life for the sheep (v. 18), that the sheep might have life through Him in abundance (v. 10). The scope of the teaching cannot be limited to the mere metaphor. The metaphor is used to help us to grasp the fullness of the truth. That Christ taught redemption here is surely beyond doubt, when He said, "Therefore doth My Father love Me, because I lay down My life that I might take it again" (v. 17; Heb. 13. 20). The Father loved the Son because He willingly obeyed this command to lay down His life for the salvation of all who would enter in at this door into the sheepfold (1 Peter 2. 25).

II. **His Sheep Hear His Voice.** "They shall hear My voice" (v. 16). Every soul who would follow Christ must individually hear His voice. That voice may be heard through the written Word, or in the preaching of the Gospel, but it will be recognised as His voice and His call to a new and separate life. Christ's first message was to the Jewish flock, but He had other sheep—multitudes of them—which were not of that flock, but which belonged to every kindred and tongue, and people, and nation, "them also," He said, "*I must bring*," for the death that He was about to die was to be "the propitiation, not only for our sins (Jews), but also for the whole world" (1 John 2. 2). This present dispensation is the time of the bringing in of the "other sheep" which He has, as the gift of the Father, and they are hearing His voice, through the preaching of the Word, and following Him. To Him is the gathering of the people to be.

III. He Knows His Sheep. "I know My sheep" (v. 14). As to the extent or limit of this knowledge, it is impossible, except by sheer presumption, to define. He knows their name, their nature, and their need. The Lord does not judge as man judgeth, by outward appearance; He judgeth the heart. He discerns the hidden spirits of men, whether they are merely carnal or Christlike. All His sheep have a love for, and a disposition like the Shepherd Himself. "If any man love God, the same is known of Him" (1 Cor. 8. 3). The Good Shepherd does not judge His sheep by their *cry*, for many will say on that day, "Lord, Lord," to whom He will say, "I never knew you."

IV. His Sheep Know Him. "And am known of Mine" (v. 14). This knowledge is akin to that which exists between the Father and the Son (v. 15). This affinity is the deepest and most sacred of all relationships. We may know Him as we know the sun that shines in the Heavens, and yet know but little of Him. The sheep knew the Shepherd because He has manifested Himself to them, so we "know that the Son of God is come, and hath given us an understanding that we may know Him that is true" (1 John 5. 20). "I know whom I have believed" (2 Tim. 1. 12). This is eternal life, to know Him and Jesus Christ whom He hath sent.

V. His Sheep are Owned by Him. "He who is an hireling, *whose own* the sheep are not" (v. 12), is here contrasted with Him who laid down His life for the sheep, as an evidence that they are *His own*. The flock of God hath been purchased by His own blood (Acts 20. 28). Jesus was speaking as the Good Shepherd when He said to Peter, "Feed *My* lambs...Feed *My* sheep" (John 21). "Ye are not your own; ye are bought with a price."

VI. He Cares for His Sheep. "The hireling fleeth because he careth not for the sheep," but the true Shepherd is very careful over *His* sheep (v. 13). The wolf-like Satan finds his greatest enemy in the Shepherd of our souls. It is the privilege of the sheep to be without carefulness, for "He careth for you," therefore cast all your care upon Him (1 Peter 1. 7). The Shepherd is most careful about the *safety* and *supply* of the sheep—about their defence and their food. His wisdom and His power are being continually exercised on their behalf. "Lo, I am with you alway, even unto the close of the age."

VII. His Sheep shall all be Gathered into one Flock. "There shall be one flock and one Shepherd" (v. 16). Meanwhile, His sheep are in every clime and country, speaking almost every language under Heaven, and divided by many sectarian folds, but all have heard His voice, and know Him, and are known by Him, having by one Spirit been baptised into one body. But when the Chief Shepherd shall appear, those who are still living on the earth shall be caught up with those who have gone to sleep, and so shall we ever be with the Lord. Wherefore, comfort one another with these words (1 Thess. 4. 16-18). In the evergreen pastures of the Heavenly Kingdom He shall lead *His flock*, and they shall follow the Lamb whithersoever He goeth. "The Lord is my Shepherd...and I shall dwell in the house of the Lord for ever" (Psa. 23. 1 and 6).

THE SAFETY OF THE SHEEP.
JOHN 10. 22-30.

IT was winter, and Jesus was walking in the porch of the temple called "Solomon's," when the Jews, who were bewildered about the character and doings of Jesus, came about Him, saying, "How long do you mean to keep us in suspense? If Thou be the Christ tell us plainly" (v. 24).

He had been telling them all along by His *words* and *works*, but they believed not (v. 25). Never man spoke more plain than He, but to those who are wilfully or judicially blind, such evidence is of little value. "Ye believe not," said Jesus, "because ye are not of *My sheep*" (v. 26). By their persistent unbelief they proved themselves unfit to enter the sheepfold of His chosen ones. "They could not enter in because of their unbelief" (Heb. 3. 19). This question of the Jews gives Him an opportunity of explaining more fully the relationship and privilege of His sheep.

I. Their Relationship. They are His by—

1. SOVEREIGN GRACE. "My sheep hear My voice, and I know them" (v. 27). "All we like sheep have gone astray; we have turned every one to his own way." The Lord might have passed us by in our waywardness and misery, but in love and in mercy He spoke. If *He* did not speak, the sheep would never hear His voice, and never follow Him. "My voice!" There is no other voice like His. To *hear it* is to turn and live, or die in sin. "By grace are ye saved through faith."

2. DELIBERATE CHOICE. "They follow Me." They hear Him, believe Him, and follow Him. They choose to obey His voice, rather than the voices of the world, or the whisperings of their own heart. To follow Christ is to renounce self and forsake all that would hinder the soul from abiding in His presence and obeying His Word.

II. Their Security. They are perfectly safe, because—

1. THEY HAVE ETERNAL LIFE. "I give unto them eternal life" (v. 28). The verb is in the present, and might be read, "I am giving them the life of the ages." This life is the *gift* of Him who laid down His life for the sheep—a gift that is continuous, running on into the endless ages of futurity. Who but the Eternal One could make such a

promise and bestow such a blessing? "The gift of GOD is eternal life" (Rom. 6. 23).

2. THEY ARE THE GIFT OF THE FATHER. "My Father... gave them Me" (v. 29). The sheep of Christ are the "elect according to the foreknowledge of God the Father" (1 Peter 1. 2). "All that the Father hath given Me shall come to Me" (John 6. 37). They are secure because they are possessed with a life suited for the ages of eternity, and because they are the chosen ones of the Father "before the foundation of the world, that they should be holy and without blame before Him in love...to the praise of the glory of His grace" (Eph. 1. 3-6). It was for such Christ prayed when He said, "Holy Father, keep through *Thine own* Name those whom *Thou hast given Me.*"

3. THEY ARE IN CHRIST'S HAND. "Neither shall any pluck them out of My hand." Of them which Thou hast given Me have I lost none (John 18. 9). His *hand* stands here for the almightiness of His power—a power as gentle as a mother's touch, as strong as the eternal God. No foe is able to wrest us from His hand. The sheep are saved by the gift of Divine life, and by the grip of Divine power. They are made partakers of a new nature and the subject of a new environment. They are in His heart of grace and in His hand of safety.

4. THEY ARE IN THE FATHER'S HAND. "None is able to pluck them out of My Father's hand" (v. 29). "My Father is greater than all...I and My Father are one." The sheep are in the all-embracing power of the Son, as the Son is in the all-embracing power of the Father. "The glory which Thou gavest Me I have given them, that they may be one, even as We are" (John 17. 22). The security of the Son is virtually the security of the sheep. As He is in the hand of the Father, so are we in the hand of the Son.

Accepted and kept in the Beloved, the *oneness* of the Son
with the Father is a powerful guarantee (v. 30).

5. THEY HAVE HIS PROMISE. "They shall never perish."
The negative here is doubly strong, and might be rendered,
"They shall *never*, NEVER perish" (v. 28). The infallible
Word of the eternal Son stands like an adamantine wall
between the helpless sheep of His fold and perdition. The
breaking of that Word would be the breaking down of His
own character. One "jot or tittle" of His Word cannot
possibly fail. Thus we have strong consolations who have
fled to Him as the Refuge and Shepherd of our souls.

LAZARUS.
JOHN 11.

THE Hebrew form of the name Lazarus is Eliezer—God my
Helper. Surely a fitting name for one who was so mightily
helped by God. The history of Lazarus is, in a spiritual
sense, the history of all who have passed from death unto
life. Note the various stages in his remarkable experience.
There was—

I. Sickness. "A certain man was sick" (v. 1). "He
whom Thou lovest is sick" (v. 3). Loved by the Lord,
yet smitten with sickness. Through some cause or other,
soul-sickness is almost invariably the prelude to enlarged
and deeper spiritual blessing. When Jesus heard of it, He
said, "This sickness...is for the glory of God" (v. 4).
Yes, blessed be His Name, for that sickness which brings us
down to the place of death, that the Son of Man might be
glorified in doing a marvellous work in us and for us. The
Holy Spirit must convince of sin before He quickens into
newness of life.

II. Death. "Jesus said unto them plainly, Lazarus is
dead" (v. 14). This sickness was not unto eternal death,

but unto that death which in a very singular way made
Lazarus a fit subject for the *resurrecting* power of the
Son of God. Real sin-sickness is only unto the death of
self-love and self-will, that the power of Christ might be
manifested. Sin, when it is finished, bringeth forth death.
When the Spirit convinces of sin, of righteousness and of
judgment, it is the passing of the sentence of death upon
the sinner. All hope of salvation from any other source
had to be abandoned. "Sin revived, and I died" (Rom.
7. 9).

III. **Life.** "He that was dead came forth" (v. 44).
The *life-giving* power of Jesus Christ could only be manifested in the case of a *dead* man. If Lazarus had only been
in a swoon, or in a sleep, there would have been no glory to
God in his awakening. Christ Jesus came into this world
to save sinners. It would bring no glory to Him to give
life or salvation to those who did not need it. Before the
Apostle Paul could say, "Now I live," he had to say, "I am
crucified." Resurrection life can only come where there
has been death. We must die to self if we would live unto
God. To share with Christ His resurrection power, we
must needs go to the Cross and the grave with Him. If
we refuse to die, we refuse to enter into the new and
fruitful life. "Except a corn of wheat die, it abideth
alone" (John 12. 24).

IV. **Liberty.** "Jesus said, Loose him and let him go"
(v. 44). It ill becomes one who has been raised from the
dead by the power of God, to be in bondage to any man,
or the customs and habits of men, especially those manners
and customs that belong to the dead. As in nature, so in
grace, where there is a fullness of life there will be the
bursting open and a breaking forth from the old dead forms
and habits. All that we can do for our dead is to bind
them and bury them, but how different when, with a loud

voice, the Son of God speaks to them. The man that has
been liberated from death and the grave, must not be
hindered by any fashion of grave clothes. Whom the Son
of God makes free are free indeed. The relatives of those
saved by Christ may do much to bind or loose their lives for
His service. The Lord's command to the friends of Lazarus
was, "Loose him and let him go" (John 11. 44). What a
crime in His sight if they had refused to obey. See that
ye refuse not.

V. Communion. "Lazarus was one of them that sat at
the table with Him" (chap. 12. 2) What a blessed
privilege to company with Him who has given us to know
in our own experience that He is the "Resurrection and the
Life." To those who have passed from death unto life
there is no fellowship to be compared with His. As like
draws to like, so must the resurrected spirit draw to Him
who is the Resurrection. Every time we sit down prayer-
fully to study His Word, we are sitting at the table *with
Him*, listening to His voice, and receiving food for our
souls. Are you one of those who *sit* at this table with Him?

VI. Testimony. "By reason of him, many of the Jews
went away and believed on Jesus" (chap. 12. 11) The
power of his testimony lay, not so much in what he was
able to say, as in what he was. The fact that he had been
raised from death and corruption by the word of Jesus
Christ, was in itself a most convincing witness to His
Divinity and Messiahship. The greater the work of grace
wrought in us by God's mighty power, the greater will
be the force of our testimony for Him. The influence of
Christ's risen life in us should be the leading of others to
"believe on Jesus."

VII. Suffering. Because of the converting power of
this new life in Lazarus "the chief priests consulted that
they might put him to death" (chap. 12. 10). His old

life brought no persecution, but now he has the happiness
of those who are reproached for the Name of Christ (1 Peter
4. 14). It is beyond the power of the enemy to kill or
destroy the resurrection life. Your life is hid with Christ
in God. "If any man suffer as a Christian, let him not
be ashamed, but let him glorify God on *this behalf*"
(1 Peter 4. 16).

JESUS.
JOHN 11.

THE Gospel of John is like the rending of the veil, it
opens up the way for us into the Holiest of all. Much of
the personal glory of the Son of God will be unseen by us,
if we fail to discern what His sayings and doings reveal
concerning *Himself*. In this chapter we have several bright
glimpses of this inner glory, glimpses such as we have
everywhere throughout the Gospels.

I. **His Divinity.** When Jesus heard of the sickness
of Lazarus, He said, "This sickness is not unto death, but
for the glory of God, that the Son of God might be glorified
thereby" (v. 4). This prophetic language is full of
meaningless mystery if Jesus Christ was nothing more than
the "best of men." Although He *emptied* Himself as the
Divine One, that He might live and die for us, He was
still *Himself*, the eternal Son, in the bosom of the Father.
He knew that this sickness had come that He, as the Son
of God, might be glorified thereby.

II. **His Love.** "Now Jesus loved Martha, and her
sister, and Lazarus" (v. 5). While Jesus Christ was
Divine, He was also perfectly and purely human. He
loved all with that love of God which is the love of pity
and compassion, for even those who are His bitterest
enemies, but the Marthas, the Marys, and the Lazaruses
are the special objects of His affection and delight. He

can only delight with His whole heart in those whose
hearts are opened with delight toward Him. It is not
possible for such love as His to rejoice in iniquity.

III. **His Faith.** "Are there not twelve hours in the
day?" etc. (vv. 7-9). These very suggestive words were
spoken to His disciples, in answer to their alarm at His
proposal to cross over from Peræa, where the Jews of late
had sought to stone Him. There were to be twelve hours
in His working day, and but eleven had passed. He must
work the works of Him that sent Him while it is day
(John 9. 4). He did believe that His life was "immortal
till His work was done," and so He would walk *in the day*
that He might stumble not. Faith in God never leads to
laziness or fatalism. He that believeth shall not make the
haste of flurried excitement, but they shall make steady
progress, despite all the oppositions of the forces of Hell.
"Are there not twelve hours in the day?"

IV. **His Joy.** "I am glad" (v.15). The conjunction
here is most remarkable. "Lazarus is dead, and I am
glad; glad for *your sakes* to the intent that ye might
believe." He was glad that He was not there to save
Lazarus from dying, that He might have the opportunity
of raising him from the dead, that they might see His
glory and believe in Him. Mark the secret of Christ's
gladness—glad to have the chance of manifesting His
power that others may *believe in Him*, so that they might
be blessed by Him. This was the joy that was set before
Him when He endured the Cross. The nature of Christ's
gladness is totally different from that which is sought
for by the sinful sons of men.

V. **His Indignation.** "When Jesus saw her wailing,
and the Jews also wailing, He was moved with indignation
in the Spirit" (v. 33, R.V., *margin*). Why all this wailing
now that HE had said, "Thy brother shall rise again," and

that "I am the Resurrection and the Life?" In the face of His words and in His presence, this wailing was surely to Him the wailing of unbelief. He groaned in Spirit with a holy anger because of their slowness of heart to believe all that He had said unto them.

VI. His Compassion. "Jesus wept" (v. 35). Those tears were as "drops of grief" from the loving heart of our Great High Priest, who is touched with the feeling of our infirmities (Heb. 4. 15). What a contrast between the hypocritical tears of those would-be mourners and the tears of the pure-hearted Son of God. The voice of these tears seems to have spoken louder than His words, for, "*Then* said the Jews, Behold how He loved Him." If these teardrops were pearls of love, what shall we say of those blooddrops wept in the Garden of Gethsemane? "Greater love hath no man than this." There is a way through Christ's tears, as well as through His words, to the heart of God the Father.

VII. His Power. "He cried with a loud voice, Lazarus come forth, and he that was dead came forth" (vv. 43, 44). This was the cry of Him who is "the Resurrection and the Life." "Resurrection," one has said, "is not an impersonal fate, but a personal effect." It is not the natural result of any known law, but the supernatural outcome of a Divine personal act. In Christ was life, and the life was the light of men. He speaks and it is done. As when Christ, who was the Life, appeared at the grave of Lazarus, Lazarus also appeared with Him, through the power of His Word; so "when Christ, who is our Life, shall appear, then shall we also appear with Him in glory" (Col. 3. 4). While on earth our Lord had to do with death in three different stages: the child on the death-bed, the young man on the bier, and the man in the grave. It was only in this last stage that He spoke with a *loud voice*. The raising of Lazarus was a

manifestation of that power that shall one day with the
voice of a trumpet awaken the dead, and as the vile body
of Lazarus was changed (v. 30), so shall it be in the
resurrection (Phil. 3. 20, 21). This corruptible must put
on incorruption. He that heareth His Word now, and
believeth on Him.. is passed from death unto life (John
5. 24).

A SUPPER SCENE.
JOHN 12. 1-8.

ACCORDING to Matthew and Mark, this supper which
"they" made for Jesus, was in the house of Simon, who had
been a leper, and may have been a united effort, with the two
families, to do honour to Jesus and His disciples because
of the raising of Lazarus from the dead, and, perhaps, the
healing of Simon. It took place six days before the passover, which meant six days before His death and burial.
It must have been a hallowed time. Let us think of—

I. **Mary, the Sacrificer.** While others rejoice to sit
at the table with Jesus, and learn of Him, Mary, who had
before sat at His feet, feels impelled by the love of her
heart to embrace this opportunity of proving her faith and
affection by personal sacrifice. To her, at that time, it was
more blessed to give than to receive. There surely must
be seasons in our lives when we shall find it more blessed
to sacrifice than to seek, to give than to take, to praise
than to pray. See the *nature* of it. "Mary took a pound
of ointment of spikenard, *very costly.*" Judas reckoned its
value at "three hundred pence"—more correctly, *shillings*
As money goes now, it would mean probably about £60.
The costlier the better for Mary's deep purpose of love.
Hypocritical worshippers are content to give the Lord the
lame and the blind, the odd coppers and the spare moments.
They never cross the threshold of the sanctuary of self-
sacrificing service.

See the *manner* in which it was given. She "anointed the feet of Jesus, and wiped His feet with her hair." It is possible to give even a costly gift in such a way as to sting the soul of the receiver. The Lord loveth a cheerful giver. Mary not only offered Him her precious treasure, but her personal glory was also laid at His feet and surrendered to His service. The ointment was all the more precious to the Saviour because the soul of the offerer was in it. See the *influence* of it. "The house was filled with the odour of the ointment." Such a self-sacrificing act could not pass without being *felt* by all who saw it. Such costly offerings, made for such a sacred purpose, are sure to betray themselves (Prov. 27. 16). A consecrated life has always a sweet odour to Christ and His faithful disciples.

II. **Judas, the Criticiser.** The only one who did not appreciate the holy deed of Mary was Judas. The "odour of the ointment" poured upon the Son of God had no sweet savour to him, "because he was a thief," and would rather have had the "three hundred shillings" in his bag for his own advantage. His hypocritical plea was, that it might have been sold and the money given to the poor. "Not that he cared for the poor." Surely the Saviour of sinners was more interested in the poor than he was. He who was rich, for our sakes became poor. "To what purpose is this waste?" (Matt. 26. 8). Judas, the son of perdition, could not see that the breaking of this alabaster box, and the pouring out of the fragrant treasure upon the Person of Christ was the consecrating of both to the greatest possible service. It is noteworthy that the word "waste" used by Judas is literally the same word used by our Lord in referring to him as the "son of *perdition*." Where the spirit of self-seeking is there is blindness to the honour and glory of the Lord Jesus Christ. Mary's vision of Jesus was such that it constrained her to surrender all. Judas could not see beyond the black shadow of his own sinful self-interest.

III. Jesus, the Justifier. "Then Jesus said, Let her alone; against the day of My burying hath she kept this." He understood the full significance of this singularly solemn service, and always puts the highest value upon such gifts. The costly offering was in no sense wasted on Him. To His soul, in view of His death and burial, it had a sweet savour. "Let her alone." The Son of God who sacrificed Himself for sinners will never put any hindrance in the way of a believing, grateful heart showing its devotion to Him to the fullest extent. He knows that such love and sacrifice will have its corresponding reward (Mark 14. 9). "Let *her* alone." Well He knew that there are so few who care to go this length in honouring Him. She broke through all the forms of etiquette, and gave to Christ exceeding abundantly above all that *they* would have asked or thought of. Such a spontaneous outburst of self-sacrificing affection was to Jesus the principal part of the feast. Love feasts on love. Here He had a meat to eat that others knew not of. "The poor," he said, "always ye have with you, but Me ye have not always." But those who reckon it waste to pour out wealth for the cause of Jesus Christ will not be likely to break *their* treasure boxes in behalf of the poor. The best friends of the poor have always been those who are the most devoted friends of Jesus Christ. The love of Christ constraineth us.

DEATH, LIFE, AND SERVICE.
JOHN 12. 20-26.

PROBABLY these Greeks who desired to see Jesus came from the same city as Philip and Andrew, and may have been personally known to them. Philip and Andrew did what they could to bring about an interview, but seemingly

failed. The closing words in verse 36 are very significant
in this connection. "These things spake Jesus, and
departed, and did *hide Himself from them.*" But while He
hid Himself from them, the things which He spake were in
themselves a new and fuller revelation of the Christ which
He wished them to see. He who would "see Jesus" as God
desires Him to be seen, must see Him as "a corn of wheat
falling into the ground and dying, and bringing forth much
fruit."

I. Death. "Except a corn of wheat fall into the ground
and die, it abideth alone." A corn of wheat *in the process*
of dying is here alluded to. As applied to His own
preparation for the Cross, the reference is full of solemn
suggestion. As a corn of wheat must *fall into the ground*
before it will die, so He had to condescend to come into the
place of death before He could reap the fruits of resurrection
life. When Christ came into this world He came into the
place of death. His coming was the falling of the corn of
wheat into the ground, but *except it die*, it abideth alone.
A seed that had lain in the hand of a mummy for 3000
years, remained alone, but when, by another hand, it fell
into the ground and did die, then it brought forth fruit.
The process of dying is the process of yielding up everything to those forces that are opposed to stationary barrenness. Just as the buried seed slowly surrenders its all, so
is its new capacity created for fruitfulness. The life of
Jesus Christ, which ended in the shameful death of the
Cross, was like the life of the corn-seed in the ground—
there was no reserve, no keeping back, the treasures of His
marvellous nature were wholly surrendered. "He came not
to be ministered unto, but to minister, and to give His life."
He died for us What was true of the Christ as "a corn
of wheat" is also true of the Christian, except he die—to
the old self-life—he abideth alone. It is by being "alway

delivered unto death for Jesus' sake, that the life also of
Jesus is made manifest in our mortal flesh" (2 Cor. 4. 11).

II. Life. "But if it die, it bringeth forth much fruit."
The life that is yielded up by the dying seed conditions and
prepares the way for another and more fruitful life. Christ
died, and therefore did not abide alone. The life that He
yielded up has been abundantly fruitful in an ever-
increasing harvest of resurrected souls. The possibilities
of Jesus Christ as seed-corn dropped, as it were, from the
hand of the Heavenly Father into the soil of humanity, are
the possibilities of GOD. He shall see His seed, because His
soul was made an offering for sin. Christ died, but like a
corn of wheat, He was born anew—begotten again in
resurrection fruitfulness. In this new life, in Him and in
us who have died unto sin, there is the abiding power of
eternity. Herein is My Father glorified, that ye bear
much fruit, but "that which thou sowest is *not quickened
except it die*" (1 Cor. 15. 36). If the seed refuses to die, the
quickening power refuses to act. The Holy Spirit, the
Quickener, can only work this *newness of life* where there is
death. This new Divine life, begotten out of the death
of the self-life, is the life that glorifies God in bearing
much fruit. He that soweth to the flesh shall out of the
flesh, as out of poisoned soil, reap corruption.

III. Service. "If any man serve Me, let Him follow
Me." To *follow Him* is the highest and holiest of all
service. To follow Him is to go on continually denying
self. We cannot be following Him in His life of perpetual
self-denial unless we are prepared daily to lose our own
life. He that loveth his (own) life shall lose it, and he that
maketh his own life of no account shall keep it unto life
eternal (v. 25). Christ loved not His own life, but yielded
it, day by day, unto the will of the Father, and so served
Him by following Him. Our service must be of the same

nature, as we have, through grace, been brought into the same privilege. Now are we the sons of God. In essence, then, this service is *self-denial* for the sake of Jesus Christ. But think of the blessedness of it. "If any man serve Me, him will My Father honour." The Father honoured the Son for such a service; He will also honour all who so follow His footsteps. They will be honoured with His presence, His peace, and His power, and "where I am, there shall also My servant be." "If any man will come after ME, let him deny *himself*" (Matt. 16. 24). To go after a self-denying Christ is impossible without the denial of self. We must deny our own thoughts, will, power, interests— everything that would hinder His will, power, and interests from being accomplished in us and by us.

THE LIGHT OF THE WORLD.
JOHN 12. 44-50.

OUR Lord's ministry on earth was first prophetic, then priestly. John's reference to the lament of the prophet Isaiah, in verses 38-41, may be regarded as the close of Christ's work as a Prophet, and here the beginning of His work as a Priest.

I. His Relationship to the World. "I am come a *Light* into the world." In Him was no darkness at all. The purity and power of ineffable light was in Him, to meet the needs and solve the problems of a guilty and benighted world. "*I* am come." There is no other light powerful enough to scatter the darkness of a world. He comes, not as a citizen to share our sorrows, or as a patron to protect our rights, but as a Light to *reveal*. This was the world's first great need.

II. The Nature of this Light. It was the light of the great Heavenly Father's will revealed in the Son. "I have not spoken of Myself," He says, "but the Father which sent Me, He gave Me a command what to say, and in what words to speak" (v. 49). The body of Jesus Christ was as a lantern, the light that was in Him was the Light of God, the manifestation was through His words and works. These words and works reveal infinite love and mercy, hand in hand with infinite power and holiness. The shining was perfect, for He could say, "He that seeth Me, seeth Him that sent Me" (v. 45).

III. **The Purpose of the Light.** "I am come not to judge the world, but *to save the world*" (v. 47). The purpose of every lighthouse is salvation. Light is a great saviour from death and destruction. There were those who were opposed to gas light, when first introduced in 1807, but it was declared that the new light had done more for the reduction of crime than all the laws of Parliament since the days of Alfred. The light of Christ is sin's greatest enemy. To see a Father's love in the life and death of His beloved Son is to see our own need and God's only remedy. He has not come as a light to shine out judgment, and condemnation, but that the world *through Him* might be SAVED (John 3. 17).

IV. **How this Light is Received.** "Whosoever believeth in Me shall not abide in darkness" (v. 46). This heavenly and saving Light shines into the hearts of those who with the heart believe in Him. This faith cometh by hearing. "If any man hear My words," etc. Hear His words, believe them, yield to them, and the light of life will possess the soul. While ye have this light, believe in it, obey it, follow it, trust it. It is as real and as free as the light of the sun. Having believed in Him as the Light of your life, *confess* Him, and be not hindered by the fear of man, or the desire for their praise (see vv. 42, 43; Heb. 11. 27). To believe in Christ is to believe also in Him who sent Him (v. 44). We honour the Father when by faith we receive the salvation, which is Christ Jesus (John 6. 40).

V. The Consequences of Rejecting the Light. If those who believe in Him "shall not *abide* in darkness," then those who believe not are *abiding in darkness*. Light has come into the world, yet men love darkness rather than the light, because their deeds are evil. To abide in darkness is to abide in death. To reject this light is rebellion against the will of God. They shall lie down in sorrow who prefer the sparks of their own kindling to the light of eternal truth. But although men reject those illuminating *words*, or message of God in Christ, and cling to the delusions of darkness, they are not done with this light, they must face it again in its more fierce and withering form, for He says, "The word (message) that I have spoken, the same shall judge him in the last day" (v. 48). The light that has been rejected, lest it should consume their sin, will become a consuming fire for sinners. As every flower reflects the colour that it rejects, so every Christ-rejecter will be manifested in that day (John 3. 19-21).

CHRIST'S LAST TOKEN OF LOVE.
John 13. 1-17.

THE passover and the supper, linked together here, is most significant. The passover commemorated deliverance from Egyptian darkness and bondage; the supper supplied the emblems of redemption from the darkness and dominion of sin. What Pharaoh was to the Israelites, Judas was to Jesus Christ, and the consequences were much alike. the sudden destruction of the enemy, and the triumph of the Lord and His people. It was here, at the supper, that Christ gave to His disciples the farewell token of His self-humiliating love to them. Let us try and think afresh of—

I. What He Did. "He rose from the supper, and laid

aside His garments, and took a towel, and girded Himself
...and began to wash His disciples' feet and to wipe
them." To wash the feet of guests, at a feast, was the work
of a *slave*. "He made Himself of no reputation, and took
upon Him the form of a servant" (Phil. 2. 7). This was the
attitude of the Lord Jesus from the beginning. "He came
not to be ministered unto, but to minister (serve) and to
give His life" (Matt. 20. 28). The Lord would have our
feet (walk), as well as our hearts, clean.

II. **When He Did It**. "When He knew that His
hour was come that He should depart...unto the Father
(v. 1)...that the Father had given all things into His
hands, and that He was come from God, and was going
to God" (v. 3). This lowly act of personal humiliation
and service was performed, as it were, in view of the awful
death of the Cross and the glory that was to follow. The
near prospect of the agony of Gethsemane, the desertion of
His washed disciples, and the eternal glory of the Father,
did not prevent Him from humbling Himself to attend to
their present need. How easy it is for us to get so taken
up with our own sufferings or successes as to become self-
centred and proud, or unsympathetic. He pleased not
Himself, but lived and died for us.

III. **How He Did It**. He did it *lovingly*. "Having
loved His own...He loved them unto the end" (v. 1).
Love beamed in His eyes, love throbbed in His words,
love dropped at His fingers. His touch was as gentle as
a mother's. He did it *voluntarily*. Neither law nor
custom required that HE should wash their feet. He did
it of His own free will and choice. It was an expression
of the reality and depth of His inventive grace and love.
He did it *perfectly*. We may be well assured that when He
washed their feet they would be well washed. All His

words are perfect. "The blood of Christ cleanseth us from *all* sin" (1 John 1. 7).

IV. Why He Did It. "I have given you an example, that ye should do as I have done to you" (v. 15). Let this mind be in you which was also in Christ Jesus (Phil. 2. 3-5). Feet-washing is a very delicate business, and must be done in the Spirit of Jesus, for it is not pleasant to flesh and blood to have our faults pointed out. There is a way of doing it that may be more offensive than profitable. To rebuke a brother or sister in an unkind manner is like washing their feet in frozen water, and let us also take heed that the water is not boiling hot with temper. Let us not forget that it is more difficult for some Christians to keep their feet (walk) clean, as in their daily calling they have more dirty paths to tread, because they are more frequently in contact with the soiling influences of the world. Humbling and painful as the work may be, Christ's example teaches us that the work at times has to be done. There will always be those who, like Peter, are ready to say, "Thou shalt never wash my feet," but a little kindly explanation may turn it into a gladsome experience. But woe unto those who refuse to accept the blessing offered through Christ's humiliation. They have no part with Him (v. 8; John 3. 5).

SELF-EXCOMMUNICATED.

JOHN 13. 21-30.

OUR Lord had just been washing the feet of His disciples; giving them a final example of His humiliation and self-forgetting service. After this, John tells us that "He was troubled in spirit."

I. The Cause of Christ's Trouble. "One of you shall betray Me" (v. 21). The cause of His perturbed spirit was not the fact that within a few hours He would be crucified, but that *"one of you,"* His chosen companions and friends, would *betray* Him. Well He knew that they were "not all clean" (v. 11). His tender compassionate heart was troubled, not on account of Himself, but because of the fearful ingratitude and guilt of that "one" who had already "lifted up his heel against Him" (v. 18). Think of all that Judas had seen and heard of Jesus, and of the place he occupied, and the confidence that was reposed in him (allowing him to carry the bag), and think also of falling from such an height of privilege into a hopeless perdition. He hath no pleasure in the death of the wicked. "He was troubled in spirit."

II. **The Token of Christ's Love.** "When He had dipped the sop, He gave it to Judas" (v. 26). In giving the morsel first to Judas, Christ was not only showing to John who should betray Him, but He was also proving to the traitor that although He knew all that was in his evil heart to do, He loved him to the end. Had He not also washed his feet? washed off the very dust contracted by that secret visit to those murderous priests. If Judas, or any others, will sin their soul to doom, they will never find any occasion in Him, whose love is stronger than death. Did the Lord Jesus hope that this humiliating act of washing the feet of Judas would soften his hard and deceitful heart? If so, how terribly suggestive are the words which follow: "And after the sop, Satan entered into him." The tokens of a Saviour's love had no effect in closing the door of his heart against the entrance of the Devil. Satan is always ready to take full advantage of every opportunity. Those who reject the grace of God, in Christ Jesus, become the willing dupes of the Devil.

III. **The Departure from Christ's Presence.** "He then having received the sop, went immediately out, *and it was night*" (v. 30). He *went* out. Christ did not cast him out. He preferred to go out into the night, rather than abide in the light. He loved the darkness rather than the light, because his deeds were evil. He went out; his choice was finally made. Think of what he went out from, and what he went out to.

1. He went out from THE BEST COMPANY ON EARTH, into the company of God-hating, Christ-rejecting murderers.

2. He went out from THE RULE AND SERVICE OF THE SON OF GOD, into the rule and slavery of Satan.

3. He went out from THE PLACE OF LIGHT AND HOPE, into the night of darkness and despair.

4. He went out FROM THE OFFER OF ETERNAL BLESSED-NESS, into the place of eternal doom.

He apparently did not go out as one in a rage; he went out quite orderly, as one who had something of more importance to *do*; something of more importance to *get*. But in turning away from the love of Christ, at this particular moment, he was rejecting his last chance of salvation. Having refused Christ's place, there is nothing for him now but "his own place" (Acts 1. 25)—perdition. Judas may have imagined that his betrayal of the Master, for thirty pieces of silver, would not seriously affect Him, as He was well able to save Himself from the hands of His enemies; but every betrayer is guilty of the body and blood of the Lord. The blood of every Christ-rejecter will be on his own head. "Ye *will not* come to Me that ye might have life" (John 5. 40).

AN INFALLIBLE CURE FOR HEART TROUBLE.
JOHN 14. 1-4.

THERE were several reasons why the hearts of His disciples became troubled or affrighted at this time. Judas had left the company; the Lord had been speaking of going away, and had just been warning Peter that before the cock

would crow he would deny Him thrice. Our hearts also
may often get troubled when we look at the signs of the
times, or when we look within at our own sins and failures.
Heart trouble is a common malady, but the word and work
of Jesus Christ is a perfect remedy. He came to bind up
the broken heart. When Jesus said, "Let not your heart
be affrighted," He at the same time poured the oil of comfort upon the troubled waters. In this prescription for a
troubled heart, given by the **Great Physician**, there are
seven comforting elements.

I. **The Power of Christ.** "Ye believe in God, believe
also in Me." GOD, ME. To "believe in Me" is to believe
in God. "I and My Father are One." What a comfort
to a sinful, sorrowful soul to know that He who suffered
and died for sinners has all the authority and power of
Almighty God. "All power," He says, "is given unto Me
in Heaven and in earth" (Matt. 28. 18). Trembling soul,
affrighted at your own guilt and at coming death and
judgment, let not your heart be troubled, believe in Him.

II. **The Many Mansions.** "In My Father's house are
many mansions" (v. 2). The "many mansions" is another
way of saying there is plenty of room. The reception
room of the Father's house is large enough for all, and there
are multitudes of private apartments for the individual
comfort of the redeemed. You may be in straights here
and now; there may be no room for *you* in the world's inns;
although, like the Master Himself, you may not have
where to lay your head—let not your heart be troubled, in
our Father's house are many mansions.

III. **The Prepared Place.** "I go to prepare a place for
you." He went to the Cross and the grave to prepare
salvation for us. He went out of the grave, rising from the
dead that He might prepare eternal life for us. He
ascended into Heaven that He might prepare a home for

us. The *prepared* place will correspond with the prepared-
ness of the soul here, by the work of the Holy Spirit. The
measure of our enjoyment of the Kingdom of Heaven will be
according to the measure of our spiritual capacity. Hence
the importance of growing in grace now, and in the
knowledge of God. The place prepared for the Apostle Paul
would not be quite the same as that prepared for the penitent
thief. Let not your heart be troubled, the place prepared
for *you* will be in every way exactly suitable to you.

IV. **The Coming Again.** "I will come again." When
He says, "*I* will come again," He surely does not mean
death. He who is the *Life* can never be compared to *death.*
Neither did He mean the Holy Spirit. The Holy Spirit
had not yet been given. He did not die "for our sins."
He meant what He said, for "the Lord *Himself* shall
descend from Heaven with a shout," therefore comfort
one another with these words (1 Thess. 4. 16-18). Let not
your heart be troubled about the loved ones who have
fallen asleep in Jesus, for in that day "them will He bring
with Him," and we shall be "caught up *together*" (1 Thess.
4. 17). Neither let your heart be affrighted at the things
that are coming to pass on the earth, for "He shall reign
till He hath put all enemies under His feet" (1 Cor. 15. 25).

V. **The Great Reception.** "I will come again and
receive you unto Myself; that where I am there ye may be
also." To be received by Him is to have the honour of the
Father and of the Kingdom conferred upon us. His prayer
on our behalf will then have its perfect fulfilment, "Father,
I will that they also, whom Thou hast given Me, be *with
Me where I am*: that they may behold My glory" (John
17. 24). "If any man serve Me...where I am, there shall
also My servant be." Let not your heart be troubled
although the world despise and reject you, there is a
glorious reception awaiting you at the Coming of the Lord.

VI. The Eternal Home. "Where I am, there ye may be also." Meanwhile the mists of earth partly blinds our eyes to the glories of that place where He is. God hath exalted Him far above all principalities and powers, and given Him a Name that is above every name. He is seated at the right hand of God, crowned with glory and honour; and where He is, there His beloved bride shall be, to behold His glory, and to glory in beholding it. The place of honour purchased by the Lord Jesus Christ, as the Redeemer, is to be shared by the redeemed. Let not your heart be troubled although your circumstances here may be mingled plentifully with trials and sorrows, all tears will be wiped away when at home with Him where He is.

VII. The Blessed Assurance. "Whither I go ye know, and the way ye know" (v. 4). Blessed be His Name, we know *where* He is gone, and also *the way* into His presence. He is gone to prepare a place for us, and He Himself is the Way (v. 6). The way to where He is is the way of faith in Him. Faith *in* Him always leads *to* Him. "The way *ye* know." There is a way that seemeth right unto men, but the end is death, instead of life and glory. Let not your heart be troubled, the way may at times be rough and thorny, and narrow, and may seem long, but five minutes at home with Jesus will abundantly compensate for all the inconveniences of our pilgrim life. The way ye know, and it should be enough for us that it is the way.

———

CHRIST AND THE FATHER.
JOHN 14. 6-21.

WHEN Philip said to Jesus, "Lord, shew us the Father, and it sufficeth us," he was giving expression to the deepest, the most secret, and mysterious longing of the human soul. The curious, critical eye can never look upon the face of God; it is the pure in heart that see Him. Philip, like multitudes in every age, was perfectly sincere in his desire, but slow to believe that Jesus Himself was the visible expression of the invisible God. "He that hath seen Me hath seen the Father" (v. 9). In this chapter our Lord dwells much upon this fact, perhaps in answer to Philip's request. Christ's relationship to the Father can only be understood, in any measure, by thinking deeply into Christ's own statements concerning it. The hypothesis of the Rationalist is of no value in the face of His own plain declarations. From His teaching we learn that—

I. He Dwelt in the Father. "Believest thou not that I am in the Father" (v. 10). The home of His soul was the bosom of God. As a Son He abode in the love of His Father, delighting in His will. He dwelt in the Father that He might be ever with Him for the glory of His Name among men (See 1 John 4. 12-16).

II. His Father Dwelt in Him. "Believe Me that I am in the Father and the Father in Me" (v. 11). The Father, in all the riches of His glorious character, abode in the Son for the edification and salvation of man. He pleased not Himself; yea, more, He *emptied* Himself, that the Father might be gloried in Him. Being in the Father, He dwelt in eternal love; the Father being in Him, the love of God was thus manifested.

III. He is the Revelation of the Father. He said to Philip, "If ye had known Me ye should have known My Father also; from henceforth ye know Him and *have seen Him*. He that hath seen Me hath seen the Father" (vv. 7-9). He is the image of the invisible God (Col. 1. 15). This is the cause of that halo of glory that surrounds the character of Jesus Christ, making it unapproachably unique

among the sons of men. The revelation of Jesus Christ
on earth was the apocalypse (unveiling) of the Father.
To know Christ in His true inward character. is to *know*
the Father.

IV. His Words were the Words of the Father. "The
word which ye hear is not Mine but the Father's which
sent Me" (v. 24). This doctrine, in one form or another,
is emphatically declared about ten times in this Gospel.
It is that deep far-reaching truth, which the critics of
Christ and His teaching so often forget or deliberately
ignore. "My doctrine" He says "is not Mine, but His
that sent Me" (chap. 7. 16). "I speak to the world
those things which I have heard of Him" (chap. 8.
26-28). To reject His words is to reject the message
of the Eternal God and Father to men, and to perish in
sin and ignorance.

V. His Works were the Works of the Father.
"That the world may know...as the Father gave Me
commandment, even so I do" (v. 31). The Father's
commandments were the secret motives of His life. Just
when He was about to finish His career of obedience unto
death, He said: "I have kept My Father's commandments" (John 15. 10). He had power to lay down His
life and to take it again, because He had received "this
commandment of His Father." His wonderful works,
as well as His wonderful words, were manifestations
of the Father's grace and power in operation through
the Son. "Believe Me that I am in the Father, and
the Father in Me; or else believe Me for the very *work's
sake*" (v. 11).

**VI. His Desire was that the Father should be
Glorified in Him.** "Whatsoever ye ask in My Name,
that will I do, that the Father may be glorified in the Son"

(v. 13). That the Father may be glorified He pleased not Himself, but spoke the words and did the works of His Father; and now promises to answer prayer in His Name, that the Father, who is represented by the Son, might be glorified *in* the Son. It is surely this Divine fact that explains the value and power of His Name in prayer (John 16. 24).

VII. **He is the Way to the Father.** "I am the Way... no man cometh unto the Father but by Me" (v. 6). To miss Christ as the Way, the Truth and the Life, is to miss the Father, for the Father is in Him and He is in the Father. "This is the true God and eternal life." He is the *Way* to the Father, because He is the *Truth* about the Father, and the very *Life* of the Father. Christ as *The Way*, must be received by *faith*, as well as Christ the Truth and the Life. To come to Him as the Way, is to forsake our own way and to trust in Him as the Truth and the Life and so come into fellowship with the Father in Him and through Him (Eph. 2. 18).

VII. **To Love Him is to be Loved of the Father.** "He that loveth Me shall be loved of My Father, and I will love him and will manifest Myself to him" (v. 21). To love the Lord Jesus Christ is to love the Father and to be loved in a very special manner by Him. The effect of this mutual love is a further and fuller manifestation of Christ Himself as the image of the Father to the heart of the loving one. What a comfort to know that because we love the Son of God we are being loved by God, and that that great love of His can find no higher reward to give His lovers than a fuller, deeper experience of His Son, Jesus Christ. Oh, the depths of the riches that are in Him. How keenly the apostle must have felt this truth when he said: "If any man love not the Lord Jesus Christ, let him be accursed at His coming" (1 Cor. 16. 22).

LOVE'S REWARD.

John 14. 21-24.

The words of the Lord Jesus Christ are as fathomless as His unsearchable nature. "God is Love," Christ is the perfect manifestation of that love. "He that loveth Me," He says, "shall be loved of My Father, and I will love him and will manifest Myself to him." In these words we have the promise and condition of the greatest spiritual inheritance that God in Christ can bestow upon a human soul.

I. **The Promise.** "I will manifest *Myself* to him." The revelation of *Himself* is the redeemed soul's greatest solace. The purpose of the Holy Spirit in us is to take the things of Christ and show them to us. The quickened spirit of man must seek and yearn for God. "My soul thirsteth for God," said the Psalmist. What Christ has *done* meets all the needs of a sinner; what Christ *is* meets all the needs of a servant. Philip may have been ignorant, but he was surely honest when he said: "Shew us the Father and it sufficeth us" (v. 8). Let me see and know the true God and then I shall be satisfied. He had not yet understood that to see Jesus Christ was to see the Father (v. 9). This is the true God and eternal life. To meet this deep spiritual need in Philip, Christ manifested *Himself* to him. What a revelation this must have been to Philip. See how our Lord answered the somewhat similar question of Judas (not Iscariot): "How wilt Thou *manifest Thyself unto us* and not unto the world?" (v. 22). The Lord's answer to this most important question is pregnant with vital teaching. He will manifest Himself in the Spirit of the Father to the man that loves Him by "coming unto him and making His—or Their—*abode with him*" (v. 23). This manifestation is not outward, or external; it is the coming of the Divine life and character in fresh and fuller power into the inner man. The *indwelling* presence of God is the most central, the most solemn and influential reality with which the Christian has to do. The craving of a pure heart is to see God. In times of sorrow, loneliness, weariness, fruitlessness, and failure, our real need is expressed in one word: "Himself." We cannot possibly make too much of this fact and privilege of grace, that Christ eagerly desires to *manifest* HIMSELF as the Healer of all diseases, the Source of all fruitfulness, and the Victor in every fight. Whenever and wherever He manifests Himself, results worthy of Himself will be accomplished. When He showed Himself after His passion it was "by many infallible proofs." Although the two men on the way to Emmaus knew Him not when He appeared, yet did He make their *"hearts burn* within them while He talked to them." When He manifested Himself to Mary, there followed confession and *commission* (John 20. 16, 17). When He manifested Himself to His unbelieving disciples, He first *rebuked* them (Mark 16. 14), then when He had showed them His hands and His feet they were *glad*, and He breathed on them, saying, *"Receive ye the Holy Ghost"* (John 20. 20-22). The result of His appearing to doubting Thomas was confession and *worship* (John 20. 26-28). His appearing to the disciples by the sea shore turned their failure into great *success* (John 21). Three times did the Lord manifest Himself to the Apostle Paul for the purpose of *encouraging* him in His service (Acts 23. 11; 18. 9, 10; 27. 23, 24). To the suffering and dying Stephen He revealed Himself as the glorified One (Acts 7. 55). In the light of all this let us seek to grasp the significance and preciousness of this promise: "He that loveth Me...I will *love him*, and *will manifest Myself to him."* The manifestation of Himself to us is His infinitely gracious way of meeting and satisfying our every need. But how will He manifest Himself unto

us and not unto the world? This brings us to the second
point, namely—

II. **The Condition.** *"He that loveth Me."* This
promise of Christ is for ever true, and this simple condition
is for ever availing. Christ *will* manifest Himself to those
who *love Him.* It is possible to be wise and scholarly,
faithful and enthusiastic, and yet destitute of that deep joy
and satisfaction which comes through the manifestation of
Himself to the *loving* heart. Thank God, this greatest of
all blessings is not promised to the learned, or the laborious,
but to the loving. "Lovest thou Me?" was our Lord's
pressing question after manifesting Himself to His disciples
by the sea of Galilee. The heart must become very sensitive that would receive and retain the image of the Son
of God as revealed by the Holy Spirit. It is love, not
knowledge, that creates capacity for Christ. Intense
loving is more pleasing to Him than deep thinking. He
who loves the Lord with all his heart will live in the continual vision of His comforting presence and matchless
glory. The condition is love; but the proof of love is the
"keeping of His words"—or teaching. "He that hath My
words and keepeth them, he it is that loveth Me...If a man
love Me, he will keep My words...He that loveth Me not
keepeth not My words" (vv. 23, 24). John, in his first
epistle, restates this truth very plainly: "Whoso keepeth
His word (teaching), in him surely is the love of God
perfected" (2. 5). The soul in which that love is perfected will be honoured with the apocalypse (unveiling)
of Jesus Christ. It was to John, the most loving of His
disciples, that the book of "The Revelation of Jesus
Christ" was given (Rev. 1. 1). The love of God can only
be perfected in that heart where love answers to love. It
is impossible to keep His words and to grow under His
teaching, as He desires we should, unless there is in us a

growing love and devotion to Christ's person and work. In these days of intellectual and moral activity, let us be diligent to keep our hearts right with God, otherwise there will be no manifestation of HIMSELF as the sum of all power, and blessing, and success.

OBEDIENCE.
JOHN 14. 23, 24.

"IF a man love Me, he will keep My words: and My Father will love him, and We will come unto him, and make our abode with him. He that loveth Me not keepeth not My sayings: and the Word which ye hear is not Mine, but the Father's which sent Me."

Obedience is the necessary consequence of love.

FRUIT-BEARING.
JOHN 15. 1-8.

ISRAEL, as a vine, was brought out of Egypt and planted in Canaan, after the heathen had been cast out like weeds (Psa. 80. 8). This vine, though noble, and of a right seed, soon degenerated into a strange plant to God (Jer. 2. 21). But Jesus Christ is the TRUE Vine, brought down from Heaven and planted in the earth. He was the faithful and true witness. There was nothing in Him to create a feeling of "strangeness" or disappointment in the heart of God. He was true to God, true to His own nature, true to His environment, and to the sons of men. But the principle thought here is that, as a Vine, He is true to those who are associated with Him as branches, so that they might bring forth fruit. Note the—

I. **Source of Fruit**. "The vine." The branch cannot bear fruit of itself (v. 4). "Apart from Me, ye can do nothing" (v. 5, R.V.). Impoverished branches in this vine is no evidence of an impoverished vine, for God giveth not the Spirit with limitations to Him (John 3. 34). All the treasures of wisdom and knowledge, of grace and power, are in Him, even the "fullness of the Godhead." "From Me is thy fruit found" (Hosea 14. 8).

II. Removal of the Fruitless. "Every branch in Me that beareth not fruit He taketh away" (v. 2). "If any man abide not in Me, he is cast forth as a branch and is withered" (v. 6). This may refer to those who are in Him *religiously*, but not *spiritually*: those who have been from their birth brought up in the form of godliness, but who have never known the power and sweetness of His fellowship. There is an outward resemblance to the vine branch, but no production of the vine fruit, so the husbandman deals with it as having no connection with the vine. Such a branch "cast forth" can do nothing else but *wither*. Apart from Christ, there is no saving or preserving power in man. It is only those whose roots are in the river of God whose leaves shall not wither (Psa. 1. 3). These withered branches are gathered, not by the angel reapers, but by *men*, who cast them into the fire of testing, and they are burned. A religious, Christless life will never be of much use to men, far less to God. Like savourless salt, they are good for nothing.

III. Pruning of the Fruitful. "Every branch that beareth fruit, He cleanseth it, that it may bear more fruit" (vv. 2, 3). There are growths about the Christian life, as there are about the vine, which do not tend to fruitfulness, shoots that show signs of a vigour which is only fit for the pruning knife. The riches of the grace of God is seen here in seeking to make the fruitful more fruitful. Those fit for His service He desires to make more fit. The process may be painful, to have *our* new-born desires and fresh efforts nipped off and thrown away as hindrances;

but His will be done. The heart life is to be kept pure by *faith* (Acts 15. 9). The pruning knife is the Word of God which is sharp and powerful...discerning the thoughts and intents of the heart. "Now are ye clean through the Word."

IV. **Nature of the Fruit**. "Bear much fruit, *so* shall ye be My disciples" (v. 8). That t ranch is a true disciple of the vine that bears much of the fruit of the vine. We are the true disciples of Christ when His character manifests itself in our lives. What the sap of the vine is to the branch, the Spirit of Christ is to the Christian. The fruit of the Spirit is love, joy, peace, etc., because the Spirit Himself is all this, and when He has free access into our hearts, and full control of them, His own personal characteristics will appear as fruit in our lives.

V. **Condition of Fruitfulness**. "He that abideth in Me and I in him, the same bringeth forth much fruit" (v. 5). The human side is, "He in me;" the Divine, "I in Him." "The branch cannot bear fruit of itself... no more can ye except ye *abide* in Me" (v. 4). "In *me*," that is, in my flesh dwelleth no good thing, but in HIM all fullness dwells. His grace will be perfected in us, as we by faith abide in Him. Constant contact with Him implies the attitude of continual receptiveness, "I in Him." To abide in Him is to abide in His Word, His will, and His work, then God works in us both to will and to do of His good pleasure.

VI. **Results of Fruitfulness**. "Herein is My Father glorified, that ye bear much fruit; so shall ye be My disciples" (v. 8). The results are twofold: the Father is glorified, and our true discipleship is proven. It is to the honour of the husbandman that the tree brings forth fruit abundantly. It is also to the credit of the tree that it so proves its good character by its works. Where there

is wholehearted discipleship there will be fruitfulness **and**
a life glorifying to the Father. Fruit is the natural
outcome of a faithful following of Christ, as well as an
evidence of it. The life lived in Christ, and for Him, is
the only God-glorifying life. "Much fruit" means much
love, much joy, much peace, etc.

BRANCHES, DISCIPLES, FRIENDS.
JOHN 15.

THESE are not empty titles, the Lord Himself is the Author
of each of them, but they are each conditioned with something else. The first with abiding, the second with
fruitbearing, the third with obedience. These three names
are suggestive of three different experiences.

I. As Branches, we Receive. "I am the Vine, ye are
the branches" (v. 5). This process and privilege of
receiving of the fullness that is in Christ cannot begin until
we as branches have been broken off the old fruitless Adam-
stock, and grafted into Him who is the second Adam, the
True Vine. The precious sap of this Vine (Spirit) will
never minister to the pride of the old selfish sinful life.
But having been planted into Christ, we now live by faith
that is in Him. The branch cannot live apart from the
vine, no more can ye. To live apart from Christ is to be
dead while we live. "Because I live ye shall live also"
(John 14. 19), if ye abide in Me. The life of the branch,
then, is a life of *continual appropriation*. The call of the
vine to the branch is to take, take, take. "Let him that is
athirst, take." "If any man thirst, let him come unto
Me and drink." This receiving of the sap by the branch
was to manifest itself in fruitfulness To be filled with the
Spirit is to be filled with the fruit of the Spirit, as it is
possible to grow apples of different quality on the same
stock, so, by the same Spirit there may be different

manifestation, according to the character of the branch.
While our union with Christ is the death of our sinful life,
it is not the death of our individuality. In every Christian
life the whole fruit of the Spirit should be found (Gal.
5. 22, 23), but, as a rule, in the lives of Christians, some
one or two aspects of this fruit are often found prominent,
this may be partly due to the nature of the recipient.
Still, "the wind bloweth where it listeth."

II. As Disciples, we Follow. "So shall ye be My
disciples" (v. 8). In continuing the metaphor of the vine
and branches here, the idea is, that the branch truly
follows the vine, when it abides in it, and when by the
power imparted to it, it faithfully carries out the purpose
for which the vine had been given. So, by an adherence
to the mind and will of our Lord, and by the bringing forth
of much of the fruit of the Spirit, we are declaring ourselves to be walking in His footsteps. "If ye continue in
My Word, then are you My disciples indeed" (John 8. 31).
This discipleship implies a readiness to sit at His feet, like
Mary, and to learn of Him who is the Great Teacher come
from God. It implies also a willingness to believe every
word He says. How can His words *abide in us* if they are
not received by faith (v. 7). How can we follow His
example if we do not live and walk by faith in the Word of
God as He did. Another mark of discipleship is love one
to another (John 13. 35).

III. As Friends, we Commune. "Ye are My friends...
I have called you friends (not patients), for all things that I
have heard of My Father I have made known unto you"
(vv. 14, 15). A friend comes closer to the heart than a
servant, "A servant knoweth not what his Lord doeth."
It is a very sacred and humbling privilege to walk among
men as the friends of Jesus Christ. As His friends, living
in communion with Him, we become—

1. Sharers of His SECRETS. "The secret of the Lord is with them that fear Him" (Psa. 25. 14). It was of him who was "the friend of God" that God said, "Shall I hide from Abraham that thing which I do?" The deep heart purposes of the Son of God are revealed to those who live in fellowship with Him. In the light of His presence they see light clearly. They walk among the gloomy shadows of a sinful world, with the secrets of life, peace, and eternal glory in their souls.

2. Sharers of His SYMPATHIES. As a devoted wife becomes a partaker of her husband's likes and dislikes, so does the friend of Jesus, through close contact with Him, becomes imbued with His thoughts and feelings. They love all that He loves and hate all that He hates. They are in real heart sympathy with Him in His desire to honour the Father, and at the same time to love, and seek to save, the sinful sons of men.

3. Sharers of His SUFFERINGS. "The world hated Me... because ye are not of the world...therefore the world hateth you" (vv. 18, 19). Christ suffered because of His unlikeness to the world. His true friends will fare little better. Christ suffered in His daily life because of His sympathy with God His Father, and His separation from the sins and false conception of His age. The more we become like Him the more shall we feel the power of those forces in the world which were opposed to Him.

4. Sharers of His CONSOLATIONS. "For as the sufferings of Christ abound in us, so our consolation also aboundeth by Christ" (2 Cor. 1. 5). To be made a partaker of His sufferings, is to become an heir of His consolations. Such consolations are neither few not small, good measure, pressed down and running over. What the Father was to the Son, the Holy Spirit, the Comforter is to us an ever present, all sufficient compensation for all the sorrows and

sufferings incurred through our sympathy with Christ, and service for Him. If we suffer, we shall also *reign* with Him, that is consolation indeed.

"I AND YOU."

JOHN 15. 12-26.

IN this chapter alone Christ uses the first personal pronoun with *studied emphasis* eleven times. In each case the chief importance of the words spoken lie in the character of Him who speaks. In these impressive I's of His there is the thought of—

I. Grace. "I have loved *you*" (v. 12). *You* who sometime were afar off, but are now made nigh: you who were once in ignorance of Me, and walked according to the course of this world. I *have loved* you with a love that can only be compared with that love wherewith the Father hath loved Me (v. 9). "Ye know the grace of our Lord Jesus Christ, that though He was rich, yet for your sakes He became poor, that ye through His poverty might be rich."

II. Separation. "I chose you out of the world" (v. 19, R.V.). "The whole world lieth in wickedness" (John 5. 19). To be chosen of Christ is to be called out of the world into His fellowship and Kingdom. In this fellowship ye shall be partakers of His sufferings, for the world that hated Him will hate you. The Cain-spirit that seeks to slay those more righteous than themselves is ever with us (1 John 3. 12). We are chosen out of the world like Noah, that we might be saved from it, and become witnesses against it. By faith, like Abraham, we must go out.

III. Friendship. "I have called you friends" (v. 15). To be called friends by Him who is God's best Friend is an honour indeed. It was a blessed day for Mordecai when

he was declared the friend of the king (Esther 6. 11).
Servants have kitchen privileges, but *friends* have parlour
opportunities. Anywhere in the Lord's house is an honour
and a blessing, but covet earnestly the best gifts. He will
call *you* friend if ye abide in Him.

IV. **Teaching.** "All things...I have made known
unto you" (v. 15). He is the great Teacher come from
God. As He sought to instil into the minds of His disciples
the things that He heard of His Father, so by the Holy
Spirit does He still make known the will of the Father, for
all things are now delivered unto Him, and the Spirit takes
the things which are His and shows them unto us.

V. **Responsibility.** "I have chosen you...that ye
should bring forth fruit" (v. 16). Having called His
disciples friends, and having instructed them in the things
concerning Himself, He expects them to be something else
than mere *patients* in a doctor's hands. The love that has
grown into friendship must go on ripening into fruitful
service. A fruitless branch never serves the purpose of the
vine. A barren Christian profession is a misrepresentation
of Christ. "*Chosen* and *ordained* to bring forth fruit"
(v. 16). If the fruit of the Spirit is not manifest
in our lives, we are falsifying both our calling and our
ordination.

VI. **Brotherly Love.** "I command you that ye love one
another" (v. 17). Love is the bond that is to hold His
people one to another amidst the hatred and opposition of
this world. It is His *command*, His *new* commandment
which is the sum of the whole law. Have this salt of love
in *yourselves*, and there shall be peace one with another
(Mark 9. 50). Not to love one another is an act of
rebellion against the rule of Christ.

VII. **Promise.** "I will send you...the Spirit of
truth" (v. 26). The word Comforter in this verse may

be translated "Helper." This promised "Helper" is the "Spirit of truth." This "Spirit of truth the devil-deluded world cannot receive, because it seeth Him not, but He shall be *in you*" (John 14. 17). In promising the Spirit, Christ promised every needful thing for life and service. He is the Spirit of truth, of grace, of burning, and of power. What a Helper He is! How fruitless our testimony without Him! "I will send Him unto *you*." "Receive ye the Holy Ghost."

THE GREAT HELPER.
JOHN 16. 7-15.

THE Lord Jesus Christ is mighty to *save* a sinner; the Holy Spirit is mighty to *help* a saint. The word "Comforter" has been variously translated. The terms "Advocate," "Paraclete," "Helper," have been used. In Romans 8. 26, we read that "The Spirit *helpeth* our infirmities"— literally *taketh hold with me*. The same word is used in Luke 10. 40, but nowhere else in the New Testament. "Bid her therefore that she *help me*." The Holy Spirit has come, as one who is willing and mighty to "take hold with me," that I might be helped in doing the will and work of God.

I. **The Condition of His Coming.** "If I go not away, the Helper will not come unto you, but if I go, I will send *Him* (not it) *unto you*" (v. 7). Christ had to go, taking humanity into the character and presence of God, before the Spirit could come, bringing divinity into the character and presence of man (Acts 2. 33). The bodily absence of the Redeemer was to ensure the spiritual presence of the Helper. The Spirit could not be given till Jesus was glorified (John 7. 39). The coming of the Helper was the proof that Christ's atoning work was perfected, and that the Father, Son, and Spirit, were all most desirous that men should be *helped* into possession

of the present and eternal fruits of the saving work of
Jesus Christ.

II. **His Mission in the World.** "I will send Him
unto *you*; and He, when He is come, He will convict the
world in respect of sin, and of righteousness, and of
judgment" (v. 8, R.V.). While the Spirit's attitude to
the Church is that of an Helper, His attitude to the
world is that of a Converter. There are three things the
world needs to be convicted of: Sin, righteousness, and
judgment.

1. "Of SIN, because they believe not on Me" (v. 9).
The great sin of the world, in the eyes of the Holy
Spirit, is unbelief—believing not the Son of God. His
mission is to glorify Christ (v. 14), and the first thing
He does is to convict of the sin of rejecting His Word and
sacrifice.

2. "Of RIGHTEOUSNESS, because I go to My Father."
Christ could not go to His Father until He had gone to the
Cross and the grave as an atonement for sin. To go to His
Father, He must rise again from the dead. His resurrection
and ascension secures for us that righteousness which His
death for our sins had prepared.   He died for our offences,
He rose again for our *justification* (Rom. 4. 25). On the
Cross He was made sin for us; now at the Father's right
hand He is made of God unto us righteousness (1 Cor.
1. 30).   This is the righteousness that the world needs,
and that the Holy Spirit seeks to convict it of. Our own
righteousnesses are as filthy rags in His sight.

3. "Of JUDGMENT, because the prince of this world hath
been judged" (v. 11, R.V.). As surely as the prince of this
world (Devil) has already been judged, and brought under
condemnation by Christ's death and resurrection, so has
every unbeliever. "He that believeth not hath been

judged already" (John 3. 18, R.V.). This is the judgment, that the light is come into the world, and men love the darkness rather than the light. The Spirit has come to convict concerning judgment. All down through these ages the Holy Spirit has been, as it were, prosecuting the world, bringing it to judgment, because of its criminal attitude toward the Son of God. How is this work done? Does the Spirit use any medium, through which He convicts the men of the world? The last clause of verse 7 should surely not be separated in thought from verse 8. "If I depart, I will send Him *unto you*, and when He is come—unto you—He will convict the world." It was when the Spirit had come with power unto Peter, that the three thousand were *"pricked* in their heart," on the day of Pentecost. A powerless Christian, or a powerless Church will never be successful in convicting the world of sin, of righteousness, and of judgment. This needed work cannot be done in any other way, but by the Holy Ghost, the Almighty Helper.

III. His Mission to the Church.

To the redeemed of God the Holy Spirit has come—

1. As a Guide into all Truth. "Howbeit when He, the Spirit of truth, is come, He will guide *you* into all the truth" (v. 13, R.V.). He is the Spirit of truth, because He has come out from Him who is "The Truth," in His person and doctrine. He guides into the truth, because the Spirit searcheth into the deep *things of God* (2 Cor. 2. 10). O soul, thirsting for the truth as it is in Jesus, receive the guidance of this heavenly Helper; ask Him, and depend upon Him to do it. This holy anointing teacheth you all things and is truth (1 John 2. 27).

2. As a Revealer of the Things of Christ. "He shall glorify Me; for He shall take of Mine, and shall declare it unto you" (vv. 14, 15). He helps us all He can,

by taking the things that *are Christ's*—by right of His
sufferings and death —things purchased for His people by
His own blood; and to declare them, or make them known
unto us, that He might glorify the Son, by filling up
and making fruitful the lives of His redeemed ones (John
15. 8). Blessed Helper, help me to enter into this most
precious inheritance. "All things are yours, for ye are
Christ's."

3. As an Example of Self-abandoned Service. "He
shall *not speak from Himself*; but whatsoever things He
shall hear, these shall He speak; and He shall declare
unto you the things that are to come" (v. 13, R.V.). His
ministry was one of entire self-abnegation. As Christ
sought, through self-emptying, to glorify the Father, so
the Holy Spirit likewise sought to glorify the Son: we
also, through self-renunciation, must honour the Holy
Spirit. The Son of God spake not from Himself (John
14. 10, R.V.). Neither did the Holy Spirit, neither
should we. Self-will, and self-wisdom, and every other
form of self-assertiveness, is a usurping of the Holy Spirit.
If we would have the help of the Spirit in our ministry for
Christ, we shall not speak from our own authority, but
whatsoever things we shall hear—from Him—these shall
we speak, and shall declare the *things that are to come*.

A LITTLE WHILE.

John 16. 16-23.

In these verses, the words, "A little while," are repeated
seven times over, as if they were of special significance.
From the fact that our Lord, in explaining the meaning of
them, used the parabolic form, we may infer that different
applications may be made of them (v. 25). "A little
while, and ye shall not see Me...and ye shall be sorrowful...

but I shall see you again, and your heart shall rejoice...
and in that day ye shall ask Me no question." These
precious words may easily have a threefold meaning.
As the

I. **Historical.** "A little while, and ye shall *not* see
Me." It was but "a little while"—a few hours—and
Christ was buried out of their sight, though in a *borrowed*
grave, yet *sealed* with the royal signet. The interval
between His death and resurrection was, indeed, to them
a time of "sorrow" and "lamenting," but to the world a
time of rejoicing (Luke 24. 17). The world's feasts go on
more merrily in the absence of the Saviour from sin, but
the Christian can find a feast nowhere where He is not.
"A little while, and I shall see you again, and your heart
shall rejoice." Their hearts did rejoice when, after three
days, they saw Him again in resurrection power and glory.
"*Then* were the disciples glad when they saw the Lord"
(John 20. 20). "They worshipped Him, and *returned* to
Jerusalem with great joy." "In that day" they did ask
Him no question. The fact of His appearing to them as
the Risen One was itself the answer to all their doubts and
questionings. He who had power to rise from the dead,
had power to perform His every promise. In a dark and
cloudy day, the relative value of other lights may be dis-
puted, but when the sun breaks out in all his glorious
majesty, there is no questioning his all-sufficiency to meet
the need.

II. **Personal.** "A little while...ye shall be sorrowful
...but I will see you again, and your heart shall rejoice...
in that day ye shall ask no question." The sorrowful
"little while" of His called-out ones is *now*, while their
Lord is absent, and the world is rejoicing. "In the world
ye shall have tribulation" (v. 33), but His "I will see you
again" is the hope of his suffering saints. Through the

gathering gloom we look for the breaking of the day, when we shall see Him face to face. Just now we may see as but through a glass darkly; there are many things that we cannot possibly understand, mysterious movements of the providence of God, and of the Holy Spirit, that at times sorely perplex our eager spirits, many things we should like explained. Yes, but *"in that day* ye shall ask Me no question." One look into the glorified face of our redeeming Lord will hush at once every restless feeling and every anxious thought. So satisfied shall we be when we see HIM, that we shall not be able to ask Him any question. So perfect will be our acquiescence to *His will* in everything.

> "Not a surge of worry, not a shade of care,
> Not a blast of hurry moves the spirit there."

III. Dispensational. These words of our Lord may also be prophetic of that time when He will come again, taking to Himself *His right* to rule and reign over this world for which He died. The Church of God is now passing through its "little while" of sorrow, this is its time to "weep and lament, but the world shall rejoice." In the latter days perilous times will come. But the Church's hope lies in His promise, "I will see you again, and your heart shall rejoice, and your joy no man taketh from you." She, like a woman in travail, hath sorrow now, but when THE MAN is born *into the world*, she shall remember no more her anguish for joy (v. 21). God's people just now are sadly divided and full of questionings, but on that day when HE *shall appear* in the glory of His power, as King of kings and Lord of lords, "ye shall ask no questions." All human questionings are for ever set at rest in the presence of the glorified Son of God. Angels ask Him no questions, but it is our great privilege *now* to "Ask that we may receive" (v. 23).

CHRIST'S GIFTS TO HIS OWN.

JOHN 17.

IN approaching this chapter we feel as if we were passing through the veil into the holiest of all. This prayer of our Great High Priest, just before He offered Himself upon the altar of the Cross as the sacrifice for the sin of the world, is in itself a great unveiling of holy things. Here every petition is a revelation, every declaration a discovery. From these—Christ's own words—we shall note first of all some of the blessings He has conferred upon His own. Observe the—

I. **Life of God.** "Thou hast given Him authority over all flesh, that...to them He should give eternal life" (v. 2, R.V.). This eternal life consists in knowing God and Jesus Christ whom He hath sent (v. 3). To know Him is to be made a partaker of His nature, to be adopted into His family as "sons and daughters of the Lord God Almighty." When Christ condescended to take upon Him the likeness of sinful flesh, God gave Him authority over *all flesh*, that He might give this life to all who believe.

II. **Name of God.** "I have manifested Thy Name unto the men whom Thou gavest Me out of the world" (v. 6). The life and work of Jesus Christ was "the Lord proclaiming the Name of the LORD, the Lord God, merciful and gracious, longsuffering, and abundant in goodness and truth." In manifesting the *Name* of God, He was manifesting His nature. He could truly say, "He that hath seen Me hath seen the Father." But only those given Him "out of the world" could receive this gracious revelation. "The world by wisdom knew not God."

III. **Words of God.** "I have given them the words which Thou gavest Me" (v. 8). This thought is frequently expressed in this Gospel (chaps. 12. 49; 14. 10). Those

who have been made alive unto God must feed upon
the words of the Living God. "Man shall not live by
bread alone, but by *every word* that proceedeth out of the
mouth of God." Christ Himself is the truth, because the
words He spake were the very words and doctrines taught
Him by the Eternal Father. "I and My Father are One."
One in nature and in purpose, One in will, in deed, and in
truth. "The words that I speak unto you are spirit and
life." As He lived by faith in those words given Him, so
shall we. "Believe, and thou shalt see."

IV. **Service of God.** "I am glorified in them" (v. 10).
As the Father was glorified in the Son (v. 4), so the Son
is to be glorified in His own. The words of God have been
given us as they were given to Jesus Christ His Son, for a
very definite and gracious purpose, that God might be
glorified in faithful and successful service (v. 4). The
privilege of working for Him is a precious gift. Alas, that
so many should neglect to stir up this gift. How is Christ
to be glorified in us unless there is whole-hearted surrender
to His will and work, as He was to the will and work which
the Father gave Him to do? Was not this what the
apostle meant when he said, "Christ shall be magnified in
my body, whether it be by life or by death?" (Phil. 1. 20).

V. **Glory of God.** "And the glory which Thou hast
given Me I have given unto them" (v. 22, R.V.). What
glory was this that Christ received from God the Father,
and passed on to His disciples? Did not this glory consist
in God's nature and Name, His words and work, which
were given to the Son, and which in grace He has imparted
to His followers? As He is, so are we. There is, besides,
the glory that is yet to be revealed when we shall be with
Him where He is (v. 24). As God gave Him the glory
of Sonship and heirship, so hath He given this glory to us
who believe (John 1. 12). The purpose of this manifold

gift is, "that *they* all may be one," even as Christ and the Father are One (v. 22). What would be the results if this glory was really witnessed by the world?

VI. Love of God. "I made known unto them Thy Name, *and will make it known* that the *love* wherewith Thou lovedst Me *may be in them*" (v. 26). Christ hath made known, and will go on making known the Name (character) of God, that His nature which is love may be continually nurtured in us. This He does by the gift of the Holy Ghost, who sheds this love abroad in our hearts (Rom. 5. 5). It is surely a heart-searching thought that our Lord should close His great unveiling priestly prayer with this testimony, that the purpose for which He had faithfully declared the Name of God was that the *love* which God had for His Son might be *in us*. Has this grace of the Lord Jesus Christ been in vain to us? Are we rejoicing in the depth, the fullness, and the eternity of this love? Is this love being revealed to others through us, as it has been revealed through Christ to us?

CHRIST'S PETITIONS FOR HIS OWN.
JOHN 17.

THIS is one of the chapters of which Baxter in his "Saint's Rest" says, "It is of more value than all the other books in the world." But the veil that is over the heart needs to be taken away, before the hidden glory can be seen. This is not a prayer for the world. "I pray not for the world." His cry for the perishing world came out of His agonised heart while hanging on the Cross (Luke 23. 34). Here He pleads for those that had been given Him out of the world. He prayed that they might be—

I. Kept by the Father. "Holy Father, keep them in Thine own Name which Thou hast given Me" (v. 11). To be kept *in His own Name* is to be kept in His own character

and likeness; is to be continually acknowledged and
claimed as His own sons and daughters. They are to be
kept in that *Name* which Christ had manifested to them
(v. 6). "The Name of the Lord is a strong tower, the
righteous runneth into it and are safe" (Prov. 18. 10).

II. **Happy in Themselves.** "Now I come to Thee...
that they may have My joy fulfilled in themselves"
(v. 13). He who was the "Man of Sorrows and acquainted
with grief," was no stranger to that joy which is in the
Holy Ghost (Rom. 14. 17). If His joy had been in Himself
alone, how could He impart it to others? But being in
the Holy Spirit, this He could and did give. The Lord's
people are not asked to put on a smiling face without
possessing a smiling heart. This holy personal joy is the
joy of true *fellowship* with the Father, and with His
Son Jesus Christ, in the *communion* of the Holy Ghost
(1 John 1. 3, 4).

III. **Protected from the Devil.** "I pray...that Thou
shouldest keep them from the evil one" (v. 15, R.V.).
Christ knew, from personal experience, the subtle dangers
that lay in being tempted of the Devil, so He prays here
that we might be kept from yielding to his illuding devices.
"When ye pray, say, Lead us not into temptation, but
deliver us from the evil one" (Matt. 6. 13, R.V.). "He
that is begotten of God keepeth *Him*, and the evil one
toucheth him not" (1 John 5. 18, R.V.). While we by
faith keep hold of *Him* who has destroyed the works of
the Devil, God will keep us by His mighty power from
the evil one.

IV. **Holy unto God.** "Sanctify them in Thy truth...
for their sakes I sanctify Myself, that they also might be
truly sanctified" (vv. 17, 19, *margin*). As He consecrated,
or set Himself apart *for us*, He prays that we may be
consecrated (set apart) *for Him*. He says, "As the Father

sent Me into the world, even so have I sent them into the world" (v. 18). He delivered the same message to His disciples after His resurrection (John 20. 21). Ye are not your own, ye are, in the purpose of His grace, separated unto Himself, "therefore glorify God in your body and your spirit, which are His."

V. Useful unto Others. "Neither pray I for these alone, but for them also which shall believe in Me through their word" (v. 20). Then Christ expected that others would believe on His Name *through* them; that the "other sheep" which were not of this little fold, were to hear *His voice* "through *their word*," and be brought into the one flock under the one Shepherd (John 10. 16). Let your light so shine—that light which He hath shined into your hearts—that others, seeing the good works of God in you, may glorify your Father which is in Heaven. He hath blessed us, that we might be made a blessing. Let us see that the Holy One is not limited in His saving grace by our unbelief (Psa. 78. 41).

VI. United One to Another. He prayed also, "That they all may be one" (v. 21). There is here a double union. His request to the Father is that as *brethren*, they might be one in themselves, and as *sons*, they might be "one *in us*...as Thou Father art in Me, and I in Thee." How blessed Christian fellowship would be, if it resembled the fellowship that exists between the Father and the Son. That *they* may be one as *we* are, is the longing of Christ's heart (Gal. 3. 28). The anticipated outcome of this is, "That the world may believe that *Thou hast sent Me*." The world still needs to know that *love* of God which sent His Son to save it (John 3. 16).

VII. Glorified with Christ. "Father, I will that they also, whom Thou hast given Me, be with Me where I am, that they may behold My glory" (v. 24). When *He*

shall appear, we shall be like Him.   Here we are more
familiar with the sufferings of Christ than with the glory
which is now His with the Father; but our afflictions,
which are light compared with His, are working out for us
as His afflictions wrought out for Him, "an exceeding and
eternal weight of glory" (2 Cor. 4. 17).   If we suffer with
Him, we shall also be glorified together with Him.   Our
eyes have often been dimmed with tears while beholding
His sufferings, but all tears shall be wiped away and every
heart questioning hushed when we behold His glory.   We
cannot say of the prayers of Christ, as with the prayers of
David, that "they are ended," for they are still being
fulfilled.   May we, through our sanctified lives, help to
give Him these desires of His heart.

THE CHRISTIAN'S RELATIONSHIP TO THE WORLD.
JOHN 17.

I. They are Taken Out of the World.   "The men
which Thou gavest Me out of the world" (v. 6).   The *world*,
as such, is a ruined mass, lying in the lap of the evil one;
being coddled by the illusions and guided by the false
principles of the god of this world; but the followers of
Jesus Christ have in spirit been lifted up out of the whole
thing, as out of an horrible pit and miry clay, and have
been established in the Kingdom of our God, and of His
Christ, which is righteousness, and peace, and joy in the
Holy Ghost.   "Ye are not of the world, even as I am not
of the world."

II. They are Distinguished from the World.   "I
pray for them: I pray not for the world" (v. 9).   As soon
as we become separated in spirit from the world, we come
under a new set of laws in the Kingdom of grace.   We are
dealt with as *children* of God, not as the mere offspring of
His creative power.   Christ loves His own with a love

which is peculiar to His own. While He has the love of pity for the world, He has the love of pleasure for His own. Because they are in heart for Him, He in heart and power is for them; so all things work together for good to them that love Him.

III. They are In the World. "But these are in the world" (v. 11). As to their spirit and purpose, they are out of the world, but as to their bodily presence and influence, they are still in the world. In the world, but not of it, even as Christ was (v. 16). In the world, not as a branch in the vine, but as a light in the darkness; not as a member in the body, but as a physician in the hospital. In the world, not as a "man of the world," but as a "man of God"; not as its slave, but as its victor.

IV. They are Hated by the World. "The world hath hated them, because they are not of the world, even as I am not of the world" (v. 14). There was no hatred until He had given them the Word of God. "I have given them Thy Word, and the world hath hated them." This God-given *Word*, when received, so revolutionised their minds and hearts that the world did not know them, and so contrary did they become to the world's ways and maxims that they hated them. The worldly wise and the worldly prudent cannot receive those precious things which God is prepared to reveal unto babes (Matt. 11. 25). The *hatred* of the world is a trifling matter to those whose hearts are filled with the *love* of God.

V. They are Kept from the god of this World. "I pray...that Thou shouldest keep them from the evil one" (v. 15, R.V.). He does not pray that we should be taken out of this world, but kept from the evil one who rules in it. We need not weary to get out of this world so long as we can be made a perpetual miracle and monument of His keeping power in it. We are surely at perfect liberty to

claim, for the honour of Christ's own Name, the daily
fulfilment of this prayer in our own lives. Our beloved
gourds may wither, but His promise cannot.

VI. They are Sent into the World. "As Thou hast
sent Me into the world, even so have I also sent them into
the world" (v. 18). Every Spirit-anointed one is sent to
preach good tidings (Luke 4. 18). As Christ was sent into
the world to seek and save that which was lost, so also are
we. As He was an ambassador for God, so also are we for
Jesus Christ (2 Cor. 5. 20). As He was not sent on His
own charges, so neither are we. As He was in the world,
not on His own account but as a *Sent One*, so are we. Those
sent by Him will be equipped by Him for the work, as He
was equipped by the Father which sent Him. "As My
Father hath sent Me, even so send I you" (John 20. 21).

**VII. They are Indwelt for the Salvation of the
World.** "I in them, and Thou in Me...that the world may
know" (v. 23). As the Father was in the Son, so the Son
desires to be in us, that the world may know the love of
God. Christ fulfilled, in a perfect manner, all required
of Him, but what miserable counterfeits many of us are.
The Son has given Himself as freely to us as the Father gave
Himself to the Son, that His great love might triumph in
us and through us. As God so loved the world that He
gave His Son, so doth the Son so love the world that He
gives His Spirit-filled followers, and for the self-same
purpose. "Christ liveth in me," says Paul (Gal. 2. 20),
and all the world knows to what a God-honouring result.
The one thing needful that this world needs to know is THE
LOVE OF GOD; not only God's love to the *world*, but His
love to *His Son*, and to them that love Him. "That Thou
hast loved them as Thou hast loved Me." May this love be
shed abroad in our hearts, and out through our hearts into
this cold Christ-neglecting world around us.

REVELATIONS IN THE GARDEN.
JOHN 18. 1-11.

EVERY circumstance in which Jesus Christ was placed, somehow or other, became the occasion of a further revelation of His wondrous character. Wherever He was, He, in His unique Personality, could not be hid. In these few verses we see some rays of His heavenly glory breaking through the dark cloud of His earthly weakness. Here is a revelation of—

I. **His Habit of Prayer.** "Judas...knew the place; for Jesus oft-times resorted thither with His disciples" (v. 2). Although Christ possessed the *spirit* of prayer, He believed also in the *place* of prayer. When one gets familiar with their surroundings, the mind is more free for intercourse with the unseen and eternal. In the matter of frequent praying, as well as in suffering, the sinless Son of God has left us an example.

II. **His Knowledge of the Future.** "Jesus therefore, knowing all the things that were coming upon Him, went forth" (v. 4, R.V.). He knew that "all things that are written by the prophets concerning the Son of Man shall be accomplished," for the Scriptures must be fulfilled (Luke 18. 31). Our knowledge of the future must be derived from the same source. If we had the faith that Jesus Christ had in those words uttered by men full of the Holy Ghost, then would we be among those wise men which discern the signs of the times.

III. **His Confession Concerning Himself.** "I am He" (v. 5). They declared that they were seeking Jesus of Nazareth. He confessed that He was that Nazarene. *Reproach* had been associated with that Name, and He willingly accepts it and bears it. It was as if they said, "Where is that despised and rejected One?" He answered,

"I am He." This solemn "I AM HE" of the Son of God may be looked upon as His answer to all who seek Him, whether through love and mercy, or hate and derision. It is with *Him* all have to do.

IV. His Power Over His Enemies. "As soon as He had said unto them, I am He, they went backward, and fell to the ground" (v. 6). It was good for them that they had the ground to fall on. The same power that drove them back might have as easily driven them into Hell. This manifestation of His power was His last convincing proof that, apart from His own will, they had no power at all against Him. "No man taketh it from Me, but I lay it down of Myself" (John 10. 18).

V. His Love for His Own. "If, therefore, ye seek Me, let these go their way" (v. 8). These words are full of solemn significance, as they reveal Christ's attitude toward the powers of darkness and the sheep of His pasture. He was no hireling to flee when the wolf cometh. What He here said to His enemies He could say with a deeper meaning to that "death and the curse" which was coming upon Him. "If, therefore, ye seek *Me*, let these go their way." As our Substitute and Surety, His chief desire was the salvation of His people. Christ is the end of the law for righteousness to every one that believeth.

VI. His Submission to His Father's Will. "The cup which My Father hath given Me, shall I not drink it?" (v. 11). He knew the Father's love too well to refuse even that awful cup of suffering that was just now being put into His hands. He was so perfectly at one with the Father's purposes that His meat was to do His will and to finish His work. As the weapons of His warfare were not carnal, neither are ours, yet they are mighty, through obedience to God, to the pulling down of strongholds. By

His surrender and obedience unto death, He triumphed in resurrection power. He hath left us an example that we should follow His steps.

CHRIST'S SUFFERINGS AT THE HANDS OF MEN.
JOHN 18.

HE suffered by being—

I. Betrayed by the Hypocritical. "Judas also, which betrayed Him, stood with them" (v. 5). He who companied with Christ, and shared the fellowship of His disciples, now takes his stand among the enemies of his Lord, and lends his influence towards His downfall. "Woe unto you hypocrites."

II. Defended by the Passionate. "Simon Peter having a sword, drew it and smote the high priest's servant, and cut off his right ear" (v. 10). The Lord had as little need for Peter's passion as for his sword. The wrath of man works not for the praise of God. There is a zeal for Christ and His cause that must be more painful than pleasing unto Him.

III. Smitten by the Unreasonable. "Jesus answered, If I have spoken evil, bear witness of the evil; but if well, why smitest thou Me?" (v. 23). It is easier for pride and prejudice to sneer and to smite than to face the truth. Self-seeking men are ever ready to justify themselves if it should be at the cost of smiting the character of the Saviour. But the clouds that would hide the face of the sun cannot hinder its progress.

IV. Denied by the Cowardly. When Simon Peter was charged with being "One of His disciples, he denied it, and said, I am not" (v. 25). The Lord and His cause still suffers much through the cowardliness of His professed followers. There are other ways than Peter's in denying Christ. He did it with his tongue; we may do it with our feet, or by our general conduct. When the act or behaviour is more in keeping with the enemies of Christ than with His Word and teaching it is practically a denial of Him.

V. Shunned by the Self-righteous. "Then led they Jesus...unto the hall of judgment...and they themselves went not into the judgment hall, lest they should be defiled, but that they might eat the passover" (v. 28). Any thing or place was clean enough for Jesus, but *they* must preserve their (supposed) ceremonial holiness. "They strain at a gnat, and swallow a camel." This is what one has called "putid hypocrisy." These, like all other self-righteous bigots, would seek the blessing without the Blesser; they would have the passover without Him who is the Passover (1 Cor. 5. 7). They are like men crying for light and closing their eyes to the sun.

VI. Questioned by the Ambitious. Pilate asked three questions of Jesus, and profited nothing by them: (1) "Art Thou the King of the Jews?" (v. 33); (2) "What is truth?" (v. 38); (3) "Whence art Thou?" (chap. 19. 9). By such questions the Christ was "oppressed and afflicted," so He "opened not His mouth." Men animated by selfish and impure motives still oppress Him, whose Divinity is clear as the sun, by their questionings regarding His character and teaching. He that *doeth* His will shall know of the teaching whether it be of God (John 7. 17).

VII. Mocked by the Frivilous. "The soldiers platted a crown of thorns, and put it on His head...and said, Hail, King of the Jews" (chap. 19. 2). These men of war set Him who is the Prince of Peace at *naught* (Luke 23. 11). To them the kingdom of Caesar is everything, the Kingdom of God nothing, material things important, but spiritual things ridiculed and laughed at. Truly they know not what they do, who trifle with the Person of the Lord Jesus Christ (Rev 1. 17, 18).

> "I have seen the face of Jesus,
> Tell me not of aught beside;
> I have heard the voice of Jesus,
> All my soul is satisfied."

MARY MAGDALENE.
JOHN 20. 1-18.

JOHN was that disciple whom Jesus loved, but Mary Magdalene was surely that disciple who pre-eminently loved Jesus. She loved much because she had been forgiven much (Luke 8. 2). Behold her—

I. **Anxiety.** She came "early, when it was yet dark, unto the sepulchre" (v. 1). The darkness without was nothing to her who had had the lamp of heavenly love burning in her heart. Was it *only* to see the sepulchre she came? Was there not a tremulous restlessness about her feelings that some unusual thing was about to happen?

II. **Disappointment.** "They have taken away the Lord out of the sepulchre, and we know not where they have laid Him" (v. 2). It never was more blessedly true than in this case, that our disappointment is God's appointment. In search for a dead Lord, she finds but an empty grave. He is "away" not that she might lose Him but that she might—to her heart's satisfaction—find Him.

III. **Sorrow.** "Mary stood at the sepulchre weeping" (vv. 11-13). Peter and John, at her report, ran together to the sepulchre and looked in and returned again to their own home, but Mary stood, as one bound to that tomb by the cords of faith and love. So intense were her desires, and so blinded were her eyes by sorrow, that "the angels

in white sitting, the one at the head, and the other at the
feet, where the body of Jesus had lain," never seemed to
awaken a suspicion in her mind that the Lord was *risen.*
Yes, it is possible to be so overwhelmed with our imaginary
loss that we fail to grasp God's greatest blessing.

IV. Mistake. "She supposing Him to be the gardener,"
etc. (v. 15). Even in resurrection power our Lord had
still the *likeness* of sinful flesh. Why did she not know
Him? The likelihood is that she was so perfectly absorbed
in thought that she was blind to all outward objects—
"Swallowed up with overmuch grief." The love of her
heart was all right, but the theory of her head was all
wrong. It will save us much sorrow and disappointment
to have a correct creed as well as a devoted life. He was
risen, *as He said*, but they believed Him not.

V. Discovery. "Jesus saith unto her, Mary. She
turned herself and saith unto Him, Rabboni" (Master)
(v. 16). She needed to have her eyes *turned* away from
herself and from the grave, to see Him who is the Resurrection and the Life. The word of Jesus caught her ear and
sunk into her heart. He called her by her name and
claimed her as His own (Isa. 43. 1). His sheep hear His
voice. No one who ever seeks the Lord Jesus Christ ever
finds a dead or powerless Saviour. The deepest cry of a
living soul is for a living God (Psa. 42. 2).

VI. Boldness. "Touch Me not" (v. 17). She evidently
fell down and was about to embrace His feet, when Jesus
stood back saying, "Touch Me not, for I am not yet
ascended to My Father." Another little disappointment
to her ardent heart and another lesson to her that she must
learn to walk by faith and not by sight. No mortal hand
was allowed to *touch Him*, who died as the sinner's Substitute, until He had presented Himself to His Father for
acceptance as our Redeemer and High Priest. Afterwards

every doubting Thomas was invited to thrust his hand into His side that he might feel the mark left by the spear wound.

VII. Obedience. "Jesus said unto her, Go to My brethren and say unto them...Mary came and told the disciples" (vv. 17, 18). She tarried in the garden until she was endued with the power of a great commission. What a message was Mary's, the Gospel of *Sonship*; "*My* Father, and *your* Father,*" in the power of the Resurrection. Her love is rewarded by being made the first herald of His resurrection power. "He that loveth Me...I will *manifest Myself* unto him." The vision of the glorified Christ makes a willing servant (Acts 9. 6).

DOUBTING THOMAS.
JOHN 20. 24-29.

THAT evening of the first day of the first resurrection week was an ever memorable one. The hearts of the disciples were full of fear and wonder at the things which had happened (v. 18). They had met with closed and bolted doors, for fear of their enemies, to reconsider the whole situation. But He who died to save them set all their doubtings and their fears at rest, by suddenly appearing among them, speaking peace and breathing into them a foretaste of Pentecostal power and blessing. All Christ's acts here are full of significance. (1) He spoke the word of "*Peace*" to them; (2) He revealed *Himself* as the Crucified One (v. 20); (3) He *Commissioned* them (v. 21) ; (4) He *Endued* them (v. 22); (5) He promised them success in His business (v. 23). Now what about Thomas? If Peter was rash with his tongue, Thomas was slow in his mind (chap. 14. 5). Observe his—

I. Lost Opportunity. "But Thomas...was not with

them when Jesus came" (v. 24). Why he was absent
is not stated, but it is at least suggestive that *he* was
absent. He must have known of the meeting, but being
incredulous regarding the resurrection of Christ, he
probably had given up all hope, feeling utterly perplexed
and ashamed. In refusing to assemble with His brethren
he only strengthened his unbelief and lost the faith-
confirming fellowship of the Lord. Those out of fellowship
with the body of believers need not expect to enjoy the
fellowship of Christ.

II. Emphatic Denial. When the disciples said unto
him, "We have seen the Lord," he said, "Except I see...
I will not believe" (v. 25). He was faithless (v. 27).
His heart was hardened against the truth of "the resurrection." His "*I will not*" reveals the desperate
antagonism that was in his nature. He would walk by
sight, not by *faith*. It is little short of madness to set one's
self against the united testimony of the disciples of Jesus
Christ. The imperious "I will not believe" of the haughty
and prejudiced mind can never make the faith of God of
none effect. "Believe, and thou shalt see."

III. Humbling Rebuke. Thomas gained nothing but
sadness and separation from his independent attitude. He
did not, however, miss the next meeting of the disciples,
"after eight days," for "Thomas was with them." Again
Jesus appeared and saith to Thomas, "Reach hither thy
finger...and be not faithless, but believing" (v. 27).
He had now, according to the grace of the Lord Jesus
Christ, an opportunity of "handling the Word of Life,"
but as soon as HE comes within touch, the hand of unbelief
is paralysed. What the disciples could not do in a week's
reasoning, Jesus Christ did in a moment by His Word.
Unbelief is the most shameful of all things when Christ
Himself is seen. How Thomas must afterward have

repented over his treatment of the testimony of his believing friends. Are *we* not losing much blessing just now for the same reason, refusing to believe those who have experienced a fullness of blessing to which we, in our unbelief, are utter strangers? May He so reveal Himself to us that every doubt will be ashamed before Him.

IV. **Confession of Faith.** "Thomas answered and said unto Him, My Lord and my God." He hath seen, and he hath believed, but the blessedness of the man who hath not seen and yet hath believed could never be his (v. 29). However, he hath believed, and that with all his heart. His words were few, but profound, and came from the uttermost depths of His soul. There was in them a confession—

1. Of His DEITY. "My *God.*"
2. Of His AUTHORITY over him. "My *Lord.*"
3. Of his PERSONAL SURRENDER to Him. "*My* Lord and *My* God."

HOW JESUS SHOWED HIMSELF.
JOHN 21. 1-14.

AFTER His resurrection no one could see Jesus through mere curiosity or by accident. Neither Mary nor the two men who walked with Him on the way to Emmaus knew Him till He *revealed Himself* to them. None but disciples ever saw Him in His resurrection body. The vision now is a spiritual one; only those who *believe* shall *see* the glory of God in the Person of the risen Christ. "On this wise shewed He Himself" on that memorable morning.

I. **The Time.** It was—

1. AFTER A NIGHT OF FAILURE. "That night they caught nothing" (v. 3). In those days of quiet testing. Peter got somewhat restless and said, "I go a-fishing. They

say unto him, We also go with thee." They followed
Peter, and they caught nothing. Disappointment and
defeat may prepare us for a new manifestation of the grace
and power of Jesus Christ To labour without His presence
and blessing is like putting our treasure in a bag with holes.
Failure in business may be a good preparation for spiritual
success.

2. AT THE BREAKING OF THE DAY. "When the day was
now breaking, Jesus stood on the shore" (v. 4, R.V.).
Sorrow may endure for the night, but joy cometh in the
morning when He appears He was there, but they knew
Him not There is always the breaking of a new day when
Christ shows Himself afresh to the weary soul. Every
vision of Him is a new and fuller dawning of the heavenly
day.

II. **The Manner.** Our Lord followed the example
of no man. He had His own unique way of showing
both Himself and His doctrine. He began to reveal
Himself by—

1. LEADING THEM TO CONFESSION. "Children, have ye
aught to eat? They answered Him, No!" (v. 5, R.V.).
This was an honest confession of failure. They had taken
nothing, so they made no attempt to make it look like
something. They had nothing, neither for themselves nor
for others, and they said so; and by so doing put themselves in a position to be blessed by the Lord. Beware
of misrepresentation and exaggeration. Christ is interested
in our reports.

2. TESTING THEIR FAITH. "Cast the net on the right
side of the ship, and ye shall find" (v. 6). They had toiled
all night to no purpose, and now that the day was breaking
they had given up all hope. But the authoritative voice of
that stranger on the shore, so full of promise, was heard,
and immediately obeyed. There is always a ring of

certainty about the Word of the Lord Jesus. To *hear* it is
to have our hearts tested by it.

3. TURNING FAILURE INTO SUCCESS. "They cast therefore, and now they were not able to draw it for the multitude
of fishes" (v. 6). They obeyed, and their faith was abundantly rewarded. By this sign which followed, John was
constrained to say, "It is the Lord." This is the *Lord's*
doing; John feels that it is so like HIM. Yes, it is just Christ-
like to turn our total defeat into unprecedented success,
through the giving of His Word and the believing of it.
It is in "this wise" that sinners are converted, and fruitless
Christians made wise to win souls.

4. PROVIDING FOR THEIR WANTS. "As soon as they came
to land they saw a fire of coals, a fish, and a loaf" (v. 9,
R.V., *margin*). Even in His resurrection body the Lord
was not unmindful of the bodies of His cold and hungry
disciples. This is another *revelation* of His love and care
for His own. It was not, perhaps, a sumptuous feast, but
it was according to His manner as the Shepherd of His
flock. "The Lord is My Shepherd, I shall not *want*."
"My God shall supply all your *need*" (Phil. 4. 19).
The Son of God is always before us in His providential
arrangements.

5. HAVING FELLOWSHIP WITH THEM. "Jesus said unto
them, Come and break your fast...Jesus then cometh
and taketh bread, and giveth them, and fish likewise"
(v. 12, 13). Now, "none of the disciples durst ask Him,
Who art Thou?" None but the Lord Himself could act
in this manner, showing such grace and power. Christ
has a way of *giving*, whereby He Himself is made known
(Luke 24. 30, 31). He gave Himself for us. The *law*
demands, but the *grace* of God that has come to us in
Christ Jesus delights to give. It is an ever memorable
experience to have our long spiritual fast broken by the

blessings provided for us, and offered to us by Him who died for us and rose again. Eat, O friends! Come and dine. "Behold, all things are now ready" (Matt. 22. 4).

"IF I WILL."
JOHN 21. 15-22.

AFTER they had dined, the Lord showed Himself in another way to Peter, when He searched the secrets of his heart with that threefold question, "Lovest thou Me?" This was Peter's final examination for the Gospel ministry. It had to do with the *heart* more than the head. It was a test of *love*. There can be no truly educated ministry without a whole-hearted devotion to the Person of Jesus Christ. It was because of Peter's confession of *love* he received his commission to serve, "Feed My lambs." After the Lord had signified to Peter by what painful death he should glorify God, Peter made no protest, accepting it at once as the good will of God, but he became anxious to know how John was to end his earthly journey, "What shall this man do?" Jesus said, "If I will that he tarry till I come, what is that to thee? Follow *thou* ME." This reply of Christ to Peter's question of curiosity is a further revelation of His unique methods and matchless character. "If *I* will." This is an *I* that stretches from the deepest depths to the highest heights; its arms reach out to all time past and to the eternity to come. These words of Christ are a revelation to us of His—

I. **Views of Life.** His eye was always on the great essentials of true existence. He allowed no place for mere personal curiosity. "What is that to thee? Follow thou ME." Here is the true centre around which our lives should move, and from which they must receive their guiding and inspiring principles. We must be more anxious to follow Christ than to contrast our experience with the experience of others, either in their life or in their death.

II. Methods of Working. "If I will that HE tarry... what is that to thee?" His dealings with His disciples is not in any stiff mechanical fashion, not after the rigid law f uniformity. The wealth of Christ's wisdom and power cannot permit of this. Each individual disciple will have His special consideration and providence. He calleth His own sheep by *name*, which means *nature*, and will deal with them for their highest good and His highest glory.

III. Divine Power. "If I will." What a WILL this is! What a refuge for the weary trembling soul! His will is not a burden for us to carry, but a pillow on which to rest. Think of the dignity, authority, almightiness, that lie in these words, like strength in a giant's limb. He has but to *will* and it shall be done, for His will is done in Heaven and among the inhabitants of the earth. If He wills to bless thee and keep thee, then thou shall be blessed and kept. How safe and right our life is when yielded to His will!

IV. Abiding Presence. "Follow thou Me." By His Word and Spirit, lo, He is with us alway, even to the end of the age. He has left us an example that we should follow His steps. "Follow thou Me." Is this possible now that He is risen in newness of life, and seated in heavenly glory? Yes. It is *His will*. Whatever is His will for us is possible to us. Think of the *privilege* of following Him whom angels delight to honour, and of the tremendous *possibilities* associated with such a life.

V. Second Advent. "Till I come" (v. 22). This is at least the third time in this Gospel that our Lord definitely refers to His coming again (chaps. 14. 3; 16. 22). Throughout the New Testament there are something like 603 references to this subject. He has come as a suffering

Saviour. He shall come as a glorious King. The hope of the Church is the *Cross* of Christ, the hope of the world lies in the *throne* of Christ When He comes again it will not be in grace, but to assert His *right* and reign. "Then the kingdoms of this world shall become the Kingdom of our God and of His Christ." Blessed hope! This heavy-laden world, staggering on through the ages with its ever-gathering burden of sin and woe into ever-deepening darkness, shall, at the coming of the Lord Jesus Christ, be saved and filled with His glory (Heb. 10. 37).

"HE HELPED ME."
PSALM 116. 3-9.

A PERSONAL TESTIMONY.

1. His CONDITION,   "The sorrows of death...the pains of Hell...I found trouble" (v. 3).
2. His CONFESSION.   "I was brought low" (v. 6).
3. His PETITION.   "I called upon the Name of the Lord" (v. 4).
4. His SALVATION.   "He helped me...He delivered my soul...mine eyes...and my feet" (vv. 6-8).
5. His RESOLUTION.   "I will walk before the Lord" (v. 9).
6. His CONSOLATION.   "Rest, O my soul, for the Lord hath dealt bountifully with thee" (v 7).

TRANSFORMING GRACE.
1 CORINTHIANS 15. 9, 10.

1. His Past: "I persecuted the Church of God."
2. His Present: "An Apostle."
3. How this great change was wrought: "By the grace of God."

BIBLE READINGS.

THE CHURCH, WHICH IS HIS BODY.
EPHESIANS 1. 22-23.

THIS is a simple statement, but it reveals a wondrous mystery. The Church is the body of Christ. How precious and beautiful is the thought that every believer—every truly converted soul—is a living member of the living mystical Body of Christ, and precious to Him as the apple of His eye. Being baptised or planted into Christ, we are made partakers of His Divine nature, and so become heirs of that eternal life. As members of His body we are part of Himself. This metaphor is very suggestive.

I. **The Church, as His Body, is the Visible Proof of His Presence.** I cannot see your spirit; you cannot see mine; but our bodies are alike visible. The presence of a *living* body is the evidence of the presence of a living invisible *spirit*. The world cannot see the invisible Christ who dwells in His Body the Church, but it can see the body. It can see you and me. Does Christ so live in us that our lives evidence the presence and power of an unseen Saviour? Every Jew is a proof that Abraham lived. Every Christian is a witness to the *living* Christ, as surely as a living hand proves a living head (Eph. 5. 23-30).

II. **As His Body, the Church is Animated by a Divine Spirit.** "You hath He quickened." The life is God-given. It is His own life. Because "I live ye shall live also." It is God who dwelleth in you. In every living human body there is a human spirit. The Church of Christ is a Divine body and is indwelt by a Divine spirit. Every branch in the vine must be possessed by the life-sap of the

vine. Do we realise that as members of His body the
source and power of our life is in Him alone? Just as the
hand is dependent on the head, and waits the energising
of the will, so our spirits depend on Christ, our Head, and
are animated by His Spirit (1 Cor. 6. 17; Eph. 4. 4).

III. **As His Body, its Members are all One.** The
head controls every member of the body, and each member
is connected with each other because of its connection with
the head. As members of Christ, we are members one of
another, and should have the same care one for another
(1 Cor. 12. 25). There are different functions for the
members, but there are in the sight of Christ, the Head, no
divisions—"all one in Christ." Oh, that, as individual
members, we may live and work under the power of this
soul-raising truth—in honour preferring one another
(Rom. 12. 5; Col. 1. 18).

IV. **As His Body, each Member is Dependent upon
the Head.** Without the head the body would be nothing
but a corrupt lifeless corpse. The body exists for the head
and not the head for the body. From the head each member
receives its authority. Child of God, remember this. If
the hand is enabled to perform any cunning workmanship
it is because the wisdom of the head has been imparted.
He is made of God unto us wisdom (Rom. 14. 7, 8; Eph.
2. 21, 22).

V. **As His Body, it is Subject to Suffering.** Christ
as "the Head once wounded" is now beyond the reach of
the smiter; but His body, the Church, is still exposed to
scorn and persecution. How sweet to know that the Head
is in deepest, closest sympathy with *each* suffering member.
"Inasmuch as ye did it unto these, you did it unto Me."
When Saul was persecuting the members of His body, Jesus
said to him, "Why persecutest thou *Me*?" O Christian,
bear patiently. If the head, who feels the pang more

keenly than the member, complains not, why should the member? These things may be permitted for edification. "Tribulation worketh patience" (2 Tim. 3. 10-12; Matt. 19. 29; Phil. 3. 8).

VI. **As His Body, its Members are His Instruments of Service.** The body is the servant of the head; the Church is the servant of Christ. The head has no way of working out its purposes but through the body. So Christ, as the living, thinking Head of His Body, the Church, is pleased to accomplish His will, and work out His gracious purposes through the members of His body. What a privilege! "Workers with Him." "Weapons of righteousness unto God" (Rom. 6. 13, *margin*). "Ye are not your own." No; ye are the hands and feet, the eyes and tongue of Christ. It is God who worketh in you, both to *will* and to *do*. If every member of His body were fully yielded to His will, what mighty things would be accomplished. Who could withstand *Him*? (1 Cor. 6. 15-20; Rom. 12. 1).

VII. **As His Body, it is Amply Provided for.** Bodies are often ruined through thoughtless heads, and sometimes great heads are hindered because of weak and deformed bodies. It is the work of the head to lay up in store for the body. What stores of grace and truth, what powers of sufficiency dwell in Christ for us, as members of His Body. A *withered* branch is no honour to the vine. A powerless, half-starved Christian is a discredit to Christ. "My God shall supply all your need according to His riches in glory *by* Christ Jesus." If ye, being evil, know how to feed, protect, and clothe your own bodies, will Jesus Christ your Lord not much more care for His? "O ye of little faith" (Matt. 6. 32; Phil. 4. 6; Psa. 34. 9-10).

VIII. **As His Body, the Church cannot see Corruption.** The Body of Jesus, which was a type of His Church, was abused, bruised, and broken, but it did not

see corruption. The Church as His body may be marred
and outwardly weak, but is indwelt by the Spirit of God.
Just as surely as the *Body* of Jesus was glorified on the
mount of transfiguration, so surely shall His body, the
Church, be transformed with resurrection beauty and
filled with the glory of God. He, as the Head of the Body,
has already ascended. The body, which is still on earth,
will likewise one day be "caught up." "We shall not all
sleep (die), but we must all be changed. It doth not *yet*
appear what we shall be, but we know that when He shall
appear we shall be like Him, for we shall see Him as He
is" (Col. 1. 21, 22; Eph. 5. 27, Cant. 4. 7; Jude 24, 25).

WALK WORTHY OF THE LORD.

"TEACH me, O Lord, the way of Thy statutes, and I shall
keep it unto the end. Give me understanding, and I shall
keep Thy law; yea, I shall observe it with my whole heart.
Make me to go in the path of Thy commandments; for
therein do I delight. Turn mine eyes from beholding
vanity; and quicken Thou me in Thy way" (Psa. 119.
33-37). "It is God who worketh in you both to *will* and to
do" (Phil. 2. 13).

I. The Christian Life as a Walk. It implies—

1. PILGRIMAGE. Here we have no continuing city; we
are pilgrims and strangers on the earth: sojourners with
the Lord (Lev. 25. 23). Our citizenship is in Heaven.

2. SELF-DENIAL. "If any will come after Me," said
Jesus, "let him deny himself" (Matt. 16. 24). Must
be prepared to give up the riches, pleasures, and honours
of the world, to find our all in Himself.

3. SEPARATION (Col. 3. 1, 2). If *we* be risen with
Christ our affections are risen out of the world with Him.

Outside the camp; not of the world. "Transformed by the renewing of your mind" (Rom. 12. 2).

4. SUFFERING (1 Peter 2. 20, 21). If any man will live godly he must suffer. The world which hated Christ will not love His friends (John 15. 15-19). *Here* we have fellowship with His suffering; by and by with His glory.

5. PROGRESS. We cannot be standing still while we are walking. "The path of the just is as the shining light, shining *more and more* unto the perfect day." The sphere of this walk is in the heavenlies. We *mount up* as on eagle wings; *then*, when we are up, we run and are not weary, walk and are not faint. Don't believe in the coming-down theory.

II. The Christian's Companion in the Walk.

It has been said, "A crowd is not company: one good companion makes good company." We have—

1. A DIVINE COMPANION (2 Cor. 6. 16). While sceptics are crying out, "Where is God?" the Christian is walking with Him day by day.

2. AN ALMIGHTY COMPANION (Gen. 17. 1). Surely these words should hush every doubt, silence every complaint, and calm every fear.

3. A PLEASANT COMPANION (Amos 3. 3). The pleasures of companionship depend largely upon our *oneness* of purpose and feeling. What a blessing to be agreed with God—one in heart and purpose.

4. AN EVER-PRESENT COMPANION (Psa. 116. 9). "Lo, I am with you always." "I will never leave thee, nor forsake thee." He is "a *present* help in the time of need" (Psa. 46. 1).

5. A CLOSE COMPANION (2 Cor. 6. 16). No earthly friend can be so near as He. Not only does He walk with us, but He dwells *in us*.

6. A FAITHFUL COMPANION (Heb. 11. 5). He takes His companions with Him. "Where I am, there shall My servants be." He is a Friend that loveth at all times.

7. A COMFORTING COMPANION (Psa. 23. 4). He knows how to speak a word to him that is weary. His rod and staff—strange comforters in the eyes of the world—comfort us.

8. AN EXEMPLARY COMPANION (1 John 2. 6). We are to walk as He walked. How did He walk? He walked by faith, and always did those things which pleased the Father.

III. The Manner of the Christian's Walk.

1. IT SHOULD BE BY FAITH (2 Cor. 5. 7). We received Christ Jesus by faith, and we are to walk in Him as we received Him. It is neither by sight nor feeling, but by faith, as He walked.

2. IN NEWNESS OF LIFE (Rom. 6. 4). As risen with Christ, we are to show forth this newness of life by seeking those things which are above, and turning not back to the sins of the old life (2 Peter 1. 9).

3. WITH HUMILITY (Micah 6. 8). If we continually realise with whom we walk, it will surely constrain us to "walk in the fear of the Lord."

4. IN THE SPIRIT (Gal. 5. 16). The best way to keep tares out of the bushel is to fill it with wheat. Abide by the law of the Spirit and you will not fulfil the lusts of the flesh.

5. IN HIS TRUTH (Psa. 86. 11). According to the truth of God. Jesus Christ Himself is the Truth; let His Word dwell in you richly.

6. IN LOVE (Eph. 5. 2). If we walk with Him who loved us and gave Himself for us, it much becomes us to walk in love.

7. In Wisdom (Col. 4. 5). This is needed, when we remember those who are without, and how they watch our steps and read the book of our lives.

8. Worthy of God (1 Thess. 2. 12). That is, worthy of God who is calling you and walking with you. One false step might bring His Holy Name into dishonour. "Hold Thou up my goings" (Psa. 17. 5).

IV. The Privileges of the Christian Walker. He is—

1. Reconciled (Amos 3. 3). There can be no fellowship without agreement. Justified, and at peace with God. Old things have passed away.

2. Cleansed (Isa. 35. 8, 9). Only the clean can walk the way of holiness. The path of the redeemed is the path of righteousness. Abiding with Him, His blood keeps cleansing (1 John 1. 9).

3. Indwelt (2 Cor. 6. 16). Possessed by Him with whom we walk. Blessed mystery; a secret the unrenewed cannot know.

4. Illumined (Psa. 84. 11). Not only walking in the light of His favour, but having the light of the knowledge of God shining in the heart. Children of the light.

5. Delivered from fears, from iniquity (Psa. 119. 3-45). In His good company we are saved from much bad company.

6. Comforted (Acts 9. 31). The comforting Spirit walks with those who walk with God, taking the things of Christ and showing them to them.

7. Happy (Psa. 128. 1). Happy is every one who walketh in His ways. His ways are ways of pleasantness. Miserable, says the wicked spirit. Happy, says the Holy Spirit.

8. Honoured (Rev. 3. 4). They that walk in the light shall walk in white. They journey to a land where there is no night. Shall they weep again? No, never; but shall reign with Him for ever (Rev. 20. 5).

FOR CHRIST'S SAKE.

OUR prayers usually end with these words, "For Christ's sake." We desire that God should look upon the face of His Beloved Son, and deal with us according to the merit of our Suffering Substitute. But this is only one side of this great truth God also desires *us* to look upon the face of His Son, and for Christ's sake, suffer, serve, and glorify the Father. This is the true motive for Christian life and work. How much will a mother suffer for her child's sake? For Jonathan's sake, David was willing to bless the house of Saul. For Christ's sake we are to—

I **Forgive** "Forgiving one another, even as God for *Christ's sake* hath forgiven you" (Eph. 4. 32). God for Christ's sake hath forgiven us, so we for Christ's sake are to forgive others, even until seventy times seven (Matt. 18. 21, 22). It is so *Christlike* to have compassion and pity, and a heart ready to bless and forgive (see Col. 3. 12, 13). For His sake we are to—

II. **Serve One Another.** "Ourselves your servants *for Jesus' sake*" (2 Cor. 4. 5). The Son of Man came not to be served, but to serve, and to give His life; so he that will be chief among the followers of Christ will be the *servant* of all Paul gloried in this, that he "made himself servant unto all, that he might gain the more" (1 Cor. 9. 19). The service of each member, when done for "Christ's sake," is done for the good of the whole body, not otherwise. Men-pleasers add nothing to the perfecting of the Body of Christ. For His sake we are to be—

III. **Always Delivered unto Death.** "We which live are always delivered unto death *for Jesus' sake*, that the life also of Jesus might be manifested in our mortal flesh" (2 Cor 4. 11). For His sake self is to be continually surrendered unto death, "Killed all the day long," that the life of the now glorified Jesus might be manifested in

us. Only those save their lives who lose them for His
sake (Matt. 10. 39). The seemingly painful and death-
like gloom of such an experience may cause some to fear
this entire abandonment of self unto death; but dying for
His sake is the way into the liberty and power of His risen
life. For Christ's sake the martyrs faced the sword, the
flaming fagots, and the floods, and entered into rest. If
we suffer for Him, we shall also reign with Him. The
muffled cry of the Christ-despising is still, "Save thyself
and come down from the Cross." Let our answer be, "I
am crucified with Christ, nevertheless I live, yet not I,
but Christ." For Christ's sake we should—

IV. **Take Pleasure in Afflictions.** "I take pleasure in
infirmities, in reproaches, in necessities, in persecutions,
in distresses *for Christ's sake*; for when I am weak, then am
I strong" (2 Cor. 12. 10). Wherever Christ is, there is
salvation and the restfulness of Heaven; therefore bring
Him into all your "infirmities," "reproaches," "necessities," "persecutions," and "distresses." This is part
of our inheritance in Christ, for "it is *given* unto us, not
only to believe, but also to suffer for His sake" (Phil. 1. 29)
For His sake we are to—

V. **Strive Together in Prayer.** "I beseech you
brethren *for the Lord Jesus Christ's sake*...that ye strive
together with me in your prayers to God for me" (Rom.
15. 30). As Christians we may differ in many things, but
surely we may all agree in this, that for the Lord Jesus
Christ's sake we will pray for one another. Yes, there
are sharp and ugly crooks in some disciples' characters,
but for *His sake* we ought to strive together in prayer.
The full depth of the possibilities of prayer has never yet
been fathomed. For His sake we must also—

VI. **Labour Patiently.** "I know...thou hast borne,
and hast patience, and *for My Name's sake* hast laboured,

and hast not fainted" (Rev. 2. 3). A fitful worker is as untrustworthy as a fitful lover. It is easy to lose patience, and to faint when the labour is not directly "for His Name's sake." The secret of perseverance and victory lies in doing all as unto Him. The work given us to do is HIS work, and must be done in His Name, and for His sake. Therefore, for His sake labour patiently for the salvation of the lost, and the sanctification of the saved. "Consider Him...lest ye be wearied and faint in your minds."

> "I will not work my soul to save;
> That my Lord hath done,
> But I will work like any slave
> For the sake of God's dear Son."

Moreover, we must be willing for His sake to be—

VII. Counted Fools. "We are fools *for Christ's sake*" (1 Cor. 4. 10). In the eyes of the world a fool is one who, perhaps through mental weakness, is incapable of entering into the business and pleasures that engross the multitude, and whose mind is occupied, perchance, with some trivial, worthless thing; or he is a man with a strong self-will that is constantly leading him into difficulties and disappointments. Those who are fools for Christ have a business, and pleasures, and prospects, that Christless eyes have never seen. Fools, because they hold lightly the material, and grasp with firm hand the eternal. The things of the Spirit of God are foolishness to the natural man (1 Cor. 2. 14). To die to live, is wiser than to die to be lost.

YOUR MASTER.

"ONE IS YOUR MASTER, CHRIST" (Matt. 23. 8).

"WHAT kind of a master have you?" asked an Irish tramp of a farm servant, who was busy in the field. "He is a good master when you give him all his own way." "Och, sure, so is the Devil," was his comment. But although

you do give the Devil all his own way he never can be a
good master; but give the Lord Jesus Christ His own way,
and you will find Him the Good Master, and His service the
best and sweetest of all. His will is the only true and
lasting good; to be in it is to be in the best of all environments, and the surest and safest way to abiding peace and
eternal success. "Good is the will of the Lord." "Ye
call Me Master...and so I am." What about the servants?

I. The Servant's Relationship. "You are not your
own, for you have been redeemed at infinite cost" (1 Cor.
6. 20, Weymouth). His servants have been bought with a
price, the value of which is for ever beyond the grasp of
man's finite mind. It does not become those bought with
His blood to be servants of men (1 Cor. 7. 23). Redeemed
by Him, and for Him, "therefore glorify God in your body
and in your spirit, which are God's."

II. The Servant's Motive. "I love my master...I will
not go free" (Exod. 21. 5). The experience of this
Hebrew is that of all those who have yielded themselves
heartily to the service of Jesus Christ, they fall in love with
their Master, and count His service the greatest liberty and
sweetest delight. The love of Christ constraineth us. We
love Him because He first loved us. *Love* is the fulfilling
of the law, not duty.

III. The Servant's Work. "The Son of Man...gave...
to every man his work" (Mark 13. 34). "To each one his
special duty" (Weymouth). The Son of Man does not lay
upon every servant the same task; the gift of work is
according to the character of the vessel, or the ability of
the worker. A vessel made meet for the Master's use will
be put by Him to the highest possible use. Let us not say
"What can I do?" but "What wilt *Thou* have me to do?"
"Christ is over His own house; whose house are we?"

(Heb. 3. 6). Therefore the ordering of the vessels and the service is in His hands. "What is that in thine hand?"

IV. **The Servant's Supply.** "He called his ten servants, and delivered them ten pounds, and said unto them, Occupy till I come" (Luke 19. 13). When He gives the work, He gives the power to carry it out. Each servant received his pound, and each pound meant a Pentecost; it was an enduement with power, to occupy his place till he should come again. "The manifestation of the Spirit is given to every man to profit withal." Let us take heed that we are trading (serving) with His gift (Holy Spirit) and not depending on our own acquirements, to the neglect of His pound and the ruin of our own testimony.

V. **The Servant's Encouragement.** "Lo, I am with you alway, even unto the end of the age" (Matt. 28. 20). This is not only the promise of His presence, it is the assurance of His co-operation. "The Lord is with thee... go in this thy might" (Judges 6. 12-14). As servants, we are His property, to do His work, using His means and enjoying His presence and help. In this holy service we have nothing that we have not received, but in this lies the secret of our confidence. We take His yoke upon us, and so learn of Him who walks in the yoke with us (Phil. 4. 13).

VI. **The Servant's Reward.** "Well done, good and faithful servant...enter thou into the joy of *thy* Lord" (Matt. 25. 21). As ye have shared your Master's service and sufferings, ye shall also be sharers of His joy. In His right hand there are pleasures for evermore (Psa. 16. 11, R.V.). None shall pluck us out of this hand. But the servant of Jesus Christ has a mighty reward *now* as well as awaiting him, for the Spirit of God is in him, and the honour of the Father upon him, as well as the joy of the Lord before him. Eternal life is a gift, but it is the overcomers who sit with Him on His throne (Rev. 3. 21). This reward is not for being saved, but for being faithful servants and sufferers for His sake. "If we suffer we shall also reign with Him."

HINDRANCES TO PRAYER.

"That your prayers be not hindered" (1 Peter 3. 7).

THERE is surely something wrong when we sow much in prayer and bring in little reward. That your prayers be not hindered, see that ye—

I. **Love the Lord.** "Delight thyself also in the Lord, and He shall give thee the desires of thine heart" (Psa. 37. 4). Is thy *heart* right with God? It is the nature of love to seek *Himself*, and to those who love Him hath He promised to manifest Himself. Delight also in His *Word* if your petitions are to be unfettered in their approach (John 15. 7).

II. **Confess Sin.** "If I regard iniquity in my heart, the Lord will not hear me" (Psa. 66. 18). Sin discovered in the heart, and unconfessed before God, remains a barrier to prayer. Such sins hide His face from you that He will not hear (Isa. 59. 1, 2). The Lord looketh upon the heart, there must be no secret controversy there with Him—no traitor in the camp. It is not a question as to what others may think of me. If I regard iniquity there, then I must deal with it if I would prevail with God.

III. **Put away Idols.** "These men have set up their idols in their heart...should I be inquired of at all by them" (Ezek. 14. 3). An idol is anything that is set up in the forefront of our affections, taking the place of God. Seen or unseen by men, it is erected before His face. It may take the form of Pleasure, Fashion, Friends, Business, Sin, or Self. There is no room *in the heart* for an idol and the Holy Spirit. The heart must be cleansed if the spirit of prayer is to prevail.

IV. **Deny Self**. "Ye ask, and receive not, because ye ask amiss, that ye may consume it upon your pleasures" (Jas. 4. 3, R.V.). The desire after our own personal pleasure strangles multitudes of prayers. The petitions are right in themselves when we plead for wisdom, power, grace, or the salvation of our friends; but if our motive is *our own pleasure*, we ask amiss. Has not our Lord said, "If any man would come after Me (in prayer), let him deny himself?" God still hides many things from such "wise and prudent" self-seekers.

V. **Be Steadfast**. "But let him ask in faith, nothing wavering; for he that wavereth...let not that man think that he shall receive anything of the Lord" (Jas. 1. 6, 7). There is no stability about a wave; it is utterly purpose-less, being driven about with the wind, a creature of mere circumstances. The prayer of persevering faith storms the fort of blessing. A prayer may be like a wave tossed up against the throne of God, through the force of some tempestuous trial, but this is not a wavering prayer. "All things, whatsoever ye ask in prayer, believing, ye shall receive."

VI. **Consider One Another**. "Likewise, ye husbands ...giving honour unto the wife as unto the weaker vessel, and as being heirs together of the grace of life; that your prayers be not hindered" (1 Peter 3. 7). What is true of husbands is true also of wives, and, in a great measure, of sons and daughters, brothers and sisters, and of the whole *household of faith*. They are *"heirs together* of the grace of life" (1 Peter 3. 7). All one in Christ Jesus, and the lack of giving honour one to another, especially the weaker vessels, acts as an hindrance to prayer, because it is a grieving of the Holy Spirit, and a dishonouring of the Father's love and the Saviour's redeeming grace. *Agree-ment* with one another is a powerful condition of prevailing prayer, so much so that, "If *two* of you shall agree on earth as touching anything that they shall ask, it shall be done for them of My Father which is in Heaven" (Matt. 18. 19).

_____

LIFTED.

"WHEN THEY CAST THEE DOWN, THEN THOU SHALT SAY, THERE IS LIFTING UP" (Job 22. 29).

YES, thank God, although we may at times be cast down, and our characters almost dismantled by merciless hands, we can still hope in God, for His hand is not shortened that it cannot save, we can confidently say, "There is lifting up."

I. **The Need.** In Luke 13. 11 we read of a poor woman who had a spirit of infirmity eighteen years, and was bowed together, and could in *no wise lift up herself*. Such were some of us, "bowed together" by the love of the world that we could in no wise lift ourselves above it, and, like the publican, we could not lift up so much as our eyes unto Heaven. At that time without strength.

II. **The Lifter.** "But Thou, O Lord, art...the Lifter up of my head" (Psa. 3. 3). When the head is lifted above the whelming flood, the life is saved. Man in his helplessness and guilt needs such a lift that only God in His infinite mercy and power can give. Christ is not only the Breaker up of the sin-closed way, but the Lifter of the sin-bound head (Psa. 27. 6).

III. **The Provision.** "I, if I be lifted up from the earth will draw all men unto Me" (John 12. 32). Our Almighty Lifter had Himself to be lifted on the Cross, lifted from the grave, and lifted to that throne that is "high and lifted up," that He might be the Lifter up of His people. His love is an uplifting power: "Thou hast loved my soul out of the pit of corruption."

IV. **The Condition**. Those whom He lifts up are described as being *needy*. "He raiseth the poor out of the dust, and lifteth the needy out of the dunghill" (Psa. 113. 7). It belongs to the character of God to choose the weak things, and to exalt the lowly. His mercy seeks the guilty, His power the weak, His wisdom the ignorant, and His love the lost. Again, He lifts up the *humble*. "Humble yourselves in the sight of God, and He shall lift you up" (James 4. 10). He that exalteth *himself* shall be abased, but he that humbleth himself shall be exalted. Wherever there is true humbling of ourselves before God, His mighty uplifting hand will be manifested in due time (1 Peter 5. 6).

V. **The Manner**. The Lord took Peter's wife's mother "by the hand and lifted her up" (Mark 1. 31). Ezekiel the prophet says, "So the Spirit lifted me up and took me away" (chap. 3. 14). There is still lifting up by the hand of faith and by the Spirit of power. It is the Spirit that quickeneth the whole man, lifting the entire character into the upper regions of faith, where as on eagles' wings we can run and walk without growing weary or faint.

VI. **The Results**. There is—

1. The uplifted FACE of reconciliation. "Then thou shalt have thy delight in the Almighty, and shall lift up thy face unto God" (Job 22. 26). Once afar off, with face earthward and Hellward, but now Godward.

2. The uplifted HEAD of confidence. "Lift up your heads, for your redemption draweth nigh" (Luke 21. 28). Saved from all fear amidst the perilous times of the later days, when men's hearts are failing them for fear when the powers of Heaven are being shaken.

3. The uplifted HANDS of supplication and consecration. "I will lift up my hands in Thy Name" (Psa. 63. 4). Hands that used to hang down in feebleness and idleness

now lifted up in holy intercession for others, and offered as
empty hands to God to be filled for His service and glory.

4. The uplifted VOICE of praise and testimony. "They
shall lift their voice, they shall sing...they shall cry
aloud" (Isa. 24. 14). The ransomed of the Lord shall
return, and come to Zion with songs and everlasting joy
upon their heads. Cry aloud, and shout, *thou* inhabitant
of Zion, for the Lord hath done great things for thee. Say
to those who are cast down, or who are wallowing hopelessly
in the sinking mire of sin: "THERE IS LIFTING UP."

THE TABERNACLE OF GOD.

EXODUS 40. 17-35.

LET us think of—

I. **The Meaning of It**. Everything here is typical of
things spiritual. Paul, in his epistle to the Hebrews,
speaks of them as "The shadow of heavenly things," "The
patterns of things in the heavens," "The figures of the true"
Those blind to spiritual things can see neither beauty nor
meaning in this wonderful arrangement. It was God's
own picture to His people of "good things to come." Open
Thou mine eyes to behold wonderful things here in Thy
Tabernacle.

II. **The Purpose of It**. It was to be a sanctuary for
God, that He might dwell among them (Exod. 25. 8). God
so loved His people, whom He had redeemed, and delivered
from the bondage of Egypt, that He desired a place for
Himself, that His presence might abide with them. Does
He not still desire to abide in every soul whom He hath
saved by His grace? Then let us make Him a sanctuary
in our own hearts, that He may dwell with us. "Ye are
the temple of God."

III. **The Time of its Setting Up.** "In the first month,

on the first day of the month, the tabernacle was reared
up" (v. 17). Is it not significant that this House of God
was to be set up on "New Year's day?" Does not this
indicate that it was to be a *new beginning* for them? They
were to begin the year with God in their midst—as a
Pilgrim with them. The only *new start* worth making is to
begin with God. If He is with us, then certainly prosperity
in the highest sense will follow.

IV. **The Structure of It.** The manner of its get-up was
simple, yet everything had to be made and set in order
according to the pattern shown to Moses on the mount.
The sockets, which formed the *foundation* (v. 18), were of
solid silver, made from "atonement money" (Exod 38),
so that these golden boards actually stood upon that which
represented "Redemption"—the price of souls. Like this
Tabernacle in the wilderness, the "Church of God" has no
other standing than on that which has been paid (the blood
of Christ) as a ransom for the soul. These boards, built
upon the sockets of "Ransom," and "fitly knit together,"
and strengthened by the "bars thereof"—as encircling
arms of power—represent our standing in Christ, and our
union one with another within the everlasting arms of
Divine strength and faithfulness.

V. **The Contents of It.** The Tabernacle was divided
into three parts: "The Holiest of all," "The Holy Place,"
and the "Court." In the "Holiest" was put the Ark which
contained the law, the lid of which formed the "*Mercy-
seat,*" where God promised to meet with them (vv. 20, 21).
Christ has *covered* the broken law, and formed a mercy-seat
for us. Then, in the "Holy Place" there was the *Table*
with its bread, meaning *fellowship* with God in Christ. The
Candlestick, with its branches (v. 24), which speaks of
testimony in the power of Christ. The *Golden Altar*
(vv. 26, 27), with its sweet incense, speaking of acceptable

prayer in the Name of Christ. Then outside the door of the Holy Place stood the *"Altar* of burnt-offering"—the place of sacrifice, indicating that the *first need* of the people in their approach to God was *Atonement* (v. 29). The altar points to the Cross of Christ. Between the Altar of Sacrifice and the door of Communion, they set the *Laver* (v. 30), with its water for cleansing, teaching the need of the Holy Spirit's cleansing by the Word of Christ. There must be Substitution before true fellowship with God.

VI. **The Glory of It**. "The glory of the Lord filled the Tabernacle" (v. 34). The glory of it was the *manifest* presence of God. As it was with the Tabernacle, so was it with the life and work of the Lord Jesus Christ. It was crowned with a supernatural manifestation. He showed Himself alive by many infallible proofs (Acts 1. 3). When the glory of His Holy Presence is seen, then men feel like Moses, "Not able to enter in" without atoning blood.

BACKSLIDING.

HEBREWS 3. 12.

I. **The Subjects**. "Take heed, *brethren!*" Only those who have been made nigh unto God can backslide from Him.

II. **The Cause**. "An evil heart of unbelief." Unbelief is in itself the fruit of an evil heart.

III. **The Manner**. "Departing from the living God." The trust of the heart turning away from God to something else.

IV. **The Preventative**. "Take heed!" Examine yourselves.

GOSPEL OUTLINES.

THE GREAT SALVATION.

"How shall we escape if we neglect so great salvation?"
(Heb. 2. 3).

I. This Salvation is Great. Great, when you think of
the greatness of Him who saves. He is the Heir of all
things, the Maker of the worlds, the brightness of the
Father's glory, the express image of His Person, who
upholdeth all things by the word of His power, and is
much better than the angels (Heb. 1. 2-4). Great, when
you think of the awful condition from which He saves,
from the guilt and dominion of sin, and delivers from that
death which is the wages of sin, and from the wrath of
God which must for ever rest upon sin and sinners. Great,
when you think of the happy position into which He
saves—brought into the family of God, justified from all
things, made sons and daughters and heirs of eternal life,
having the promise for the life that now is, as well as the
life which is to come. Great, when you think of the
unspeakable price He paid for our salvation. Not corruptible things, as silver and gold, but His own precious
blood. It took the *sacrifice* of Himself to purge our sins
and He willingly, lovingly, gave His all.

II. This Salvation may be Neglected. It is neglected
every time the opportunity of being saved is let slip. We
ought to give the more earnest heed to the things which we
have heard, lest at *any time* we should let them slip.
Because to let the chance slip *any one* time may be letting
it slip for the *last* time. Many neglect salvation by
neglecting the Lord's day. To neglect the Word of God,

the Gospel of God, the strivings of the Spirit of God, and the Providence of God, is to neglect salvation. The process of neglecting, like the process of drifting, may be painless and unconscious, but it is the more dangerous on that account. You may neglect it without hating it or denying it. The Osbtinates, who refuse to go forward, and the Pliables who turn back, equally neglect salvation.

III. This Salvation, if Neglected, Leaves no Escape. This question, "How shall we escape if we neglect?" is one which the wisdom of God cannot answer, although some men in the pride of their own hearts have attempted it. How shall the merchant escape ruin if he neglects his business? How shall we escape hunger if we neglect food? How shall we escape darkness if we neglect the light? How shall we escape the wages of sin if we neglect the Atonement for sin? How shall we escape the wrath of God if we neglect the Gift of God? How shall we escape the doom of the lost if we neglect the Saviour of the lost? How shall we escape the condemnation of Hell if we neglect the salvation of Heaven? "Behold, now is the accepted time." One of the most melancholy sights of earth is a Christless old age.

DECISION.

"How long halt ye between two opinions? If the Lord be God, follow Him; but if Baal, then follow him" (1 Kings 18. 21).

It is sometimes needful to "halt between two opinions," if the proper course of action is not quite clear, but when the right and the wrong stands out in naked reality indecision becomes sin. It is with spiritual things, as with the temporal, the wavering and the lukewarm cannot succeed. The young man who cannot make up his mind as to what business he should follow is in danger of being

ruined. In religion, as in politics, no progress can be
made, no definite testimony can be given, so long as the
mind is not clear, and the will emphatic. In these, and
other matters, a halting man is a useless man, worse than
useless, for he is a stumbling-block to others. The scene
on Mount Carmel is an object lesson on the need of instant
decision for God. Elijah's call is needed now as much
as then.

I. **Where the People Halted.** "Between *two*
opinions." To them this simply meant—

1. BETWEEN TWO RELIGIONS. There were only two.
The religion of Baal and that of Jehovah. The one was the
product of man's darkened imagination, the other was a
revelation from Heaven. The heart of man and the heart
of God are the only two possible sources of religious
thought. Here is the halting ground of multitudes—
between the thoughts of men and the thoughts of God. To
halt here is to halt—

2. BETWEEN TWO MASTERS. Between Baal and
Jehovah, between the false and the real, between superstition and revelation, between the tyranny of ignorance
and fear, and the freedom of light and truth. The one
represents the prince of darkness, the other the Prince
of Peace. The design of the one is to destroy, the purpose
of the other is to save. His servants ye are to whom ye
yield yourselves. Let not sin have dominion over you.
There is no communion between these two masters: no
fellowship between light and darkness, between Christ
and Belial. There is no agreement between the temple of
God and the house of idols. Ye cannot serve these two
masters; your choice lies between them.

II. **Why the People Halted.** Some thing, or things,
must surely have been hindering them from confessing the

Lord as their God. They may have been deterred as many in our day are—

1. BECAUSE OF THEIR NUMBER. Their name was legion who had entered the broad road of God-rejection. It is comparatively easy to go right, or wrong, while going with the multitude, but a man is his own miserable comforter when he tries to console himself by saying, "If I am not right there are a great many like me." Though hand join in hand, the wicked shall not go unpunished. "Broad is the way that leadeth to destruction, and many there be which go in thereat." It is poor comfort, when on a sinking ship, to know that *many* are perishing with you. To remain undecided for Christ because many are doing it is a sad betrayal of moral weakness. Although Baal and the groves had 850 prophets, and Jehovah only one, yet to be with Him was to be in the majority and on the side of victory and blessing.

2. BECAUSE OF THEIR FEAR OF MAN. Some halted, doubtless because they feared the wrath of the king. It was very different with the parents of Moses (Heb. 11. 23). Ahab was the enemy of God, and the troubler of Israel. He sought to banish the worship of Jehovah out of the land, and because of him many were afraid to acknowledge the Lord. They *halted*, perhaps because they were convinced that the policy of Ahab and Jezebel was base and revolutionary, but they had no courage to take their stand for Jehovah. The fear of man bringeth a snare. When Luther was told that all the world was against him, he said, "Well, I am against the whole world." "Why halt ye? If the Lord be God, follow Him." Better is it to grieve and forsake the enemies of God than remain an enemy to God.

III. **The Unsatisfactory Nature of such a Position.** "*How long* halt ye?" Every moment one halts between holiness and sin, between Christ and the world, is likely to weaken the will power and reduce the life to a waste heap for God and a coming eternity. To remain undecided for God and righteousness to say the least—

1. IT IS FOOLISH. It is like the donkey in the fable, which died of starvation because it could not decide which of the two bundles of hay to eat first. Moses was wise when he "chose rather to suffer affliction with the people of God, than to enjoy the pleasures of sin for a season." Rebekah was wise when she said, "I will go." The poor Indian woman knew in whom she had believed when, after having been robbed of all her goods, she said, "I would rather die a poor Christian than a rich heathen."

2. IT IS DANGEROUS. Indecision has been the ruin of many. Remember Lot's wife. To *decide* means literally "to cut off" that which is unnecessary. Then "cut off" from that state of sin and doubt, and, like Mary, choose the better part. The undecided are always easily overcome. When Charles I., after having been defeated at the Battle of Naseby, was about to make another charge upon the troops of Cromwell, one of his courtiers caught the bridle of his horse and turned him aside from the path of honour. Charles had not the courage to rebuke him. Who would have dared to have done this with Cromwell?

CONVERSION.

"VERILY, I SAY UNTO YOU, EXCEPT YE TURN AND BECOME AS LITTLE CHILDREN, YE SHALL IN NO WISE ENTER INTO THE KINGDOM OF HEAVEN" (Matt. 18. 3, R.V.).

THIS was Christ's answer to some of His own *disciples*, who had been asking that somewhat half-curious, self-confident question, "Who is the greatest in the Kingdom of Heaven?" They are not all properly converted who are the professed followers of Jesus Christ. Three things here should be noted—

I. The Need of Conversion. "Except ye turn and become as little children, *ye shall in no wise enter the Kingdom of Heaven.*" We may be disciples, in a sense, and yet be unfit for the Kingdom of God. Those who don't need to be converted are those who, at some time or other, have been converted, for "All we like sheep have gone astray." There may be an outward conformity where there is an inward deformity. The tree needs to be made good before the fruit can be good; the fountain of the heart must be cleansed if the streams of thought and feeling are to be pure. The Kingdom of Heaven cannot be entered by those who selfishly seek their own good, and not the glory of God. Not to submit to the will and purpose of God is to rebel against this Kingdom, which is the "rule of the Heavens."

II. The Nature of Conversion. "Except ye *turn.*" It is a turning about—a turning from self-confidence and self-rule unto the rule of God. Saul was thoroughly converted when he said, "Lord, what wilt Thou have me to do?" He had turned from His own self-made plans and purposes to the will of his Lord and Saviour. In one sense we need to be converted very often, for every time we turn aside, like Bunyan's pilgrims, into any By-Path Meadow that leads us out of fellowship with the Lord, we need another conversion, another *turning back*, if we would enter again into the peaceful Kingdom of Heaven. Christ "suffered for us, the Just for the unjust, that He might bring us to God." If we have not been *turned unto God* we are yet unconverted; and if we have been thus converted, and are not now walking in the light and joy of His presence, it is quite clear that we need another turning about. "Turn ye, turn ye, why will ye die?"

III. The Evidence of Conversion. "Become as little children." The little child which "Jesus set in the midst of them," was for them an object lesson of self-abasement and trustfulness. Those who are wholly turned to God are as open minded and submissive as little children. They are very conscious of their own weakness, and free from all unholy ambition and secret intrigue. They are harmless, affectionate, and sincere, without duplicity and hypocrisy. To become as a *little child* is to have the past blotted out and forgiven, and to begin life anew after another and more heavenly fashion. It is only when a man gets converted, and becomes again a little child, that he can have all the prospects and opportunities of a lifetime before him. He has not yet begun to live in a real, true sense, if he has not been *turned to God*. "God is angry with the wicked every day; if he turn not, He will whet His sword" (Psa. 7. 11, 12).

ASSURANCE.

"THESE THINGS HAVE I WRITTEN UNTO YOU THAT BELIEVE ON THE NAME OF THE SON OF GOD, THAT YE MAY KNOW THAT YE HAVE ETERNAL LIFE" (1 John 5. 13).

I. **The Persons to be Assured.** "You that believe." To believe on the Name of the Son of God in John's day was to take up the ignominy of the Cross. The object of faith is not Christianity as a system, or the Bible as a book, but the Son of God as a living, abiding Personality. It is not written, "*Believe* and be saved," but "Believe *on the Lord Jesus Christ* and thou shalt be saved" (Acts 16. 31). The faith that does not take hold of Christ is a dead faith. To be assured of salvation we need more than faith in things, we need faith in HIM.

II. **The Blessing to be Assured Of.** "Eternal life." This is something different from, and something better than, mere eternal existence. Devils know about eternal existence, but they know nothing experimentally of eternal life. This life stands for the sum of all good, here and hereafter. As the acorn seed contains within itself, potentially, all the power and majesty of the oak, so does this life, begotten in us by the Holy Spirit, contain the fullness of joy and glory that is yet to be revealed.

III. **The Blessedness of Being Assured.** "Ye may know." This word "know" is a favourite one with John. In these few verses (13 to 20) he makes use of it seven times. If you are a believer in Jesus Christ and don't know that you have eternal life, "ye may know." It is not only a possibility, but it is your privilege to know. This assurance is needful for the comfort and joy of salvation. How can we thank God for the gift of eternal life, if we are not sure that we have it?

IV. **The Ground of this Assurance.** "These things have I *written* unto you...that ye may know." Assurance does not come through any special revelation from Heaven, apart from the *written Word*. "He that hath the Son hath life" (v. 12). These words, inspired by the Holy Spirit, and penned by the apostle, are for you who believe, that ye may know that ye have eternal life. Not to receive this testimony is to make God a liar, and rob your soul of this blessed confidence. A little orphan girl, happy in the knowledge of Christ as her Saviour, was asked how she knew that she was saved, said, "He says it, and that's enough for me." Is it not enough for you?

THE NEW CREATION.

"IF ANY MAN IS IN CHRIST, HE IS A NEW CREATION; THE OLD THINGS ARE PASSED AWAY: BEHOLD, THEY ARE BECOME NEW" (2 Cor. 5. 17, R.V., *margin*).

I. **The Condition of It.** "In Christ." "If any man is in Christ he is a new creation." This implies that we have fled to Him for shelter and salvation—as the man-slayer

fled to the City of Refuge—taking refuge in His atoning
work. In Christ, as the branch is in the vine, for strength
and supply; in Christ, as the member is in the body, for
sympathy and service.

II. **The Nature of It.** "A new creation." It is a
reformation in a very radical sense. "We are *His workmanship*, created in Christ Jesus" (Eph. 2. 10). There is a *new
life*. Born, not of blood, nor of the will of the flesh, nor of
the will of man, but of God. There is a *new mind*.
"Renewed in the spirit of the mind" (Eph. 4. 23), and able
now to comprehend something of the character and power
of God in Christ Jesus. There is a *new heart*. The
affections that were alienated from God are now centred in
Him. There is a *new spirit*. The Spirit of God now bears
witness with our spirits, implying oneness of purpose in
service and testimony. There is a *new song*, because there
has been a new revelation of Divine mercy and grace
(Psa. 40. 1-3).

III. **The Results of It.** "The old things are passed
away; behold they are become new." With the new
creation then comes new views of *sin*. Sin is now seen to
be a crime and a curse, and the old view of it being a debt,
or a misfortune, passes away. There comes also new
views of *self*. Self is now seen to be a worthless, unclean
thing, and it too becomes an "old thing" only fit to pass
away. The old unscriptural views of *Christ* pass away, and
new Spirit-inspired views take their place. Jesus Christ
is no longer a Saviour waiting for us at a death-bed, but a
present, living reality in the daily life. The old things
which used to interest us in the *world* are passed away, and
behold, new interests have been awakened. In the old life
the pleasures and profits of the world were the objects of
our desires, but now the desire is for the salvation of the

world. It used to be the place of amusement for self, but now it is a workshop for Christ.

IV. The Privilege of It. "If any man." The door into this new and better life stands open for all. "Any man," no matter how weak and helpless, no matter how sad and sinful, "any man," no matter how old and forgetful if he steps out of sin-ruined self into Christ, will instantly become a new creation. For, in Christ, God is reconciling the world unto Himself.

GRIEVE NOT THE HOLY SPIRIT.
EPHESIANS 4. 30.

IT is solemnly possible to grieve the Holy Spirit, because He is a gracious, loving, tender *Personality*. It is not possible to grieve or vex a mere influence. The *wind* bloweth where it listeth, you cannot grieve the wind; but the breath of the Holy Spirit is the breathings of the very heart of God. All the attributes of God are attributed to the Holy Spirit. He is the Spirit of truth, of wisdom, of life, and of power. To grieve Him is to hinder His loving and merciful operations in the heart, and thereby impoverish our lives, and stultify our most earnest efforts in the service of Christ.

I. By Unholy and Profitless Talk (see vv. 29 and 31). Communications that are not "to the use of edifying," but which have a *corrupting* influence must be a grief to Him who is "Holy," and who has come to take the things which belong to the incorruptible Christ and show them to us. The Spirit of Truth can have no fellowship with frivolous talk and evil speaking.

II. By Ignoring His Presence. If our earthly friends dealt with us as we often deal with the Holy Spirit, we would be sorely offended. To live in the same house with

one and be seldom recognised must be a great hardship.
Mutual recognition is absolutely essential to the main-
tenance of real friendship.   Don't grieve Him by the
coldness of forgetfulness.

III. **By Rejecting His Teaching.**   It was by rebelling
against His leading that Israel "vexed His Holy Spirit"
(Isa. 63. 10).   The Spirit is ever seeking to lead us into the
truth as it is in Jesus, that we might be sanctified and made
meet for His use.   We grieve the Spirit, when through
prejudice or unbelief, we refuse to accept His teaching,
or to obey His leading.   If we are not *growing* in
grace, and in the knowledge of God, we may well
suspect ourselves of disobedience to the Lord the Spirit.
It must be a great grief to Him that His gracious work
should in any way be hindered in us or through us, as
Christ is dishonoured thereby, and His chief purpose is
to glorify Him.

IV. **By Conniving at Things which He Hates.**   The
Holy Spirit is opposed to sin in every form.   All worldli-
ness and self-seeking are antagonistic to His nature and
mission.   If we found any of our personal friends winking
secretly at things which they knew our souls abhorred,
how deeply we would be grieved at such a discovery.   Are
we more sensitive than the Holy Spirit is?   If we are
ashamed to rebuke what He rebukes, and to exalt what He
exalts, then we are not in the fellowship of the Spirit.
Grieve not the Spirit by encouraging the ungodly in their
sin.   Remember Samson.

V. **By Grieving the Children of God.**   Uncharitable
thinking which leads to uncharitable *speaking*, must grieve
Him who is the Spirit of *love* and of *unity*.   Whatever tends
to alienate the affections of God's people, one from another,
is a striving against the workings of the Holy Ghost.
"That they all may be one," was the prayer of Christ.

"That they all may be one," is the purpose of the Spirit.
To hinder this *oneness* is to grieve the Spirit by marring
the unity of the Body, which He is so eager to maintain.

VI. By Serving the Lord in Our Own Strength.
The Holy Spirit has come that we might have power to
witness for Christ; to speak and labour in *our own* strength
is a denial of His mission, and must be a great grief to His
heart. How very sad it must be to the mighty Holy Spirit
to see the servants of Christ, whom He has come to
empower, substituting fleshly energy and worldly policy for
His subduing, quickening presence. When the Spirit is
grieved by such self-assertiveness, the evidence of it is
apparent in a formal, fruitless life. A grieved Spirit not
only means a powerless testimony, but also a lack of the
enjoyment of the love of God in the heart. If this love is
to be shed abroad in our hearts, we need the *communion*
of the Holy Spirit; this we cannot have if our manner of
life and service is opposed to His mind and will. We may
have our lamps, and we may have a measure of light, like
the foolish virgins, but if we have not that reserve of oil
which is to be found in the presence of an ungrieved Spirit,
we will be ashamed before Him at His coming.

"I OBTAINED MERCY."

1 TIMOTHY 1. 16.

I. He needed mercy. According to his own confession,
he was the "chief of sinners" (v. 15). He was a ringleader
among the enemies of Christ. Nothing but *mercy* could
meet his need. He did not need more worldly wisdom
or a better man-pleasing life; he needed the mercy of God
to forgive his sin and save his soul from death. Divine
mercy covered all his deep, dire need.

II. He obtained mercy. He did not obtain it by any

work or merit of his own. *He* obtained it just because God in His infinite grace *gave* it to him. He obtained it because he readily *accepted* the gift when offered to him. There is no other way for us to obtain mercy than by receiving it.

III. He obtained mercy **through Christ Jesus** (v. 15). There is none other name under Heaven, none other channel between Heaven and earth, through which the stream of God's forgiving and saving mercy can flow. The only price by which we can obtain the mercy of God is the precious Blood of Christ. When the Lord said to Saul, "It is hard for thee to kick against the pricks," it was His merciful call to surrender. The mercy and the victory came when Saul answered, "Lord, what wilt thou have me to do?" God is rich in mercy through Jesus Christ His Son.

IV. He obtained mercy **that Jesus Christ might shew forth all longsuffering in him.** Not only that he might be saved from a life of rebellion and coming wrath, but that he may become a lantern through which the long-suffering goodness and patience of Christ might shine forth. The longsuffering Christ was revealed to him and in him, that He might be revealed through him. The obtaining of mercy has to do with the honour and glory of God, as well as with our own salvation.

V. He obtained mercy, **that he might be a pattern to them which should hereafter believe on him.** In obtaining mercy, he not only became an exhibition of the grace of God, but an example to encourage all those who desired to trust Jesus Christ, with the view of obtaining that mercy which means "life everlasting." Seeing, then, that the conversion of Saul is to be taken as a *sample* of the saving mercy of God, what great encouragement there is for sinners of every age to believe on the Lord Jesus Christ. It is said that Abraham Lincoln gave orders to his doorkeepers never to turn away anyone petitioning for life. All the doorkeepers of the House of God have the same instructions. If you are seeking life, eternal life, here is mercy for you. Have you obtained it?

DARKNESS AND DAWN.

"THE PEOPLE WHICH SAT IN DARKNESS SAW GREAT LIGHT; AND TO THEM WHICH SAT IN THE REGION AND SHADOW OF DEATH, LIGHT IS SPRUNG UP" (Matt. 4. 16).

"DARKNESS" as emblematic of an unsaved state, is very frequently referred to in the unerring Word of God. Salvation is represented as a being "called *out of* darkness *into* His marvellous light." Those who have experienced this change, cannot but be perfectly conscious of it. In this verse there is a description of—

I. **Man's Condition without Christ.** "The people which sit in darkness."

1. Darkness implies a state of IGNORANCE. Christ is the Light of the World; to be ignorant of Christ is to be in darkness about the Father, for "no man knoweth the Father but the Son, and he to whom the Son will reveal Him."

2. Darkness implies SUPERSTITION. Where there is no light there is sure to be false and exaggerated views of things. The light of God's truth always reveals the foolishness of man's wisdom. His darkened mind cannot think the thoughts of God, and so he builds castles which have no foundation but in the air of his own fancy.

3. Darkness implies DANGER. The position is described in the text as being "*in* the region and shadow of death." To be in the malarial region of unforgiven sin, is to be in the shadow of the second death. Those who are in darkness cannot see the shadow; this makes their condition all the more perilous. To be in ignorance of Christ the

Saviour is to be already in the region of death, having no
fitness for the regions beyond, of eternal life and glory.

4. Darkness implies a condition of HELPLESSNESS.
"They *sat* in darkness." When the light dawned upon
them they were *sitting* in darkness, as if they did not know
where to go or what to do. This is the attitude of those
who have, through failure and disappointment, come to
an utter end of themselves. All the sparks of their own
kindling only made the darkness the more dense. It was
when they discovered their own helplessness and hopelessness, that the "great light sprung up" (Matt. 4. 16). The
darkest hour is the hour before day-break.

II. **God's Effectual Remedy.** "The people which
sat in darkness saw *great light.*" The light that has come
through the appearing of Jesus Christ is indeed a "great
light." Those who are not satisfied with sunlight will
never be satisfied with any light, for there is no greater
than this. Those who do not find the light of Christ
sufficient for the darkness of their hearts and lives, will
for ever remain in darkness, for there is no greater light
than this. There is nothing like light for overcoming
darkness. Christ is that light, and this true light now
shineth.

As darkness is emblematic of ignorance, superstition,
danger and helplessness, so light is emblematic of knowledge, truth, safety and power. This light has come as
God's message of hope "To them which sit in the region
and shadow of death" (Matt. 4. 16). Alas, that so many
should condemn themselves, by preferring the darkness to
the light, because they love the deeds that are evil (John
3. 19). There be many who have *seen* this "great light,"
but there are few who follow it. While ye have the light,
believe in it, and ye shall not walk in darkness, but shall
have the light of life.

RESCUE WORK BY ANGELS.

GENESIS 19. 1.

"THERE came two angels to Sodom." *Angels* in *Sodom!* What a contrast. The brightest and holiest of servants in the darkest and wickedest cities. Even slumwork may become angelic. These messengers of mercy and of judgment are examples to all who desire to rescue the perishing. Notice—

I. **Where they Went.** They went to "Sodom" (v.1). A city reeking with iniquity, and they went conscious that their eyes and ears must see and hear things that would pierce their souls with an agony of pain and distress, but they were prepared to suffer, they were willing even to "abide in the street all night" (v. 2). Those who would seek the salvation of others must be ready to sacrifice their own comfort and ease.

II. **Why they Went.** They went because the Lord sent them (v. 13). They did not go because they felt that the wickedness of the city demanded that *something* should be done, or because they had nothing else more urgent to do. No. They went with a definite commission at the bidding of the Lord. They realised that the work was not theirs, but God's. They had come in His Name, and in His strength, to do His will among them, and it would be done. The servants of Christ will soon grow weary in well-doing if they have not this perfect assurance, that they are in the very place and doing the very work He has sent them to do.

III. **What they Went to Do.** They went to preach instant salvation and coming judgment. "Up, get you out of this place, for the Lord will destroy this city" (v. 14). They had no scheme of social reform to propose. Those Sodomites were condemned already. There was no alternative left them but to escape or perish. The eyes of these Heaven-sent messengers were wide awake to the real facts of the case, so that they could do nothing else but press home their one message of warning and hope. They spoke and acted as those who believed in the "wrath to come," and who saw the peril of those who were disposed to "linger" through indecision (v. 16). There was no time like *"now"* to them: "Behold, now is the day of salvation." So urgent were these evangelists that they literally laid hold of Lot, his wife, and his two daughters (v. 16). *Personal* dealing they felt was a pressing necessity if souls were to be rescued from the approaching doom. Why should preachers of the Gospel not be as earnest and as urgent as these two heralds were? Have they not as definite a message to deliver? Is there not the same danger of destruction awaiting those who believe not, nor obey the Gospel? (1 Thess. 5. 3). "This one thing I do" which characterised these "sent ones" is a special feature in all those who have been called of God and sent. He maketh His ministers a *flame* of fire.

THE TRUE AND THE FALSE REFUGE.

"A MAN SHALL BE AN HIDING PLACE" (Isa. 32. 2).
"THE REFUGE OF LIES" (Isa. 28. 17).

Two hiding places are brought before us here. The one is the refuge of truth, the other is a refuge of lies. The one is a *Man*, the other is an imagination. The first is a revelation from God, the second is an invention of man. All men feel their need of a refuge of some kind or other, but all men are not equally safe in their place of refuge. It is of vital importance that we should know now the true from the false. It will be too late for the self-deceived to find out this distinction when their "refuge of lies" is being swept away. Here then are some of the features of the true, God-appointed refuge. The true refuge is the place of—

I. Conscious Safety. "A man shall be an hiding place *from the wind*, and a *covert from the tempest.*" Those who have fled to the Man Christ Jesus, as a refuge for the soul, are now being sheltered from the wind and tempest of sin and judgment The wind round about them may be as bitter and terrible as ever, but they *are being saved* from its power, and they know it. Their refuge saves them. Is your refuge saving you from being turned aside by the sudden blasts of sin and the pressing storms of iniquity. If your hiding place—that in which you trust—is not sheltering you day by day, then your refuge is a refuge of lies.

II. Friendship and Communion. "A *man* shall be an hiding place." This is the man who is God's fellow (Zech. 13. 7). All those who have fled for refuge to the true hiding-place are in the fellowship and friendship of the Lord Jesus Christ. They are reconciled to God, and rejoicing in Him. They know assuredly that *God* is their refuge and strength. Does your hiding-place bring you into contact and communion with God? Does that in which you trust for salvation make Christ unspeakably precious to your soul? If your refuge is not *in Him*, it is a refuge of lies that the judgment of hail shall sweep away, and the waters of desolation overflow. God's only refuge for the sin-smitten souls of men is the MAN who was smitten for sin. "Other refuge have I none." "I flee to *Thee* to hide me" (Psa. 143. 9).

III. Rest and Refreshing. "A man shall be...as rivers of water in a dry place." Those who have found the true refuge of the soul know of it and enjoy it, for they now drink the living waters of satisfaction. In their place of hiding they find the source of abiding blessing. Their Rock of refuge has become a fountain of delight. Here everlasting springs abide, and never-withering flowers. They heard the Divine call, "If any man thirst, let him come unto *Me* and drink;" they obeyed, and found in Him salvation from the wind and the tempest of sin and wrath, and waters of cleansing and refreshing. Does your hiding place bring cleansing for your soul, and yield refreshing streams for your thirsty heart. If you are not happier and holier through that in which you trust for salvation, your hiding place is, in the sight of God, only a "refuge of lies." If that so-called *faith* of yours is not saving you from your sins, and bringing refreshing and gladness into your life, then it is a delusion; it is not faith in Jesus Christ, for all that believe in Him are justified from all things. A dying infidel was exhorted by his companion to "Hold on." "I am quite willing to hold on," said the dying man, "if I knew what to hold on by." He had no Christ, and so had no hope, for all refuges of lies will be swept away.

> "Jesus, Lover of my soul,
> I will to Thy bosom fly "

GOD-SHINE.

"GOD HATH SHINED IN OUR HEARTS" (2 Cor. 4. 6).

WHEN the blessed sunshine breaks out from behind the thick clouds of darkness, there is no mistaking the fact that a great change has taken place. This is just such a change as takes place in the benighted soul of man when the *light* of the knowledge of God breaks through the darkness.

I. The Source of this Shining. "GOD hath shined." This light is not of man's kindling. Out of the darkness within no such light could ever be produced. Only He who could "command the light to shine out of darkness" could cause such a light to shine in the sin-darkened hearts of men. The light of the knowledge of God is the light of God Himself. It is a definite and direct act of the infinite mercy and goodness of God upon the individual soul. "God hath shined." God, who is Light, and in whom is no darkness at all, is still shining through His Son Jesus Christ, by His Word.

II. The Place of this Shining. "God hath shined *in our hearts.*" The brightest thing in Heaven is the darkest place on earth. This God-shine in the heart brings with it a double revelation. It shows by way of contrast how dark the heart by nature was, and how hopeless it was for it in itself to create such a soul-satisfying light. It is also a revelation of the character and presence of God in the heart. This is not so much a light created by God, as it is the light of the *presence* of God in the heart. Into every dark crevice of the soul this shining has come. It is the nature of light to cast its influence over everything that is anywhere within its reach. In shining into the *heart* this light enters into every act and deed of the life, into every thought and feeling and motive of the soul's activities. *God* hath shined His light, and wisdom has come to take the place of our darkness and ignorance. The god of this world had *blinded* the mind, but the God of Heaven hath shined in our hearts to give the light of the knowledge of God (v. 4).

III. The Purpose of this Shining. "To give the light of *the knowledge of the glory of God, in the face of Jesus Christ.*" This shining of God, in His glorious grace, upon and in the heart, gives us to know something of that glory that has come to God in and through His Son Jesus Christ. God hath shined in our hearts in answer to the atoning death of His Son, by which His Holy Name has been glorified. This shining assures us of much more than the *existence* of God, it is the manifestation of His glory—the glory of His *saving* grace—in the face or character of Jesus Christ. As all the colours of nature are in one single ray of pure white light, so all the attributes of God are perfectly harmonised and embodied in this revelation of Himself. *Knowledge* is light, but the knowledge of the glory of God which is radiant on the face of Jesus Christ, is the brightest and most effectual light that ever pierced the darkness of a human heart. It is a light that transforms the whole inner man, and that adorns with the beauty of the Lord; it is the dawning of that great eternal day upon the soul, which will never be followed by the darkness of night but which will brighten as the hours and years go by, until the *perfect* day of perfect likeness, face to face. God hath shined. Walk in the light and ye shall not stumble.

A DREADED BLESSING.

"FOR THE MORNING IS TO ALL OF THEM AS THE SHADOW OF DEATH" (Job 24. 17, R.V.).

THE moral nature of any man must be sadly perverted, when the bright rays of the morning dawn are to him as the shadows of death. All rebels against the light are lovers of iniquity (v. 13). "Men love darkness rather than the light, *because* their deeds are evil."

I. **The Contrast.** "The morning...the shadows of death." The difference is that of day and night, life and death, good and evil.

1. The "morning" is suggestive of PLEASURE. "Light is sweet, and it is a pleasant thing for the eye to behold the sunshine." How beautiful and fresh is the morning dawn, with all its new revelations and silent benedictions. What a lovely emblem of the dawn of spiritual life in the soul.

2. The "morning" is suggestive of PRIVILEGE. With the morning light comes all the opportunities and possibilities of a new day. The darkness as a difficulty in the way of general labour is removed and the generous sunshine pours

its cheering beams into every needy corner where its progress is not obstructed The voice of the morning is, "Awake, awake, put on strength." Behold now is the day of salvation. "The night cometh when no man can work."

3. The "shadow of death" is suggestive of GATHERING DARKNESS. The bright, hopeful light has died away, and the thick gloomy clouds of darkness are spreading quickly over the sky. Those who have been thankfully using the daylight have entered into rest, while those who have been idling away their time have lost their opportunity. Spiritually, this is a very melancholy condition to be in.

4. The "shadow of death" is suggestive of FUTURE HOPELESSNESS. It is that awful shadow which is the certain forerunner of eternal separation. *Death* is not far away when its shadow has come. What prospect can a man have of re-establishing his lost character when the shadow of death is already upon him? While death does not end all, it is the end of all opportunity, as far as this life is concerned.

II. **The Anomaly.** "The morning is to them *as* the shadow of death." This is a most unnatural and wretched state to be in. It betrays a condition of perfect moral disorder; an inherent unfitness for the enjoyment of God's order of things. Why should God's brightest gifts be to them as the darkness of doom? Why should the light of *the Gospel* be to some as the shadow of death, instead of the morning dawn of the light of life? The more brightly this light of truth shines, the more dark does the sky of their self-created hopes become; so, to them the "morning" of God's light of salvation is as the shadow of death—

1. Because it awakens the FEAR OF DISCOVERY. Like the thief, the murderer, and the adulterer, they love the darkness better than the light, because it is better suited

for their vile purposes. The morning light is as it were the death blow to their ungodly prospects. That which is good very good, is to them bad, because it exposes and condemns their own badness. Those who wrap themselves up in the garment of self-righteousness cannot bear the glare of God's unsullied truth, because it reveals their boasted righteousness to be nothing but filthy rags. They would rather have the pleasures of darkness, the delusive joys of sin, to the pure delights of holiness that comes to us through the shining of His Word. The man who is afraid of Heaven's light is an enemy to God at heart. He that loves the light comes into the light that his life and character might be tested and purified. To them who love not the Lord Jesus Christ, His coming again, as the Bright and Morning Star, will be to them indeed as the shadow of death, for they will be consumed by the brightness of His coming.

A DIVINE COMPLAINT.

"My people doth not consider" (Isa. 1. 3).

THOUGHTFULNESS about the things of the world, and thoughtlessness about the things of eternity, is a very common sin among the people of God. Superficial thinking leads to superficial living. The ox knoweth his owner, and the ass his master's crib, but how often the Lord's people fail to recognise their Owner, or the blessings He provides for them. Inconsiderateness is a great hindrance to the growth of spiritual life and to usefulness because it is dishonouring to God. Mere talk and mechanical action will never be a substitute for solemn heart reflection. If we would take time to meditate until the fire burns, our testimony would not be so powerless and fruitless. "My people doth not consider." This is the language of wounded love. Think on some of those things which *we* fail to

consider as we ought, and of which God might justly
complain. "My people doth not consider"—

**I. The Pit out of which they have been Digged, or
they would be more Humble.** How ready we are, like
Israel, to forget our bondage in Egypt, and as we look
upon other worldly, sin-sodden lives, fail to remember
that such were some of us.

**II. The Cost at which they have been Redeemed,
or they would be more Thankful.** Not with silver and
gold, but with that blood which speaks of the sacrifice
of Divine love and of life. Have I considered it sufficiently
that the peace which I now enjoy was purchased by the
blood of Christ's Cross, and that it is mine, not for any
good in me, but because of His infinite mercy and grace?

**III. Their Relationship to Him who Saves, or they
would be more Restful.** "Ye are not your own." Ye
belong to Christ. Have we thought deep enough into
this blessed truth? As members of His body, will He
not be very careful over us? Why take anxious thought
about your physical life; does not your Father know that
you have need of these things? "Let not your heart be
troubled, ye believe in God, believe also in *Me.*"

**IV. Their Privileges as Sons, or they would be
more Joyful.** Because ye are sons, God hath sent forth
His Spirit into your hearts, that ye might cry "Abba—
My Father," and that He might in answer to that cry
"supply all your need."

**V. Their Responsibility as Servants, or they would
be more Watchful.** *Now* is the acceptable time for self-
sacrificing service, as well as the day of salvation. To-day
if ye will hear His voice, harden not your hearts. All who
have received the Gospel become custodians of it, and are
responsible to the Master for it. Watch ye, therefore.

VI. The Gift of the Holy Spirit, or they would be more Fruitful. "Know ye not that your body is the temple of the Holy Ghost in you, which ye have of God." Do you reckon on Him as a Teacher and Comforter, and as the Endurer of power? Do you consider Him all-sufficient for you in the work of God?

VII. The Glory that is Coming, or they would be more Praiseful. The glory that is yet to be revealed in and through the redeemed of God, is the glory that belongs to the eternal Son of God. They shall *see* His face, they shall be *like* Him, and shall be *with* Him where He is. Consider your ways, and consider Him, for a book of remembrance is written before Him for them that *thought upon* His Name.

———

"SPRING UP, O WELL!"

NUMBERS 21. 17.

At the beginning of the journeyings of the children of Israel, Moses was commanded to *smite* the rock in Horeb that water may flow forth for the thirsty people. Now, nearly forty years after, he is told to *speak* to the rock, but in anger he smote it twice, for which disobedience he was prevented from entering the promised land (20. 10-12). That Rock was Christ, says the Apostle (1 Cor. 10. 4), and as such it was not the purpose of God that it should be smitten *twice*. He suffered *once* in the end of the age to put away sin. Now we have but to *speak* to the Rock that the refreshing stream may spring up. This sweet little word—"Spring up, O well"—contains—

I. A Suggestive Metaphor. "A *well*." A well within a rock. This rock is Christ, the Fountain of living water. Like Jacob's well, it is *deep*, deep as the fathomless fullness of God. The waters in this well represent the unsearchable riches of Christ—that, which is abundantly able to satisfy all the needs of a human soul.

II. A Felt Need. *"Spring up*, O well.*"* Spring thou up in my thirsty soul, for I have been to the broken cisterns of earth, and am disappointed, and perishing of thirst. Spring up, O well, in this desert life of mine, that has hitherto brought forth no fruit unto God. My heart thirsteth for God, yea the living God.

III. A Great Encouragement. This well can "spring up," so that its life-giving stream may be within the reach of every needy one. There is a tremendous pressure in this spring. It is the pressure of infinite love, a force that can send its influence into the deepest depths of need, and up to the highest heights of satisfaction and spiritual attainment.

IV. A Simple Means. "Spring up." *Speak* ye to the *rock.* This rock is waiting to yield its treasures to those who ask. *Speak*, you don't need to shout. Your speech need not be eloquent. Prayer is a very simple thing when it is real. The remedy for soul-thirst is to speak to the rock. *Speak* to it when your heart is smitten with barrenness and death. *Speak* to it when burdened with the dying need of others. Speak to it believingly, and the waters will gush out, then ye shall be able to *"Sing* unto it."

THE DIVINE VISITOR

"Behold I stand at the door and knock" (Rev 3. 20).

Christ *knocking* at the door is a proof that He has come very *near*, and that to bless us. It also implies His *willingness* to come in, and the heart's reluctance to let Him in. Man's nature is like a house with many rooms. The Lord knocks at the door of each apartment that He might have access to the whole house of Mansoul.

I. He Knocks as a Redeemer *that He might save.*
Save the sleeping conscience from sleeping the sleep of
death.   As the One who paid the ransom for the soul, He
knocks that He might get into possession of His blood-
bought property, that it might be saved from the
destructive hands of the enemy.   "If any sinful man opens
the door I will come in to Him" (Rev. 3. 20).

II. He Knocks as a Physician *that He might heal.*
He knows that all the inmates of this house of Mansoul are
sick and in need of His healing touch.   The whole head is
sick, the heart faint, and the hands and the knees are feeble.
There is, in fact, "no soundness," the whole inner life
has been polluted with the poison of sin.   Behold, thy
Healer is at the door.   "If any sin-sick man opens the
door I will come in to him" (Rev. 3. 20).

III. He Knocks as a Teacher *that He might instruct.*
He is the great Teacher come from God who can anoint the
eyes of His pupils with the heavenly eye-salve, that they
may see and understand heavenly things.   The minds,
blinded by Satan, can be beautifully illumined by Him
who is the Wisdom of God.   "If any unlearned man opens
the door I will come in to Him" (Rev. 3. 20).

IV. He Knocks as a King *that He might rule.*   A life
that is self-centred is a ruined one.   As Lord He knocks
that He might so get into that life which He hath redeemed
by His life as to govern and control it for its own good and
His glory.   Until the King is enthroned within, the soul is
under the bondage and tyranny of foolish and presumptuous
self.   He wishes the government of your life to be upon
His shoulders, that there might be no mismanagement in
the affairs of the soul.   Although He is "King of our
lives," He does not compel, He knocks.   "If any man
opens the door I will come in to him" (Rev. 3. 20).

V. He Knocks as a Merchantman *that He might enrich.* He knows the poverty of those who say that they are rich and have need of nothing. Unsearchable riches are in *Himself*, and infinite mercy and love has brought Him to the very door of your impoverished life that you might be filled out of His fullness. "I counsel you to buy of ME gold refined in the fire, that you may become rich" (Rev. 3. 18). You buy without money when you let the Merchant in. "If any poor man opens the door I will come in to him" (Rev 3. 20).

VI. He Knocks as a Bridegroom *that He might woo.* His desire is not only to save, heal, teach, rule, and enrich, but to have the *fellowship* of those whom He hath blessed. He knocks at the door of the heart because He seeks admission into the affections. Three times Peter heard this knock, "Lovest thou Me" (John 21. 15). Because He loves us so much, He is very jealous of our affections. If you have admitted Him as Saviour and King, surely you will give Him with your allegiance the love of your heart and the fellowship of your life. His love constrains Him to knock that our love might constrain us to open, so that every barrier between the soul and Christ may be removed, and unbroken communion enjoyed. "If anyone listens to My voice and opens the door I will come in" (Rev. 3. 20).

CHRIST THE END OF THE LAW.

"FOR CHRIST IS THE END OF THE LAW FOR RIGHTEOUSNESS TO EVERY ONE THAT BELIEVETH" (Rom 10. 4)

I. What is the Law? As God's revealed standard it is "holy, just, and good," therefore a revelation of His holiness, justice, and goodness. The source of the law is holy, the character of it is just, the purpose of it is good.

II. What is the End of the Law? "Christ is the end of the law." This blessed fact may be interpreted in different ways. The end of the law, for a thief, is the prison; for a murderer, it is the rope. The end of the law for all sinners, is condemnation or Christ. The end of a book is to instruct; of a watch, to keep time; or a lamp, to give light; the end of the law is to bring us to Christ. It came as a tutor (slave) for this very purpose (Gal. 3. 24). The end of the avenger of blood is to kill, and in seeking to do so he often chased the manslayer into the city of refuge.

III. Why did Christ become the End of the Law? It was "for righteousness." He did not come to act in defiance of the law, but to fulfil it. He was made under the law, that its holy and just claims might be perfectly satisfied in Him. He became obedient unto death, and so brought to an end the righteous demands of the law against all those who are in Him. He is now made of God unto us *"righteousness"* (1 Cor. 1. 30).

IV. To Whom is Christ the End of the Law? "To every one that believeth." "By Him all that believe are justified from all things" (Acts 13. 39). The end of an unalterable law to Daniel, in the eyes of his enemies, was the *lions' den*, but to him *God* was the end of that law for deliverance. To those who are out of Christ, there is no end to the demands and threatenings of that offended and insulted law. Only those who are ignorant of the righteousness of God would ever go about seeking to establish their own. To submit to the *righteousness* of God is the only wise thing to do, and you do this when you cease from your own works and believe on the Lord Jesus Christ, who made an end of the law, and brought in for you everlasting righteousness.

PULLED OUT OF THE FIRE.

JUDE 23

WHAT is more alarming than an outbreak of fire? What excitement! What consternation! What strenuous, self-sacrificing efforts to save the perishing inmates from the blazing tenement. The fire of sin broke out in Eden, and has spread over the whole world. The only way of escape is by that ladder which Jacob saw, which reaches from earth to Heaven (John 14 6) Think of the—

I. **Nature of Sin** It is compared here to "fire." Fire is an element that can neither be weighed nor measured. Who can set a boundary to the workings of sin, or reckon up its capabilities and effects? The nature of sin, like fire, is to mar or destroy all that comes within its grasp that is not able to resist its mighty influence. Sin is an unquenchable fire, as far as the wisdom and power of man is concerned.

II. **Danger of the Sinner**. As he needs to be "pulled out" of the fire, it is clear that he must be *in the fire*. He is living under the power and dominion of sin, therefore, *in* sin. He may be utterly unconscious of his awful position, but the end is destruction all the same. To be in a state of sin is to be in a state of condemnation. Sin, like fire, when it is finished, bringeth forth death.

III. **Work of Rescue**. "Pulling them out of the fire." There are only two ways whereby a brand can be saved from the burning: either put out the fire, or pull out the brand. Men cannot put out the fire of sin, so sinners must be pulled out of the fire. In this world of sin the Church is God's fire brigade—a rescue party sent to pull men out of the fire. There is no escape from sin's destructive power but by being *separated* from it. The love of Christ is the constraining motive.

FIRE IN AN ASYLUM.

On the 27th January, 1903, fire broke out in a London lunatic asylum. Of the 300 inmates, 50 perished and 250 had to be literally *pulled out of the fire.* While the work of rescue was going on, these poor insane creatures behaved in such a way as to remind us very forcibly of how insane sinners behave when their salvation is earnestly sought after by others. It was reported that—

"Some laughed at the mention of fire." Only fools could laugh at a calamity like this. Fools make a mock at sin. Only those who are morally insane would dare to trifle with the fire of sin.

"Some said they would not leave their bed in the night and go out." They would not consent to leave their present enjoyment, even to save their lives. There are many like this, who prefer the pleasures of a condemned state to the joys of salvation. Their madness is self-evident by the choice they make.

"Some were found hiding under the bed from the fire." In their refuge of lies, they said, "Peace, peace, when there was no peace." No one but a fool can suppose that a bed of ease or of indifference is any protection against a consuming fire. Be sure your sin, like a fire, will find you out.

"Some seemed to fancy that the rescuers had made the fire." They were blamed for trying to "burn them up." You would think, to hear some people speak, that preachers were the makers of Hell, and the disturbers of the peace, by seeking to convince men of sin and to pull them out of their perishing condition. Of course in making a charge like this they only prove that they are beside themselves.

"Many of them fought against their rescuers, biting and tearing their hair out." What a melancholy picture; what a sad proof of insanity—warring against those who were

sacrificing themselves for their deliverance. It is no uncommon experience for those who seek to pull men out of the fire of sin to have their Christ-like efforts gnashed upon with their teeth, and to have their merciful motives torn to pieces. Only spiritual lunatics could behave in this fashion.

"Some were heard knocking at a closed door to get out, when it was too late." It must have been a terrible awakening to come to their senses and find themselves imprisoned in a devouring fire. Those who refuse to be pulled out of the fire of sin will perish in it. "How shall ye escape, if ye neglect so great salvation?"

"Every sane man and woman went to the rescue." The time was short; the doom of the unsaved was certain; the work was great and urgent; every other interest was set aside; the one thing needful was the salvation of souls. All sane Christians make it their chief business to get souls pulled out of the fire of sin. Are you out or in?

"ASK FOR THE OLD PATHS."
JEREMIAH 6. 16.

IN these days the spiritual pilgrim comes to many a cross road, so that there is need for *standing* and *asking* for the old paths if there is any doubt in the mind as to their real whereabouts.

I. **Why ask for the Old Paths?** Because the *new* ones are delusive and destructive. The new paths are men's miserable substitutes for the grand old "highway" of God, which only beguile the unwary into Doubting Castle, the habitation of Giant Despair. Even though an angel from Heaven should preach a new Gospel, let him be accursed. Ask for the old paths, and be steadfast therein.

II. **What are the Old Paths?** The old paths are the

paths that were trodden by Abel, Abraham, Moses, David, Elijah, and all the prophets and apostles, who believed God and accepted His Word as a lamp to their feet, and the testimony of His Son as the sure foundation of their hope. The *revealed will* of God is the old unerring path that leads to peace and paradise. This is the old light that is as trustworthy as the sun; the new lights are mere "will-o'-the-wisps" dancing about the bogs. The old paths are sprinkled with the blood of atonement; the new with the rose-water of men-pleasing.

III. **Why we should Walk in the Old Paths.** Because there we find—

1. THE BLOOD OF CHRIST TO JUSTIFY. All pilgrims in the "old paths" are forgiven, and justified through the blood of His Cross; the new path wanderers know nothing of this.

2. THE WORD OF GOD TO SATISFY. They have not followed cunningly-devised fables, but the true light that shineth in this dark place. The testimony of Jesus is the spirit of prophecy. The plausible theories and philosophies of men may beguile for a time, but they cannot bring abiding satisfaction to the heart and conscience.

3. THE POWER OF THE SPIRIT TO SANCTIFY. The makers of the new paths have no place for the quickening, sanctifying, enduing power of the Holy Ghost. Along their new and tardy way there is no missionary enthusiasm, no felt need of being filled with the Spirit, no joy in the Holy Ghost, no glorying in the Cross of Christ, no conversions from sin and self to God. The old paths are the paths of peace, pleasure, and power, because they are the paths in which the Son of God still walks in company with His followers. "Ask for the old paths, where is the good way, and walk therein, and ye shall find rest for your souls."

AN OPEN DOOR FOR YOU.

"BEHOLD, I HAVE SET BEFORE THEE AN OPEN DOOR" (Rev. 3. 8).

WHEN out of work, honest tradesmen have often to say, with heavy heart and weary feet, "I can't get an opening." How sad a world it would be if there was no opening for weary, sin-burdened souls in the love of God, or the grace of Jesus Christ. The work of Christ was the work of an Opener. Sin had closed the door into every spiritual privilege, but He who has now the keys of death and of hades hath set before us—

I. The Open Door of Salvation. "I am the Door, by Me, if any man enter in, he shall be saved." This is a door of escape from the wrath 'of God, from the guilt and pollution of sin, from the fear of man, and the tyranny of self. It is for you, therefore you may have boldness to enter in by the blood of Jesus. Come now.

II. The Open Door of Instruction. The privilege of being "taught of God" is open for all. If any man lack wisdom, let him ask; the door into the Divine audience chamber is now open through the Name of Jesus. He can not only "open to you the Scriptures," but also anoint your eyes with such an eye-salve as shall make you see wonderful things in His Holy Word. He can also make you of quick understanding, wise in Christ.

III. The Open Door of Prayer. Others have won great victories by prayer. The same door by which they entered into fullness of blessing and triumph is open for you. "If ye ask anything in My Name." Moses, Elijah, David, Daniel, Paul, Luther, Knox, Muller, Quarrier, and hosts of other mighty ones, owed almost everything to this open door. Who can tell all the profit you shall have if you pray unto Him? (Job. 21. 15). Enter now.

IV. The Open Door of Fellowship. This is another

glorious privilege that is open to all saints. "If ye draw
nigh unto Me, I will draw nigh unto you" (James 4. 8).
The Lord needs no very urgent constraint to come and
abide with us. The deepest yearning of His loving heart
is that we should "abide" in Him. His difficulty with us
is our closed door against Him. "Behold, I stand at the
door and knock."

V. The Open Door of Power. Undoubtedly some have
more spiritual power than others. How? Have they got
into special favour with God through some hidden private
door? Hath He not declared that "All power is given
unto *Me*, go ye therefore" (Matt. 28. 18, 19). Go ye
therefore to Him and for Him. "He giveth power to the
faint, and to them that have *no might* He increaseth
strength" (Isa. 40. 29). He hath set this open door before
you. Wait upon Him, and ye shall change strength.

VI. The Open Door of Service. If you are a son, go
work to-day in His vineyard; the door is open for you, and
your work is waiting on you. What can I do? Do what
you are told, "Go, and work." Christ does not compel us
to serve or follow Him, but He commands and invites.
Who then is willing to consecrate his service to the Lord,
service of heart and voice, of mind and means? In every
foreign mission field, wide doors, and effectual, are set
open before us.

VII. The Open Door of Heaven. "I go to prepare a
place for you." Those who are Christ's have no fear of
ever getting this door closed against them. He has opened
it, and no man shutteth. Let us be faithful now, taking
full advantage of the privileges offered us, that so an
abundant entrance shall be ministered unto us on that day,
when we come to enter through this gate into the city.
Beware of acting the part of the foolish virgins who were
outside when "the door was shut."

THE DEATH OF CHRIST.

ISAIAH 53. 10, 11.

WHAT the sun is to the Heavens and the earth, the death of Christ is to the Bible and to Christianity. Look at—

I. **The Nature of It.** "It pleased the Lord to bruise Him, He hath put Him to grief." The Rationalist can only see in Christ's death a martyr to Jewish malice and Roman contempt; but it pleased Jehovah to bruise Him. "He spared not His own Son, but delivered Him up for us all." He was bruised between the upper and nether millstones of God's justice and man's guilt. He could say, "No man taketh My life from Me, I lay it down of Myself." His was a voluntary, God-ordained sacrifice.

II. **The Purpose of It.** "To make His soul an offering for sin." What an infinite depth of difference there was between *"His soul"* and *"sin."* Only God can fully judge the value of the one and the demerit of the other. The greatness of the price reveals the awfulness of the condition. He poured out the treasures of His soul, that the sin of my soul might be taken away. The price was all-sufficient in the sight of God, and so the redemption is eternal.

III. **The Result of It.** "He shall be satisfied." A woman forgetteth her travail, for joy that a man is born into the world. He shall see of the travail of His soul, but shall He ever forget it? He shall rejoice that a bride has been born into the world, and shall be satisfied when she is safely brought home to the marriage festival and to His eternal glory. We also shall be satisfied when we awake in His likeness. Meanwhile, by life and lip we are to show forth the saving, sanctifying, satisfying power of His death till He come.

THREE ASPECTS OF SALVATION.

LUKE 15.

IN this chapter we have three parables, representing three conditions of the lost, and showing three persons seeking the lost. These parables were spoken to the Pharisees and Scribes, who murmured, saying, "This man *receiveth* sinners." They show the kind of sinners He does receive, and how He does receive them. We observe—

I. A Threefold Aspect of the Lost. The—

1. LOST SHEEP—representing those who are lost to *safety*. Outside the fold means outside the count. There were ninety and nine—the lost one was not counted. The lost sheep was in danger, exposed and helpless, typical of those who are *thoughtlessly* lost, unconscious of their condition.

2. LOST MONEY—representing those lost to *usefulness*. As long as this piece of silver was lost, it was unfit to be used—good for nothing. It was not lost out in the desert, but in the house. It is possible to be in the house of God and yet lost to usefulness, like the Scribes and Pharisees, to whom these words were spoken. It is possible to have a saved soul and yet have a lost life. To be out of the hand of Him to whom we belong as redeemed ones, is to be in a condition of uselessness. When a piece of money is lost it is not only the base metal that's lost, but all the good that money might do.

3. LOST SON—representing lost *fellowship*. Out of communion with the Father: a condition of degradation and dishonour brought about by a deliberate choice and wilful separation from His presence. Thus is the backslider lost to fellowship with God through his love of the world.

II. A Threefold Salvation. In these three parables we may see the desires and longings of the Father, Son, and Holy Spirit toward the lost ones.

1. THE SHEPHERD SEEKS THE LOST SHEEP TO SAVE IT. Here we have the work of the Son revealed. He goes *after* the lost, leaving His all behind, in order that He might find it. At great *sacrifice* He seeks to save.

2. THE WOMAN SEEKS THE LOST SILVER TO USE IT. This suggests the mission of the Holy Spirit. The money is lost in the house. She lights a candle and sweeps the house. Dust and darkness usually are the causes why the Holy Ghost cannot get hold of our lives to use them. The light of the truth has to be brought from without, and the dust of inward corruption stirred up within, that confession and surrender may be made. The unsaved one has just to be outside the fold to be a lost soul; the saved one has just to be outside the control and touch of the Holy Spirit to be a lost life. He, like this woman, seeks to save those lost to a life of service for God.

3. THE FATHER SEEKS HIS LOST SON TO HAVE FELLOW-SHIP WITH HIM. The Father does not go forth to seek; He *waits* and longs for the coming prodigal. The loss of love is a great loss. He calls on the backsliding ones *to return*, and promises healing to such. It is sad to find Christians in this terrible plight—out of fellowship with God. For such two things are needed: (1) To come to themselves. (2) To come back to their Father.

III. **A Threefold Rejoicing.** There is joy in Heaven over the salvation of—

1. A LOST SOUL. The value is unspeakable, the joy is never-ending.

2. A LOST SERVANT. Grieve not the Holy Spirit. Yield yourselves unto God. Ye are bought with a price.

3. A LOST SON. Love restored, and the peace and fellowship enjoyed. In this threefold salvation—the heart of God the Father, God the Son, and God the Holy Ghost—one heart, is made glad.

SEED THOUGHTS.

METAPHORS OF BELIEVERS
IN 2 CORINTHIANS.

Epistles, chap. 3. 3; Ministers, chap. 3. 6; Vessels, chap. 4. 7; Workers, chap. 6. 1; Temples, chap. 6. 16; Sons and Daughters, chap. 6. 18.

FELLOWSHIP WITH ONE ANOTHER.
1 JOHN 1. 7.

HERE are several powerful reasons why believers ought to keep in fellowship with one another:—

1. All are born of the same Father (John 1. 13).
2. All are bought with the same Price (1 Cor. 6. 20).
3. All are members of the same Body (Col. 1. 18).
4. All are taught by the same Spirit (John 16. 13).
5. All are walking in the same Path (2 Cor. 5. 7).
6. All are serving the same Master (Matt. 23. 8).
7. All are heirs of the same Inheritance (Rom. 8. 17).

SEVEN GREAT FACTS IN JOHN 3.

1. The gift of God (16), ... *Love.*
2. The mission of Christ (17), ... *Salvation.*
3. The work of the Spirit (8), ... *Quickening.*
4. The need of man (3), ... *New Life.*
5. The way of life (14, 15), ... *Believing.*
6. The consequence of unbelief (18, 19), *Condemnation.*
7. The evidence of faith (21), .. *Works.*

CHRIST'S SEVENFOLD PRAYER FOR HIS PEOPLE IN JOHN 17.

1. That they might be *kept through His Name* (11).
2. That they might have *His joy in themselves* (13).
3. That they might be *sanctified* (17-19).
4. That they might *all be one* (21, 22).
5. That they might be a *blessing to others* (20).
6. That they might *possess the Father's love* (26).
7. That they might *behold His glory* (24).

DIVINE THOUGHTFULNESS.

"THINK UPON ME, MY GOD, FOR GOOD" (Neh. 5. 19).

I. GOD DOES THINK UPON US.

1. He thinks upon our *Past*, .. Jer. 2. 2.
2. He thinks upon our *Present*, .. Ezek. 16. 60.
3. He thinks upon our *Future*, .. Ezek. 16. 62.

II. GOD DOES THINK UPON US FOR GOOD.   It is good for us that:

1. His thoughts are *Great*, .. Isa. 55. 9.
2. His thoughts are *Many*, .. Psa. 40. 5.
3. His thoughts are *Peaceful*, .. Jer. 29. 11.
4. His thoughts are *Comforting*, Hosea 2. 14.

COURAGE.

HAVE the courage—

1. To *Obey* like Abraham,   Gen. 12. 4; Heb. 11. 8.
2. To *Suffer* like Moses, ... Heb. 11. 25.
3. To *Flee* like Joseph, ... Gen. 39. 12.
4. To *Stand* like Elijah, ... 1 Kings 17. 1.
5. To *Persevere* like Daniel, ... Dan. 6. 10.
6. To *Venture* like Peter, ... Matt. 14. 28, 29.
7. To *Testify* like Paul, ... Acts 26. 22, 23

THE CHRISTIAN'S ENVIRONMENTS.

THEY are seen—

1. Among Lions, ... Psa. 57. 4.
2. Among Thorns, ... S. of S. 2. 2.
3. Among Scorpions, ... Ezek. 2. 6.
4. Among Wolves, ... Luke 10. 3.
5. Among Tares as Wheat, ... Matt. 13. 30.
6. Among the Heavenly Host,   .. 2 Kings 6. 17.
7. Surrounded by the Lord Himself,   Psa. 125. 2.

THE WAY TO GOD.

1. A Needed Way, ... Psa. 63. 1.
2. A New Way, ... Heb. 10. 19, 20
3. A Finished Way, ... 1 Peter 3. 18.
4. A Personal Way, ... John 14. 6.
5. A Safe Way, ... Heb. 7. 25.
6. A Free Way, ... Heb. 10. 20-22.
7. A Blessed Way, into all needed help, Heb. 4. 14-16.
8. An Unfailing Way, ... James 4. 8.

THE SAVING CALL.
LUKE 19. 5.

THE Call of Jesus Christ is—

1. A *Gracious* Call,   ..   He might have passed by.
2. A *Personal* Call,   ..   "Zaccheus."
3. An *Urgent* Call,   ..   "Make haste."
4. A *Humbling* Call,   ..   "Come down."
5. An *Affectionate* Call,   "Abide at thy house."
6. An *Assuring* Call,   ..   "I must."
7. An *Effectual* Call,   ..   "He made haste."

FAITH.

1. The Ear of Faith, ... 1 Kings 18. 41.
2. The Eye of Faith, ... 2 Kings 6. 17.
3. The Feet of Faith, ... Genesis 5. 24.
4. The Hand of Faith, ... Acts 3. 7.
5. The Heart of Faith, ... Rom. 10. 10.

CONDITIONS OF FELLOWSHIP.

LUKE 24. 29.

1. Consideration, "The day is far spent."
2. Invitation, .. "Abide with us."
3. Importunity, "They Constrained Him."
4. Result, .. "He went in to tarry with them."

A GREAT OPPORTUNITY.

ISAIAH 53. 6.

1. Whom? "Seek ye the Lord." 2. Why? "Because He is near." 3. When? "While He may be found." 4. How? "Seek...call." Who? "Ye."

FAITH AND SIGHT.

"HE who pinneth faith to bodily sight, to the earthly and visible, doth himself expose it to change, since all things visible are temporal, and only the invisible is eternal" (2 Cor. 4. 18).—*Gerlach.*

ORIGINAL ILLUSTRATIONS.

DISAPPOINTED WORKERS.

IT has been proved that when a bird's nest has been robbed several times she builds her last nest in a more slovenly fashion. So much is she influenced by disappointment, and such results are very natural to all who are depending upon their *own works*. However things may turn out, the Christian worker must never become slovenly in his or her service for Christ. Do the last as carefully as the first, and the least as heartily as the greatest. "Whatsoever thy hand findeth to do, do it with all thy might," for ye serve the Lord Christ. Angels are never disappointed, neither are they at any time slovenly in their work. They obey and worship. "Go thou and do likewise."

SELF-APPROBATION.

THE peculiar, self-conceited manners of the turkey cock are very generally known. It is so cowardly that it will fly from the most insignificant animal that dares to face it boldly; but if it can only succeed in frightening a child or a little pet dog, it will strut about the yard displaying its plumage with as much pride as if it had conquered a bull. Did you ever see what might be vulgarly called a turkey cock Christian worker? He is one who will do nothing for the Lord that implies self-sacrifice, or is likely to damage the plumage of *his own* good name in the eyes of worldly men, but who, when he does accomplish anything with seeming success, makes such an ado about it that everybody within a mile must know of it. They think others should praise them, while they are glorying in their own self-conceit.

CRABBED.

A CRABBED person is one who is usually tormented or avoided—one who is supposed to be crab-like. Yet who has not at times been ensnared in the toils of this crab? It appears that hermit-crabs are extremely *crabbed*. They will fight almost to the death with each other over a few empty shells, not a whit more suitable for them than the one they already possess. Self-seeking and covetousness always lead to crabbedness. Put off the old man with his deeds, and put on the new, and be content with such things as ye have.

THE ENCHANTMENT OF NEARNESS.

DISTANCE does not always "lend enchantment to the view." Wordsworth said, on looking at a cataract two miles off, that it was "frozen by distance." The matchless love of God, the joys of salvation, and the service of Christ are to a great many "frozen by distance." In the spiritual Kingdom nearness always lends enchantment to the view. The altogether loveliness of Christ grows increasingly as we grow in nearness to Him. It is those who are *afar off* that see no beauty in Him, and who are not enchanted by Him. "Let us draw near."

PERFECT SOUNDNESS.

IN an American locomotive shed there is an instrument something like a piano, for testing engines. The sound of each part of the engine, when in a perfect state, is in unison with the corresponding note in the testing machine. The slightest flaw in any of the parts will cause a discord, and so reveal its weakness. The Word of God is a perfect testing instrument for man's character and life. If our thoughts and acts are not in harmony with it, it is because there is some defect in us somewhere. The character that is perfectly sound will be in perfect accord with this Divine instrument.

CONVERSION.

THE emigrant sailing-ship, in passing from Europe to Australia has to go through a region called by seafaring people the "Equatorial Doldrums." This region is noted for rains and clouds, perplexing calms, and baffling winds; but the sunny land lies beyond. The emigrant soul, in passing from death to life, must go through the equatorial doldrums of conversion. The experiences here are not always the same. To some it may be a distressing calm— the painful stillness of unanswered prayer. To others it may be a region of tempest and fearful agitation. Some go quickly through, while others lie helpless for weeks and months. Anyway, don't be content to abide there. Press on to the sunny land of assured salvation (Rom. 7. 24, 25).

LOST OPPORTUNITY.

IT is said of Sir I. Newton that once having dismounted from his horse to lead him up a hill, the horse slipped his head out of the bridle, but Newton, oblivious to what had happened, went on holding the bridle till he reached the hill top, and turned to remount. While he, in his mind, was busy here and there, the horse was gone. Let us take heed, lest—while we are engrossed with other things—the opportunity of salvation does not slip away from us for ever.

THE NEW LIFE.

IT is a singular characteristic of the cuckoo that it never lays its eggs in its own nest. It deposits them in the nests of other smaller birds, where they are hatched. When the young cuckoo is strong enough it hoists the other occupants of the nest outside, and takes entire possession. This conduct seems very selfish and ungrateful, but it illustrates the process of the new life in the soul. "The expulsive power of a new affection," as Dr. Chalmers termed it. The new life, like the young cuckoo, has come from a different source—born from above. It is expected to take entire control of the whole being, and is to become a herald of the spring-time of salvation, bringing gladness and hope to others.

POWER OF CIRCUMSTANCES.

A MAN went down from Jerusalem to Jericho and fell among thieves. If you or I had gone down that way at that time we would likely have met with the same fate. We have not fallen among thieves, just because we have not been brought up among them. "In a vacuum," says Ganot, "liquids fall like solids, without separation of their molecules." Where there is no resistance, every material thing falls with the same rapidity—a feather as quick as a stone. Who can tell how much we owe to the restraining circumstances into which we have been born. Might not many of those thieves and drunkards have been as moral and religious as we are if they had got the same chance? Let this awaken thankfulness and sympathy.

REGENERATION.

IT is a well-known fact, although it is an ever-increasing wonder, that a caterpillar changes into a butterfly. There is certainly very little resemblance between the two, yet every butterfly has been a caterpillar. The butterflies can truthfully say, as they look at the poor caterpillars, "Such were some of us, but we are changed." So every saint has been a sinner, but a wonderful work has been wrought in them. The caterpillar sinner knows nothing of the delights of the butterfly saint. The only way a caterpillar can enter into the joys of the butterfly life is by being made a "new creature"—by being, in a sense, "born again." The cabbage-loving caterpillar has no capacity for the new-born movements and delights of the butterfly. No more can the carnal nature of man enter into the enjoyment of the things of God without being born again.

SHAM PROFESSORS.

THE fox is said to be the prince of all schemers. When it sees that escape is impossible it will sometimes feign death, and allow itself to be kicked and carried by the tail over one's shoulder without showing any signs of life; but as soon as opportunity offers itself it will scamper with all haste back to its old quarters. Foxy professors are not uncommon. They mingle with God's people, sing and talk as they do. You imagine them all right, but as soon as an opportunity comes in the form of some worldly amusement they decamp. It is not altogether impossible for even a Christian to feign himself dead to the world, and sin, while attending a holiness convention, and then, after these holy restraints are withdrawn, to play the fox and scamper back to the old life of selfishness.

A WARNING TO IDLERS.

TAKE heed, lest there be in any of you an evil heart of *laziness*! When bees have finished the business of swarming, and the workers have discovered that there are no lack of queens, then they with one accord fall on the drones, who are massacred without mercy. Thus Nature, in these busy bees, passes the sentence of death upon the useless idler. This is also a law in the spiritual world. Those Christians who will not work for the good of Christ's cause among men will be visited with the blight of death upon their spirits. No idler in the vineyard can possibly live in health and prosperity of soul. "Son! go work to-day!" He that will not do the work of God should not eat the food of God.

IMAGINARY GREATNESS.

FROUDE tells us that "Pompey was a weak man, ignorant of himself; and unwilling to part with his imaginary greatness, he was flung down by the cruel forces of the world." The forces of this present evil world are always too mighty for those clothed in the armour of "imaginary greatness." Only in the "armour of God" can we *stand*.